PC LEARNING LABS TEACHES EXCEL 4.0 FOR WINDOWS

4567890

1234567

8901234

2345678

PC LEARNING LABS
TEACHES EXCEL 4.0
FOR WINDOWS

LOGICAL OPERATIONS

Ziff-Davis Press
Emeryville, California

Writer	Richard P. Scott
Editor	Janna Hecker Clark
Technical Reviewer	Mark D. Hall
Project Coordinator	Ami Knox
Proofreader	Kayla Sussell
Cover Designer	Ken Roberts
Book Designer	Laura Lamar/MAX, San Francisco
Series Illustrators	Peter Tucker and Tony Jonick
Word Processors	Howard Blechman and Cat Haglund
Page Layout Artists	Tony Jonick and Anna Marks
Indexer	Valerie Haynes Perry

This book was produced on a Macintosh IIfx, with the following applications: FrameMaker®, Microsoft® Word, MacLink®Plus, Aldus® FreeHand™, Adobe Photoshop™, and Collage Plus™.

Ziff-Davis Press
5903 Christie Avenue
Emeryville, CA 94608

ISBN 1-56276-074-2

Manufactured in the United States of America
10 9 8 7 6 5 4 3 2 1

CONTENTS AT A GLANCE

TABLE OF CONTENTS

INTRODUCTION

Welcome to *PC Learning Labs Teaches Excel 4.0*, a hands-on instruction book designed to help you attain a high level of Excel fluency in as short a time as possible. And congratulations on choosing Excel 4.0, a powerful and elegant program that will greatly simplify your tasks of accounting and database management.

We at PC Learning Labs believe this book to be a unique and welcome addition to the ranks of "how-to" computer publications. Our instructional approach stems directly from a decade of successful teaching in a hands-on classroom environment. Throughout the book, theory is consistently mixed with practice; a topic is explained and then immediately drilled in a hands-on activity. These activities employ the included Data Disk, which contains 40 sample Excel files.

When you're done working your way through this book, you will have a solid foundation of skills in Excel's primary areas of expertise:

- *Electronic accounting*   The manipulation and calculation of numeric data in spreadsheet form.

- *Database management*   The systematic arrangement of information which allows it to be easily searched, extracted, and rearranged.

- *Charting*   The visual display of numeric data in graph form.

You will learn how to enter, modify, save, and retrieve numeric and text data in spreadsheet and chart form. You will also learn to prepare presentation-quality screen displays and printouts of your spreadsheets, databases, and charts.

Note: We strongly advise you to read through the rest of this Introduction before beginning Chapter 1. If, however, you are anxious to dive in, work through the section below, "Creating Your Work Directory," as it is crucial to every activity in the book.

WHO THIS BOOK IS FOR

This book was written with the beginner in mind. While experience with spreadsheets and personal computers is certainly helpful, little or none is required. You should know how to turn on your computer, monitor, and printer; how to use your keyboard; and how to move your mouse. Everything beyond that will be explained in the text.

HOW TO USE THIS BOOK

This book is designed to be used as a learning guide, a review tool, and a quick reference.

AS A LEARNING GUIDE   Each chapter covers one broad topic or set of related topics. Chapters are arranged in order of increasing Excel proficiency; skills you acquire in one chapter are used and elaborated on in subsequent chapters. For this reason, you should work through the chapters in strict sequence.

Each chapter is organized into explanatory topics and step-by-step activities. Topics provide the theoretical overview you need to master Excel; activities allow you to immediately apply this understanding to specific, hands-on examples.

AS A REVIEW TOOL   Any method of instruction is only as effective as the time and effort you are willing to invest in it. For this reason, we encourage you to review the more challenging topics and activities presented in this book.

AS A QUICK REFERENCE   General procedures (such as copying a range of cells or printing a worksheet) are presented as a series of bulleted steps; you can find these bullets (•) easily by skimming through the book.

At the end of every chapter, you'll find a quick reference listing the mouse/keyboard actions needed to perform the techniques introduced in that chapter.

WHAT THIS BOOK CONTAINS

The 15 chapters of *PC Learning Labs Teaches Excel 4.0* are divided into the following four sections:

Chapters 1–7	Electronic accounting
Chapters 8–11	Database management
Chapters 12–14	Charting
Chapter 15	Advanced printing features

In addition, there are four appendices:

Appendix A	Installation
Appendix B	Keystroke Reference
Appendix C	Exchanging Data between Excel and Other Applications
Appendix D	Upgrading from Excel Version 3.0 to Version 4.0

To attain full Excel fluency, you should work through all 15 chapters. The appendices are optional.

The following features of this book are designed to facilitate your learning:

- Carefully sequenced topics that build on the knowledge you've acquired from previous topics

- Frequent hands-on activities, designed to sharpen your Excel skills

- Numerous illustrations that show how your screen should look at key points during these activities

- The Data Disk, which contains all the files you will need to complete the activities

- A quick reference at the end of each chapter, listing in easy-to-read table form the mouse/keyboard actions needed to perform the techniques introduced in the chapter

WHAT YOU NEED

To run Excel 4.0 and complete this book, you need a computer, monitor, keyboard, and mouse. A printer is strongly recommended, but optional.

 A COMPUTER AND MONITOR

You need an IBM or IBM-compatible personal computer and monitor that are capable of running Microsoft Windows (version 3.0 or higher). A 286-based system is technically sufficient, but both Windows and Excel 4.0 will tend to run somewhat slowly on it; for this reason, we recommend that you use a 386 or higher (486, 586, and so on) computer. You need a hard disk with at least 6 megabytes—preferably, it should have 12 megabytes—of free storage space. Finally, you need an EGA or higher (VGA, SVGA, and so on) graphics card and monitor to display Windows and Excel at their intended screen resolution.

Windows must be installed on your computer; if it is not, see your Windows reference manuals for instructions. Excel 4.0 must also be installed; for help, see Appendix A.

 A KEYBOARD

IBM-type computers come with various styles of keyboards; these keyboards function identically, but have different layouts. Figures I.1, I.2, and I.3 show the three main keyboard styles and their key arrangements.

Figure I.1   **The IBM PC–style keyboard**

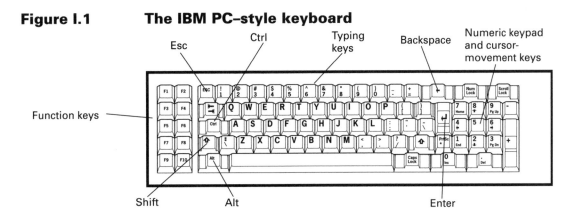

Esc   Ctrl   Typing keys   Backspace   Numeric keypad and cursor-movement keys

Function keys

Shift   Alt   Enter

Figure I.2   **The XT/AT–style keyboard**

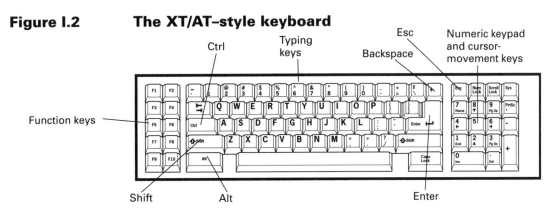

Ctrl   Typing keys   Esc   Backspace   Numeric keypad and cursor-movement keys

Function keys

Shift   Alt   Enter

Figure I.3   **The PS/2–style Enhanced Keyboard**

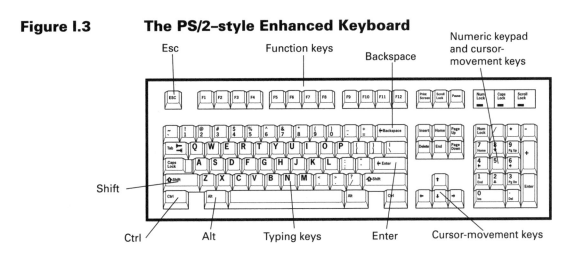

Esc   Function keys   Backspace   Numeric keypad and cursor-movement keys

Shift

Ctrl   Alt   Typing keys   Enter   Cursor-movement keys

Excel uses three main areas of the keyboard:

- The *function keys*, which enable you to access Excel's special features. On the PC-, XT-, and AT-style keyboards, there are ten function keys at the left end of the keyboard; on the PS/2-style Enhanced Keyboard, there are 12 at the top of the keyboard.

- The *typing keys*, located in the main body of all the keyboards. These include letters, numbers, and punctuation marks, as well as the Shift, Ctrl, and Alt keys, which you will need to access several of Excel's special features.

- The *numeric keypad*, which groups the numbers (the same ones found across the top row of the typing keys) for convenient entry of numeric data. The numeric keypad also contains the screen-movement keys: Up, Down, Left, and Right Arrows; Home; End; PgUp (Page Up); and PgDn (Page Down). To enter numeric data using the numeric keypad, *Num Lock* must be on. (Pressing the Num Lock key will toggle Num Lock on/off.) To use the screen-movement keys on the keypad, Num Lock must be off. To enter numeric data when Num Lock is off, use the number keys on the top row of the typing area.

The Enhanced Keyboard has an additional screen-movement keypad to the left of the numeric keypad. This allows you to use the numeric keypad for numeric data entry (that is, to keep Num Lock on) and still have access to screen-movement keys.

 A MOUSE OR TRACKBALL

You need a mouse or trackball to work through the activities in this book. Any of the standard PC mice or trackballs will do.

(Note: Throughout this book, we direct you to use a mouse, not a trackball. If you have a trackball instead of a mouse, simply use your trackball to perform all the tasks that involve mouse techniques: dragging, clicking, and so on.)

 A PRINTER

Although you aren't absolutely required to have a printer to work through the activities, we strongly recommend it. A PostScript-type laser printer is ideal, but a non-PostScript laser or dot-matrix one is acceptable. Your printer must be selected for use with Excel; for help, see Appendix A.

If you have no printer, use the Print Preview command instead of the Print command in the relevant activities. This will cause your document to be "printed" on the screen.

The printed examples shown in this book were all printed on a Post-Script laser printer. Your printouts may differ somewhat, depending upon which printer you are using.

CREATING YOUR WORK DIRECTORY

In the course of this book, you will be creating, editing, and saving several files. In order to keep these files together, you need to create a *work directory* for them on your hard disk. A directory is like a filing cabinet in which a group of related files is stored. Your work directory will also hold the sample files contained on the Data Disk at the back of this book.

Follow these steps to create your work directory:

1.   Turn on your computer. After a brief internal self-check, your *operating environment* will automatically load. If you are in Windows, please continue with step 2. If you are in DOS, please skip to step 3. If you are in a non-Windows, non-DOS operating environment (for example, OS/2), exit from this environment to DOS and skip to step 3. (For help exiting to DOS, see the reference books for your operating environment.)

2. Within Windows, locate Program Manager, an on-screen window with "Program Manager" in its overhead title bar. (If Program Manager is running as an icon—a small picture with "Program Manager" beneath it—instead of as a window, use the mouse to move the on-screen pointer to this icon. Double-click—press the left mouse button twice in rapid succession—to open the icon into a window.) Move the mouse pointer to the *Control Menu button*, the small square button in the upper-left corner of the Program Manager window. Double-click on the dash in this box. A box entitled "Exit Windows" will appear in the middle of the screen. Click the mouse pointer once on the **OK** within this box. You have now exited from Windows to DOS. Skip to step 9.

3. You may see this prompt:

```
Current date is Tue 1-01-1980
Enter new date (mm-dd-yy):
```

(Your current date will be different.) If you do not see a date prompt, skip to step 6.

4. If the current date on your screen is wrong, type the correct date. Use a dash (-) to separate the month, day, and year (e.g., 3-25-93).

5. Press **Enter**. After you type a command, you must press the Enter key to send this command to the computer.

6. You may see this prompt:

```
Current time is 0:25:32:56
Enter new time:
```

(Your current time will be different.) If you do not see a time prompt, skip to step 9.

7. If the current time on your screen is wrong, type the correct time. Use

the format *hh:mm*. Most versions of DOS use a 24-hour clock (e.g., 10:30 for 10:30 a.m., and 22:30 for 10:30 p.m.).

8. Press **Enter** to send the time you specified to the computer's internal clock.

9. The DOS prompt will appear

    ```
    C:\>
    ```

    (Your DOS prompt may differ somewhat from this.)

10. Type **dir** and press **Enter**. The contents of the current directory are displayed, followed by a final line reporting the number of free bytes on your hard disk. If you have 1,000,000 or more bytes free, skip to step 11. If you have fewer than 1,000,000 bytes free, you will not be able to create your work directory and perform all the hands-on tasks in this book. Before you proceed, you'll have to delete enough files from your hard disk to bring the free-byte total up to 1,000,000. If you need help doing this, please refer to your DOS reference manual. (Note: Make sure to back up all important files before deleting them!)

11. Insert the enclosed Data Disk (label up) into the appropriately sized disk drive and close the drive door, if necessary. Determine whether this is drive A or drive B. (On a single floppy-disk system, the drive is generally designated as A. On a double floppy-disk system, the upper drive is generally designated as A and the lower as B.)

12. Type **a:** if the Data Disk is in drive A, or type **b:** if the Data Disk is in drive B. Press **Enter** to change the current drive to the Data Disk drive.

13. Type **install c: ex4work**. (If you wish to create your work directory on a hard disk that is *not* designated as drive C, substitute your hard-disk drive letter for the "c" in this command—for example, to install onto a drive-D hard disk, you would type install d: ex4work). EX4WORK is the name of your work directory. Press **Enter** to begin the installation.

14. If all is well, the message

```
Installation begun.
Copying files .....
```

appears. When the procedure is complete, the message

```
Installation finished!
```

appears, followed by a line reporting the name of your work directory (c:\ex4work). In some cases, however, the message

```
Installation aborted! Work directory naming conflict
```

may appear. This message is displayed if a directory with the same name as your proposed working directory (EX4WORK) already exists on your hard disk. If this happens, repeat step 13, substituting a new work directory name of your choice for the suggested directory ex4-work. For example, you might type install c: mywork, or install c: ex4-files. Your work-directory name can be up to eight letters long. Do not use spaces, periods, or punctuation marks. Do not use the name "excel," as it is already taken by the Excel program.

Note: The hands-on activities in this book refer to your work directory as EX4WORK. If you've chosen another name, please remember to mentally substitute it for the name EX4WORK throughout the book.

CONVENTIONS USED IN THIS BOOK

The conventions used in this book are designed to help you learn Excel 4.0 easily and efficiently. Each chapter begins with a short introduction and ends with a summary that includes a quick-reference guide to the techniques introduced in the chapter. Main chapter topics (large, capitalized headings) and subtopics (headings preceded by a cube) explain Excel features. Hands-on activities allow you to practice using Excel's features. In these activities, menu choices, keystrokes, and anything you are asked to type are all presented in boldface. Here's an example from Chapter 2:

4. Type **=B1*B2**. Click on the **enter box** to calculate the product of numbers in the two cells (125000).

Activities adhere to a *cause-and-effect* approach. Each step tells you what to do (cause) and then what will happen (effect). From the example above,

Cause   Type =B1*B2 and click on the enter box.

Effect   The product of the numbers in the two cells is calculated, and 125000 is displayed on the screen.

A hyphen (-) is used with the Shift, Ctrl, and Alt keys to denote a multi-key keystroke. For example, Ctrl-F10 means, "Press and hold the Ctrl key, then press the function key F10, then release both."

To help you distinguish between steps presented for your general knowledge and steps you should carry out at your computer as you read, we have adopted the following system:

- A bulleted step, like this, is provided for your information and reference only.

1. A numbered step, like this, indicates one in a series of steps that you should carry out in sequence at your computer.

BEFORE YOU START

The activities in each of the following 15 chapters are designed to proceed sequentially. In many cases, you cannot perform an activity until you have performed one or more of the activities directly preceding it. For this reason, we recommend that you allot enough time to work through an entire chapter in each session.

You are now ready to begin. Good learning and ... *bon voyage!*

CHAPTER 1: GETTING STARTED

Welcome to Excel 4.0 and the world of electronic accounting. Excel provides you with sophisticated business tools for calculating, projecting, and analyzing your financial data. It also offers tools for creating attractive, concise documents and charts incorporating this data.

This first chapter gets you up and running in Excel, introduces you to the electronic spreadsheet working environment, and reviews your mouse skills. When you're done working through this chapter, you will know

- How to start Excel
- About worksheets and the Excel environment
- How to use the mouse with Excel
- How to exit Excel

THE EXCEL PROGRAM

Anyone who has ever managed a business or personal budget is well aware of the challenges inherent in such a task: filling out and making corrections to the ledger sheet; calculating the necessary totals, averages, maximums, and minimums; recalculating these values if one or more numeric entries change; redesigning the ledger sheet to add or delete rows or columns; preparing the finished ledger sheet for presentation; and so on. The beauty of Excel lies in its ability to eliminate or reduce the difficulty of these tasks.

Beyond its financial-management capabilities, Excel offers a number of useful features, including:

Database management	The systematic arrangement of information, so that it can easily be searched, extracted, and rearranged
Charting	The visual display of numeric data as graphs

Let's begin by examining a sample paper ledger sheet, or *spreadsheet*. Observe the design of Figure 1.1. Note the following features:

- Information is arranged in columns (vertical) and rows (horizontal).
- Text identifies the numbers ("Rent," "JANUARY," etc.).
- Totals and averages have been calculated.
- Some numbers have "$" and "," to make them easier to read.
- The first column is wider than the others.

- The data are neatly arranged: titles are centered, headings are properly positioned, and numbers are decimal-aligned.

Figure 1.1   **A sample paper spreadsheet**

```
                        PERSONAL BUDGET for the First Quarter
                        (excluding food and miscellaneous expenses)


                                                              QUARTER
                          JANUARY      FEBURARY      MARCH     TOTALS


   1. Rent               500.00        500.00       500.00   1,500.00
   2. Telephone           48.35         24.98        35.57     108.90
   3. Utilities           67.27         75.92        62.89     206.08
   4. Charge Cards       135.75         59.89        89.55     285.19
   5. Heating Oil        125.52        150.57        50.32     326.41
   6. Auto Insurance     113.50                                113.50
   7. Cable TV            30.25         30.25        30.25      90.75



   MONTHLY TOTALS      $1,020.64      $841.61      $768.58

   GRAND TOTAL (QUARTER)                                    $2,630.83

   AVERAGE MONTHLY EXPENSE                                    $876.94
```

Observe the data of Figure 1.1 and consider these questions:

- How would you determine that the calculations are correct?
- How would you change a number?
- How would you then update the calculations?
- How would you add columns for the second, third, and fourth quarters?
- How would you add more expenses?

All of the above tasks are relatively involved and time-consuming. Figures must be erased and reentered, calculations must be redone, rows and columns must be added, causing, in turn, the entire page layout to be revamped.

In Excel, you will work with an electronic version of a paper spreadsheet, called a *worksheet*. What you would normally type or write by hand on paper, you will now enter on your computer screen. Working electronically will make tasks like those listed above surprisingly easy to perform.

STARTING EXCEL

Before you start Excel, it must be installed on your hard disk. If Excel is not already installed, see Appendix A for directions. Windows must also be installed (version 3.0 or higher). For directions, see your Windows reference manuals. Finally, you need to have created a work directory on your hard disk and copied the files from the enclosed data disk to this directory. If you have not already done this, please do so now (see Introduction, "Creating Your Work Directory").

Follow these steps to start Excel:

1. Turn on your computer. After a brief internal self-check, your *operating environment* will automatically load. If you are in Windows, please skip steps 2 through 9, and continue with step 1 of the next activity. If you are in DOS, continue with step 2 of this activity. If you are in a non-Windows, non-DOS operating environment (for example, OS/2), exit from this environment to DOS and continue with step 2. (For help exiting to DOS, see the reference books for your operating environment.)

2. You may see this prompt:

    ```
    Current date is Tue 1-01-1980
    Enter new date (mm-dd-yy):
    ```

    If you do not see a date prompt, skip to step 5.

3. If the current date on your screen is wrong, type the correct date. Use a hyphen (-) to separate the month, day, and year (e.g., 3-25-93).

4. Press **Enter**. Remember that after you type a command, you must press the Enter key to send this command to the computer.

5. You may see this prompt:

```
Current time is 0:25:32:56
Enter new time:
```

(Your current time will be different.) If you do not see a time prompt, skip to step 8.

6. If the current time on your screen is wrong, type the correct time. Use the format *hh:mm*. Most versions of DOS use a 24-hour clock (e.g., 10:30 for 10:30 a.m., and 22:30 for 10:30 p.m.).

7. Press **Enter** to send the time you specified to the computer's internal clock.

8. The DOS prompt will appear:

```
C:\>
```

(Your DOS prompt may differ somewhat from this.)

9. Type **win** and press **Enter** to start Windows. After a few moments of furious hard-disk activity, Windows will appear on your screen.

In order to start Excel 4.0, you must locate the program icon entitled "Microsoft Excel." An *icon* is a small on-screen picture that represents a program or a group of programs.

Windows is a *customizable* program. Its screen appearance and overall setup can vary significantly from computer to computer. For this reason, we at PC Learning Labs cannot know exactly how your version of Windows is set up; please bear with us as we search for the Microsoft Excel program icon:

1. Look for the program icon depicted in Figure 1.2, a three-dimensional XL with the title "Microsoft Excel" beneath it. If you see this icon on your screen right now, please skip directly to step 5. If the icon does not appear on your screen, please continue with step 2.

2. Program icons are stored in *program groups*. Program groups are, in turn, stored in a Windows application called *Program Manager*. If Program Manager is running as an icon (a small picture with the title "Program Manager" beneath it), double-click (press the **left mouse button** twice in rapid succession) on the icon to open it into a window. If Program Manager is running in a window (as in Figure 1.2), click on the title bar of the window to activate it.

Figure 1.2   **The Microsoft Excel program icon**

Program Manager, running in a window

Control Menu button

Microsoft Excel program icon

Program-group window

Program-group icons

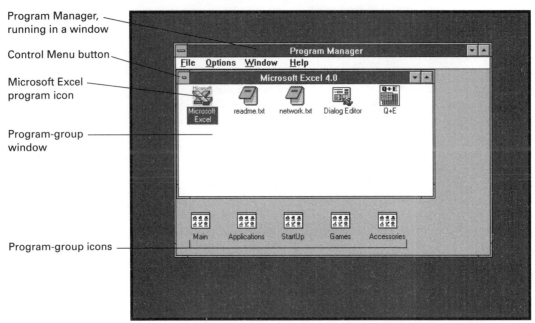

3. Within Program Manager, program groups can appear as icons ("Main," "Applications," "StartUp," "Games," and "Accessories" in Figure 1.2) or as windows ("Microsoft Excel 4.0" in Figure 1.2). Normally, the Microsoft Excel program icon is stored in a program group entitled "Microsoft Excel 4.0." If you see a program-group icon with this title, double-click on the icon to open it into a window, and skip directly to step 5.

4. If you do not have a Microsoft Excel 4.0 program group in your Program Manager window, you will have to search further for the Microsoft Excel program icon. Double-click on a program-group icon that seems appropriate for an application program like Excel ("Applications" or "Windows Applications" would be good candidates). The program-group icon will open into a window. If you see the Microsoft Excel program icon somewhere inside this window, skip to step 5. If not, double-click on the program-group window's Control Menu button (the small button in the upper-left corner of the program-group window, as shown in Figure 1.2) to close the window. Repeat this step as many times as you

need to find your elusive Microsoft Excel program icon. Don't despair: If Excel 4.0 is installed on your computer, its program icon must be stored somewhere! It just may take a while to find it.

5. Double-click on the **Microsoft Excel** program icon to start Excel 4.0. Your screen should now match Figure 1.3.

Figure 1.3   **Excel 4.0, after start-up**

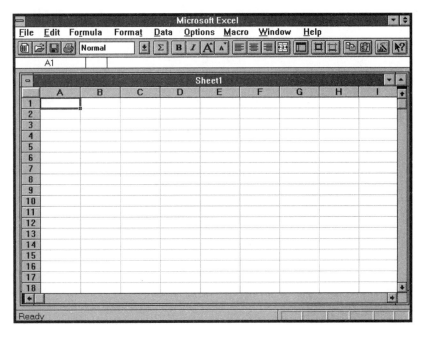

Excel, like Windows, is a customizable program. Depending upon how it has been set up, (by you or, perhaps, a colleague), your screen may differ significantly from the one shown in Figure 1.3. Please perform the following steps to ensure that your Excel setup matches, as closely as possible, the setup we use in this book. (Note: In order to walk you through these steps, we had to "jump the gun" and use some technical terms you may not understand. Again, please bear with us; these italicized terms will be explained later in the book.)

1. Click on the word **Options** in the *menu bar* at the top center of the screen; a *drop-down menu* appears.

2. In the drop-down menu, click on **Workspace...** . A *dialog box* appears showing Excel's current Workspace options.

3. Observe the options grouped together under the heading "Display." When an option is selected (active), an X appears in the box to the left of the option name. Use your mouse to set the display options as follows:

Selected	**Deselected**
Status Bar	R1C1
Scroll Bars	Info Window
Formula Bar	
Note Indicator	

   To select an option, click the mouse on the empty box to the left of the option name; an X will appear in the box. To deselect an option, click on the X in an option box; the X will disappear.

4. Now observe the four options at the bottom of the dialog box. Use your mouse to set these options as follows:

Selected	**Deselected**
Cell Drag	Alternate Navigation Keys
and Drop	Ignore Remote Requests
	Move Selection after Enter

5. Click on the **OK** *button* in the upper-right corner of the dialog box to accept the current Workspace options.

6. Click on **Options** in the menu bar to display the drop-down Options menu.

7. In the drop-down menu, click on **Toolbars**.... A dialog box appears, listing all of Excel's different *toolbars*.

8. Click once on the first toolbar in this list (**Standard**) to select it. Observe the top *button* on the right side of the Toolbars dialog box. If it reads "Hide," skip to step 9. If it reads "Show," click on this **Show button** to show the Standard toolbar on your screen.

9. If the Toolbars dialog box is no longer displayed, click on **Options** and then click on **Toolbars...** to display it. Click once on the next toolbar in the list to select it. Observe

the top button on the right side of the dialog box. If it reads "Show," skip to step 10. If it reads "Hide," click on this **Hide button** to remove the Formatting toolbar from your screen.

10. Repeat step 9 for all the remaining toolbars in the Toolbars dialog box. You should end up with only the Standard toolbar visible, as shown in Figure 1.3.

11. If the Toolbars dialog box is still displayed, click on **Close** to remove it.

THE WORKSHEET ENVIRONMENT

A *window* is a rectangular area on the screen through which you view a document (worksheet or other application). After starting Excel, you see two windows, one within the other. The outer window is the *application window*, and the inner window is the *document window*.

THE APPLICATION WINDOW

The Excel application window is like a program manager: it provides you with tools, commands, and status messages to use with your worksheets. Note these elements, shown in Figure 1.4:

Title bar	The bar at the top of the window. The title bar contains the Control Menu button, the application title, the Minimize button, and the Maximize button or Restore button.
Control Menu button	A large, shadowed dash in the far left corner. It provides a list of commands to change the size and position of the application window or to close it.
Application title	The program title (Microsoft Excel), centered within the title bar.
Minimize button	The downward arrow on the right. Shrinks the application window to its smallest form, a symbol called an *application icon*.

Figure 1.4   **The Excel application window**

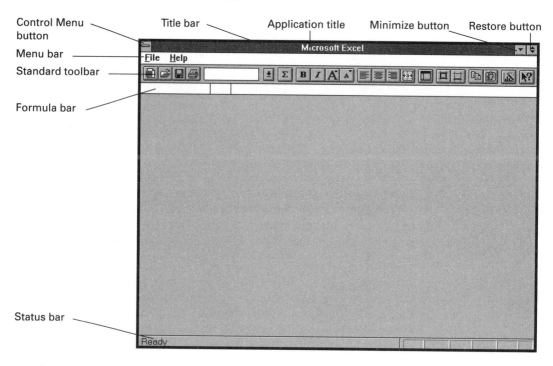

Control Menu button — Menu bar — Standard toolbar — Formula bar — Status bar — Title bar — Application title — Minimize button — Restore button

Restore button	An up- and downward arrow on the far right, displayed after you maximize the application window. It returns the window to the size and place it was before being maximized.
Maximize button	An upward arrow on the far right (not shown in Figure 1.4 because this window is already maximized). It enlarges the Excel application window to fill all available screen space.
Menu bar	The area immediately below the title bar which displays the names of the *drop-down menus* available for the current application. These menu names change, depending on the type of document window that is active. (In Figure 1.4, the only available drop-down menus are File and Help.)

Standard toolbar	The area below the menu bar. Excel's Standard toolbar includes several tools and buttons (small pictures representing options for the current application) that you will use to quickly apply graphic elements, such as styles and formats, directly to the worksheet. (See Chapter 6 for more information.)
Formula bar	The area below the toolbar. It displays the contents of the active cell in the worksheet.
Status bar	The area at the bottom of the window. It displays information about a selected command and about the current state of the worksheet.

THE DOCUMENT WINDOW

The Excel document window displays the worksheet that you are currently creating or modifying (see Figure 1.5). Familiarize yourself with the features in the following list:

Title bar	The bar across the top of the window. The title bar includes a Control Menu button (a shorter, shadowed dash, on the far left), the document's title in the center (Sheet1), and a Maximize or Restore button (on the far right).
Scroll bars	The bars framing the right and lower borders of the document window. The scroll bars, along with the *scroll boxes* and *scroll arrows*, are used to change the area of the worksheet displayed in the window.
Split bars	The small black dashes located above the vertical scroll bar and to the left of the horizontal scroll bar. They are used to split the window into *panes* that can be scrolled separately, enabling you to view several areas of the worksheet at once.
Window borders	The borders of the worksheet. They are used to change the size and shape of the document window.
Column headings	The letters at the top of each column.
Row headings	The numbers at the left of each row.

Figure 1.5 **The Excel document window**

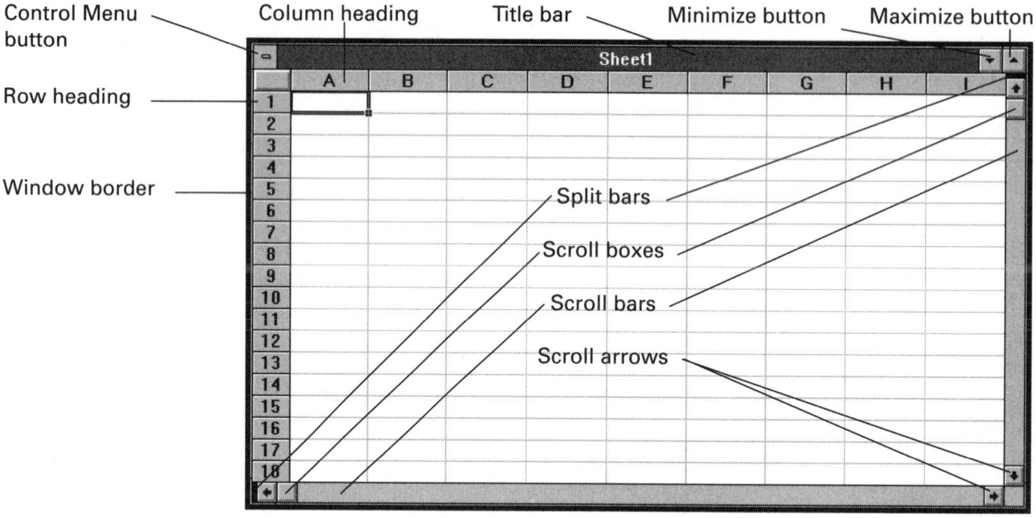

Control Menu button
Column heading
Title bar
Minimize button
Maximize button
Row heading
Window border
Sheet1
A
B
C
D
E
F
G
H
I
1
2
3
4
5
6
7
8
9
10
11
12
13
14
15
16
17
18
Split bars
Scroll boxes
Scroll bars
Scroll arrows

THE WORKSHEET

The Excel worksheet is an electronic version of a paper spreadsheet, a tool used for numerical analysis (see Figure 1.6). Data are arranged in rows and columns, just as on an accountant's ledger sheet. As you add or change data, the worksheet recalculates the relationships among the data.

An Excel worksheet is a grid of 256 columns by 16,384 rows. Columns are designated by letters running across the top of the worksheet, and rows by numbers running down the left border. Column *headings* begin with the letter *A* and continue through the letter *Z* (columns 1 to 26). After the 26th column, headings become double letters, from *A A* to *IV* (columns 27 through 256).

The intersection of a column and a row is called a *cell.* A single worksheet contains over four million cells (256 multiplied by 16,384). Data (text or numbers) are entered directly into any cell that is *active*. The active cell is identified by a thick, dark border.

The *formula bar* is the area below the toolbar. It displays the contents and name of the active cell. Data being entered into a cell appear in both the cell and the formula bar. The name of that cell appears in the *cell-reference area* on the far left of the formula bar.

Figure 1.6   **The Excel worksheet**

Formula bar

Cell-reference area

Active cell

Status bar

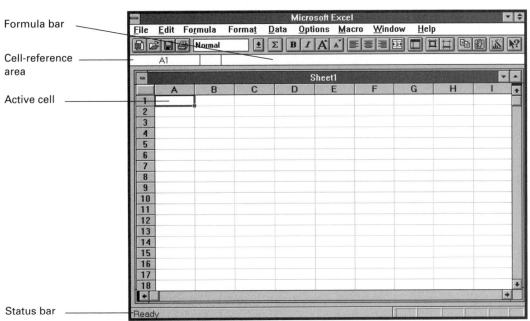

For example, the formula bar might display the cell reference A1 on the far left and 500 (the value in cell A1) on the right.

As you begin typing data into a cell, a boxed checkmark (the *enter box*) and a boxed X (the *cancel box*) appear in the formula bar. Once data have been entered into the cell, these boxes are no longer displayed.

A *status bar* frames the bottom of the window. It displays information about a selected command and about the current state of the workspace (the area of activity inside the application window). When you first open a worksheet, the status bar says "Ready."

Note the appearance of several new drop-down menu items in the menu bar (File, Edit, Formula, Format, and so on). The basics of working with the Excel menu will be covered in Chapter 2.

Let's take a look at some basic features of a new worksheet:

1. Observe the new worksheet on your computer screen. Note that it resembles an accountant's ledger paper. What you see represents a small portion of the available worksheet space.

As mentioned, Excel will allow you to create a worksheet up to 256 columns wide and 16,384 rows long.

2. Observe the column headings (across the top of the worksheet). Columns are labeled by capital letters in alphabetical order: A to IV for a total of 256 columns. Each column extends down through all 16,384 rows of the worksheet.

3. Observe the row headings (down the left side of the worksheet). Rows are numbered from 1 to 16384. Each row extends across through all 256 columns of the worksheet.

4. Observe a cell (the intersection of a column and a row). Cells are named by their column and row locations: A1, B89, IV16384, and so on.

5. Observe the cell reference (in the cell-reference area, on the far left of the formula bar). The reference identifies the current, or active, cell.

6. Identify the active cell (surrounded by a bold border, or outline). Examine the reference to verify the location of the active cell. Whenever a new worksheet is created, A1 is chosen as the first active cell.

7. Press → to select B1 as the active cell. Note that B1 is now outlined. The name of the cell in the cell-reference area has also changed to B1.

PRACTICE YOUR SKILLS

1. Select cell B2 by pressing ↓. Examine the reference.

2. Select cell A2 by pressing ←. Examine the reference.

3. Select cell A1 by pressing ↑. Examine the reference.

QUICK REVIEW OF MOUSE SKILLS

The mouse is a hand-held data-input device. It enables you to interact with Excel by manipulating on-screen images. When you move the mouse on the surface of your desktop, a screen symbol called the *mouse pointer* moves in relation to the direction and speed of the mouse. The mouse pointer changes shape according to the area of the screen in which it is located.

On top of the mouse, you will find one or more buttons. Using a *mouse button* allows you to interact with the screen in a number of ways (see Table 1.1). For the remainder of this book, "mouse button" indicates the left button on a mouse with two or more buttons.

Table 1.1   **Mouse Techniques**

Technique Name	Description
Check	To click on a check box to turn on that option.
Choose	To pick a menu command or dialog-box button by pointing to it and clicking once.
Click	To press and quickly release the mouse button.
Double-click	To press and release the mouse button twice in rapid succession.
Drag	To press and hold the mouse button while moving the mouse.
Point	To move the mouse until the tip of the mouse pointer is correctly positioned.
Press	To press and hold down the mouse button.
Scroll	To click on a scroll arrow or in the scroll bar, or to drag the scroll box.
Select	To point at and click (or drag) to highlight the portion of the document you wish to work with.
Uncheck	To click on a check box to turn off that option.

Note: You can execute each of Excel's commands by using either the mouse or the keyboard. In general, this book will teach you to use the mouse; only the most convenient keyboard commands are mentioned. Those who would like to learn more about keyboard commands should see Appendix B, "Keystroke Reference," or the Excel reference manuals.

Perform the following steps to acquaint yourself with the mouse:

1. Move the mouse. Note the direction and speed of the mouse pointer in relation to the movements of your hand. Also, note the changing shape of the mouse pointer as it moves across different areas of the screen.

2. Place the mouse pointer on cell **D1**. Note that the pointer is a cross.

3. Click the **mouse button** (press and immediately release the button on the left). The cell is *selected* (outlined).

4. Place the mouse pointer on cell **B2**. Press and hold the **mouse button** down. While holding the button, drag the mouse pointer to cell **D5**. Release the mouse button: all cells bounded by B2 and D5 are selected (see Figure 1.7). To select a range of cells, drag the mouse pointer over them. Note that the active cell (B2) is outlined and the rest are *highlighted*.

Figure 1.7   **Selecting a range of cells**

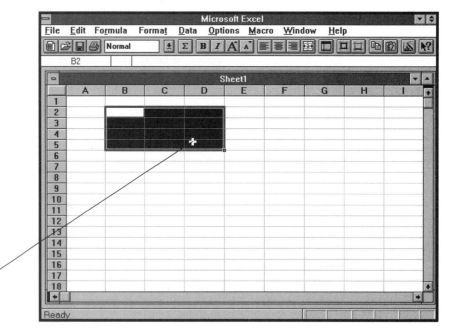

Mouse pointer

PRACTICE YOUR SKILLS

1. Select cell **F5**. (Note that when you select a cell, the previously active cells are *deselected*.)

2. Select cell **G13**.

3. Select cell **A1**.

4. Select cells **A4** through **G12**.

EXITING EXCEL

When you finish an Excel work session and wish to turn off your computer or start up another program, you must first exit Excel. Let's practice exiting from Excel.

1. Move the mouse pointer to the **Control Menu button** in the upper-left corner of the Excel application window (see Figure 1.4).

2. Double-click (press the **left mouse button** twice in rapid succession) on the **Control Menu button**.

3. You are returned to the Windows environment. You may now start up another program from Windows, exit to DOS, or turn off your computer. For more information, see your Windows reference manuals.

CHAPTER SUMMARY

In this first chapter, you've acquired some important Excel basics. You've learned to start the Excel program and to identify the primary features of a new worksheet. You've also become familiar with the Excel/Windows environment and reviewed your mouse skills.

In Chapter 2, you will expand your knowledge of Excel basics. You'll be provided with the mechanics needed to enter and correct data and to save a worksheet to a file on disk. In addition, you'll learn how to close a worksheet and begin the worksheet-building process again.

Congratulations! You're well on your way to Excel mastery.

CHAPTER 2: BASIC WORKSHEET MECHANICS

Entering Data

Saving and Closing
a Worksheet

Creating a New
Worksheet

This chapter introduces the basic procedures used to enter and correct data in Excel, and to save an electronic worksheet to a file on your hard disk.

When you're done working through this chapter, you will know

- How to enter and revise text, numbers, and formulas

- How to save a worksheet and clear the screen

- How to create a new worksheet

ENTERING DATA

Worksheet cells can contain two types of data: *constant values* and *formulas*. Constant values are text or numbers that, once entered, do not normally vary (for example, an employee's name or a fixed sales commission rate). Formulas are sets of instructions designed to perform specific calculations (determine totals, averages, projected profits, and so on).

To enter data in a cell,

- Select the cell in which you want the data to be displayed.

- Type the data.

- Click on the *enter* box (the boxed checkmark in the formula bar), or press the Enter key.

If you are not currently running Excel on your computer, please follow the steps in Chapter 1 under "Starting Excel" to load the program. Let's begin this chapter's activities by entering some text in a worksheet:

1. Select cell **A1**.

2. Type **cases** in the cell. Note that the word appears in both the cell and the formula bar, but it is not entered yet.

3. Observe the *insertion point* (the flashing vertical line in the formula bar). It marks where the next character will be inserted as you type.

4. Observe the cancel box and the enter box (the boxed letter *X* and the checkmark). Used for entering data with the mouse, they appear in the formula bar as you type, as shown in Figure 2.1.

5. Click on the **enter box** (the enclosed checkmark) to enter the data into the cell. The cancel box and the enter box disappear. The text is entered into the cell and aligned to the left.

Figure 2.1   **Entering text into a cell**

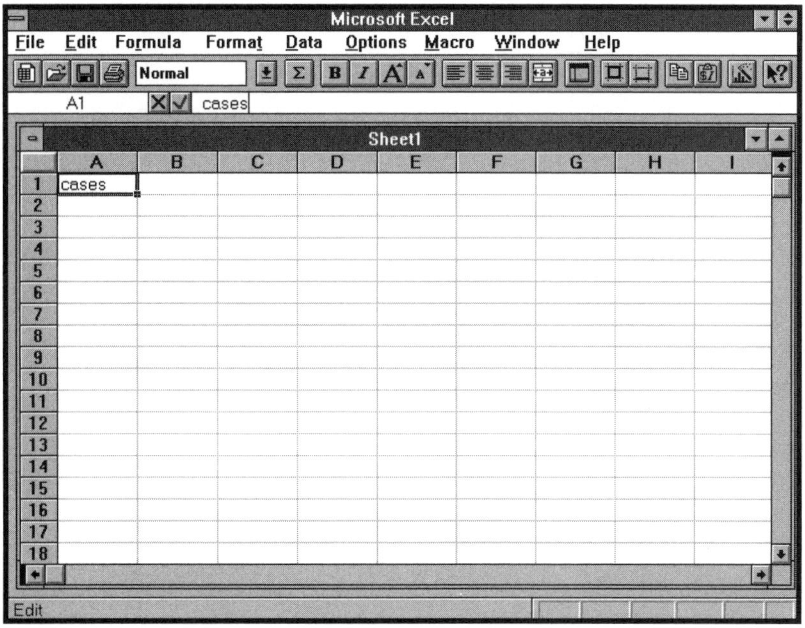

![Microsoft Excel screenshot showing the cell A1 containing the text "cases"]

CORRECTING DATA

If you make an error before entering the data in a cell, you can press the Backspace key, click on the cancel box (the boxed *X*), or press the Escape key to correct it. Pressing Backspace erases one character at a time to the left of the insertion point; clicking on the cancel box or pressing the Escape key erases the entire entry.

To correct an item *after* it is entered into a cell, retype the item and enter it again. The new data replaces the old.

Let's correct some data before you enter them into the worksheet:

1. Select cell **A2**.

2. Type **boxs**. This word is misspelled.

3. Press the **Backspace** key to delete the "s," which is the character to the left of the insertion point. Now the text is "box."

4. Type **es** and hold down the **s** key. Note that several *s*'s appear in a row. Holding a key as you type repeats the keystroke.

5. Click on the **cancel box** (the boxed *X*) to clear the entire entry.

6. Type **boxes**. This is now correctly spelled.

7. Click on the **enter box** to enter the corrected item into the same cell.

FORMULAS

A formula is a set of instructions designed to perform a specific calculation (for example, multiply 5 by 100, or add 300 to 700). No matter how complex it may be, a formula generates a single value (in these cases, 500 or 1,000). You create a formula in Excel by preceding the desired calculation with the equal sign (=).

Formulas can be written using numbers (=300+700). However, it is more efficient to enter the numbers into cells and then to construct formulas which refer to those cells. In this way, the results of the formulas will be updated (recalculated) automatically when you change the numbers.

For example, if you entered 300 in cell B1, 700 in cell B2, and =B1+B2 in cell B3, the value 1000 (300 + 700) would appear in cell B3. If you then changed the values in cell B1 or B2, Excel would automatically recalculate the value of cell B3.

When building a formula, use

+ for addition

– for subtraction

* for multiplication

/ for division

Let's enter a few numbers into the worksheet:

1. Select cell **B1**.

2. Type **500**.

3. Click on the **enter box**. The number is entered and aligned to the right side of the cell. In Excel, numbers are automatically right-aligned and text left-aligned.

4. Select cell **B2**.

5. Type **100**.

6. Click on the **enter box** to enter the number into the cell.

Now let's enter a formula using numbers:

1. Select cell **B4**.

2. Type **500+100** (do not type any spaces) . Click on the **enter box**. Excel treats this entry as text, because it does not start with the = sign (as formulas must).

3. Type **=500+100** in the same cell. Click on the **enter box** to replace the contents of cell B4 with the correct data. The formula =500+100 is entered into the cell, and the result of the calculation (600) is displayed, as in Figure 2.2.

Figure 2.2   **Using formulas with numbers**

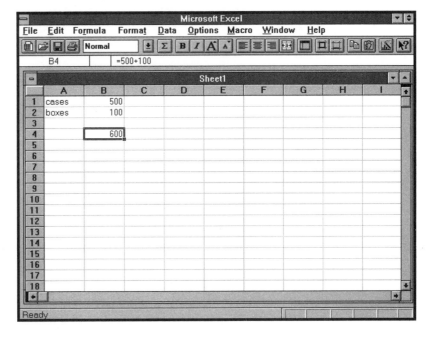

4. Select cell **B6**.

5. Type **=B1+B2**. Click on the **enter box** to add the values in cells B1 and B2 and display the sum in the active cell B6 (see Figure 2.3).

6. Select cell **B5**.

7. Observe the figures in the worksheet. Numbers (in cells B1 and B2) cannot be distinguished from the results of calculations (in cells B4 and B6).

8. Select cell **B2**. The formula bar contains a raw number or constant value. The value 100 is displayed in both the formula bar and the worksheet itself.

9. Select cell **B6**. The formula bar contains a formula (=B1+B2) and the worksheet displays the result (600).

Figure 2.3   **Examining a formula**

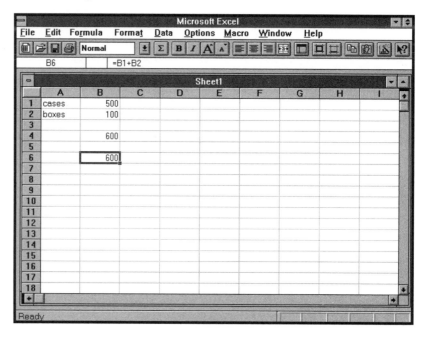

AUTOMATIC RECALCULATION

One of the chief advantages of an Excel worksheet over a conventional paper ledger sheet is Excel's ability to perform *automatic recalculation*. Whenever you change a number in an Excel worksheet, the value of every related cell in the worksheet (totals, averages, etc.) is automatically recalculated. Working with the same data that you just entered, follow these steps:

1. Observe the contents of cells B2, B4, and B6. B2 contains the number 100. Cells B4 and B6 contain the calculated result, 600.

2. Select cell **B2**.

3. Type **400**. Click on the **enter box** to replace the old cell contents (100) with the new cell contents (400).

4. Observe the contents of cells B4 and B6. Cell B4 still contains the result 600. Cell B6, however, now displays 900.

5. Select cell **B6**. The formula bar displays the formula =B1+B2, while the worksheet displays the result (900). When you changed the number in cell B2, Excel recalculated any formula that referred to the contents of that cell.

6. Select cell **B4**. The result is still 600 because its formula, =500+100, simply adds the values 500 and 100.

7. Select cell **B2**.

8. Type **250**. Click on the **enter box** to replace the current contents of the cell (400) with the new entry (250). Cell B4 still displays 600 (the result of 500+100). Cell B6, which adds the numbers in cells B1 and B2, has been updated to 750 to reflect the new number in cell B2 (see Figure 2.4).

Figure 2.4   **Cell B6 (750), automatically recalculated**

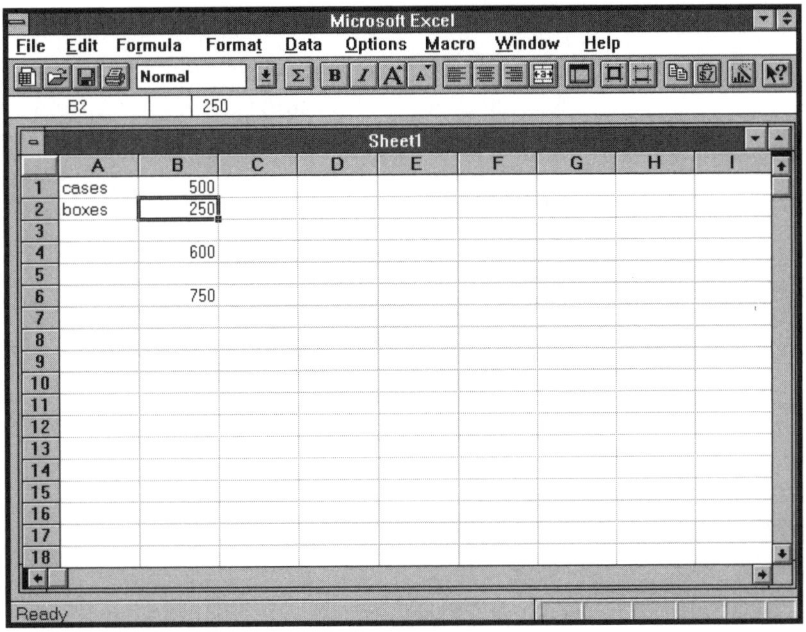

Use cell addresses in formulas (B1, B2, etc.) to create a *dynamic work-sheet:* a worksheet in which results automatically change whenever a cell referred to in a calculated formula is altered. Practice using formulas in a worksheet by completing and updating the worksheet:

1. Select cell **B7**.

2. Type **=B1-B2**. Click on the **enter box** to calculate the difference between the numbers in these two cells (250).

3. Select cell **B8**.

4. Type **=B1*B2**. Click on the **enter box** to calculate the product of numbers in the two cells (125000).

5. Select cell **B9**.

6. Type **=B1/B2**. Click on the **enter box** to divide the number in cell B1 by the number in cell B2 (2).

7. Select cell **B2**.

8. Type **750**. Click on the **enter box**. All cells that contain formulas referencing cell address B2 have been automatically recalculated (cells B6, B7, B8, and B9). The formula containing only values, entered in cell B4 (=500+100), remains unchanged (see Figure 2.5).

By default, numbers greater than 999 do not contain commas as separators (for instance, 1250 and 375000), negative numbers are preceded by a minus sign (-250), and as many decimals as will fit in the cell are displayed (.666667). As you will learn, default settings can be changed according to your needs (for example, 1,250, $375,000.00, ($250), .67).

SAVING AND CLOSING A WORKSHEET

After you complete a worksheet, you must *save* it to a disk for permanent storage. After saving the worksheet, you must *close* it to remove it from the screen. In order to accomplish these tasks, you need to learn some Excel menu basics.

WORKING WITH THE EXCEL MENU

The Excel menu allows you to execute tasks by choosing them from a "drop-down" list. The menu consists of a series of *submenus* which branch out from the Main menu, much like roots spread out from a plant. Some submenu items lead directly to an activity, while others branch into additional submenus. Choosing a submenu item that is followed by an ellipsis (...) opens a *dialog box*, in which you are offered another set of options.

Figure 2.5   **The completed worksheet**

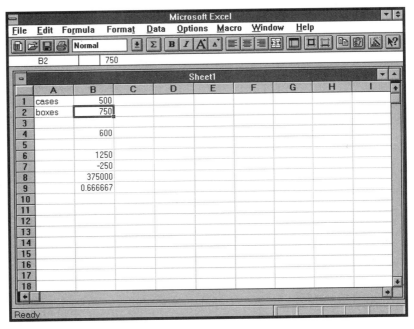

Use either of the following procedures to choose a menu item with the mouse:

- Position the mouse pointer on the desired item in the menu bar.

- Click the mouse button to drop the menu. It stays down even after you release the button.

- Position the mouse pointer on the desired submenu item.

- Click the mouse button to choose the item.

Or:

- Position the mouse pointer on the desired item in the menu bar.

- Drag (hold down the button while moving the mouse) to the desired submenu item.
- Release the mouse button.

 SAVING A WORKSHEET

Until it is saved, a worksheet exists only in computer memory, which is only a temporary storage place. When you turn the power off, computer memory empties and the worksheet is lost. For permanent storage, a worksheet must be saved to a file on a disk.

If you revise a worksheet, you must also save the revised version to a disk, or your revisions will be lost. For this reason, it is crucial to save files frequently, every 10 to 15 minutes. In the event that your computer ever shuts off accidentally due to a power outage or a pulled plug, the most recent revision of your on-screen worksheet will have been saved to disk—and you will lose only 10 to 15 minutes of work.

Save As...

The *File, Save As* command is used to save a worksheet for the first time. It is also used to save a revised worksheet under a different file name or to a different disk location.

To save a file using the Save As command,

- Choose File, Save As... from the menu to open the Save As dialog box.
- Type a file name in the *File Name text* box.
- Change the specified drive in the *Drives list box*, if necessary.
- Change the specified directory in the *Directories list box,* if necessary.
- Click on OK.

Before you save a file, you must give it a name. File names can contain from one to eight characters (letters, numbers, and some symbols), but cannot contain spaces. Name files descriptively to help you remember the file contents (SEPT91, MYACCTS, and so on). Excel automatically adds the extension .XLS to all worksheet file names.

Now follow these steps to save your worksheet as a file on your hard disk, using the Save As command:

1. Move the mouse pointer to **File** on the menu bar.

2. Click the mouse button to drop the File menu (see Figure 2.6). The File menu allows you to open, close, save, or print a document.

Figure 2.6   **Using the File menu**

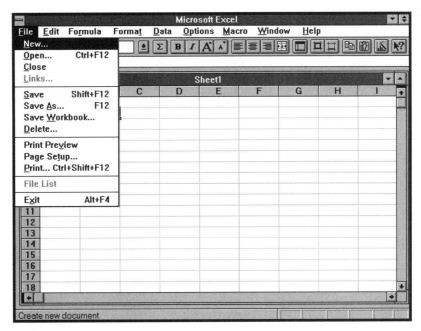

3. Position the mouse pointer on the **Save As...** option. An ellipsis (...) after a menu item indicates that this item, when chosen, will open up a dialog box.

4. Click the mouse button to open the Save As... dialog box. Observe that a dialog box is a smaller box within the larger frame of the current document. Move the mouse pointer outside the borders of the dialog box and click—the computer beeps, but nothing else happens. When you open a dialog box, you must complete all your work inside the box and then close it before returning to your document.

5. Note the highlighted file name, SHEET1.XLS, in the File Name text box at the top of the dialog box. This is Excel's standard name for a new file. You can choose to overwrite this with a more descriptive name.

6. Type **mysheet**. Note as you begin typing that your new file name replaces Excel's standard name. (Capitalization is ignored; Excel considers Mysheet to be the same as MySheet or MYSHEET.)

7. Observe the current directory under the highlighted file name. You must change this to your work directory. To do so:

   a. If the Drives list box does not show c: (or whatever drive you created your work directory on—d: or e:, for example), click on the **down arrow** to the right of the Drives list box, and then click on the correct drive.

   b. In the Directories list box, double-click on the **c:** directory icon.

   c. Locate the **ex4work** directory icon. (It may be necessary to scroll down through the list to see this; if so, place the mouse pointer on the **down scroll arrow** and click as many times as needed.)

   d. Place the mouse pointer over **ex4work** and double-click. The current directory should now read **c:\ex4work**, your work directory.

8. Click on **OK**. Excel saves a copy of the worksheet on your screen to the specified directory, EX4WORK, on your hard disk. The original worksheet remains on screen, which allows you to continue working on it. The title bar of the document window displays the new name, MYSHEET.XLS. Note that Excel has automatically assigned the extension .XLS to your worksheet.

Save

File, Save As is used to save a worksheet for the first time. *File, Save* is used to save this same worksheet on all subsequent occasions (unless you want to rename the file or save it to a new disk location). File, Save causes Excel to save the on-screen worksheet to the permanent file name and location that you assigned it to previously. No dialog box is displayed, since no additional filing information is needed.

To modify your worksheet and save it to disk using File, Save:

1. Select cell **A6**.

2. Type **total** to add identifying text to the worksheet.

3. Press **Enter** to enter the text into the cell. As mentioned earlier in this chapter, you can either click on the enter box or press the Enter key to enter data into a cell.

4. Move the mouse pointer to **File** in the menu bar.

5. Click the mouse button to drop the File menu.

6. Move the mouse pointer to the **Save** item.

7. Click the mouse button to update the file by saving it with the same name (MYSHEET.XLS) and location (your work directory, EX4WORK).

Be aware that using File, Save to save a file causes the on-screen worksheet to take the place of, and thus permanently erase, the previously saved version of the same worksheet.

In this case, your previous version of MYSHEET.XLS (the one without "total" in cell A6) was erased when you used File, Save to save the revised version of MYSHEET.XLS (the one with "total"). If you had wanted to preserve both versions, you could have used File, Save As... to save the revised worksheet under a different name (such as MYSHEET2.XLS), leaving the original version (MYSHEET.XLS) intact.

 CLOSING A WORKSHEET

Closing a file removes the document from memory and erases the document window from the screen. If only one file is open, closing that file leaves the Excel application window alone on the screen.

To close a file, choose *File, Close* from the menu. If you have changed the file since you last saved it, Excel will ask you whether or not you wish to save those changes. If you choose to save the changes, then Excel updates the current file without allowing you to change the file name and location. (If a new file has not been previously saved, Excel will prompt you to assign a file name and location.) Any files that you do not close remain in memory until you exit Excel or turn off your computer.

Follow these steps now to close your file:

1. Move the mouse pointer to **File** in the menu bar.

2. Click the mouse button to drop the File menu.

3. Point to **Close**.

4. Click the mouse button to close the file and the document window. Note that File and Help are the only items available in the menu bar. This stripped-down set of menu options is referred to as the *Null menu bar*, as shown in Figure 2.7.

Figure 2.7   **The Null menu bar (all documents closed)**

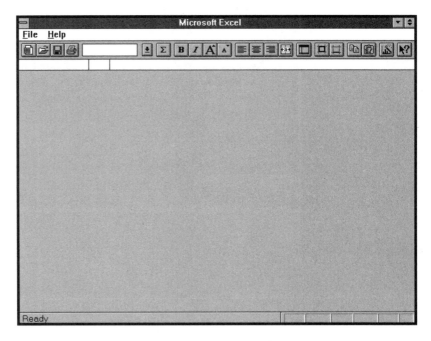

CREATING A NEW WORKSHEET

To create a new worksheet,

- Choose File, New... from the menu. The New dialog box appears.

- Select (click on) Worksheet.

- Click on OK.

Excel will create a new worksheet, assigning it the name "SheetN," where N is the number of new worksheets you have opened during the current work session ("Sheet1" will be assigned to the first new worksheet, "Sheet2" to the second, and so on).

Follow these steps to open a new worksheet:

1. Choose **File, New...** by clicking the mouse on **File**, and then clicking on **New**.

2. Select (click on) **Worksheet**, if it is not already selected.

3. Click on **OK** to open a new worksheet. Note that this worksheet is named "Sheet2," because it's the second new worksheet you opened during this work session. ("Sheet1" was opened automatically when you started Excel.)

Now let's create a worksheet that keeps track of the money collected for a breakfast-club fund (who paid and how much):

1. Select cell **B2**.

2. Type **Alice**. Enter the data (click on the **enter box** in the formula bar, or press the **Enter** key).

3. In cell **B3**, type **Sam**. Enter the data.

PRACTICE YOUR SKILLS

1. Using Figure 2.8 or the following list as a guide, complete the worksheet. The contents of the cells are

	B	C
2	Alice	1.25
3	Sam	3.75
4	Harry	2

2. Calculate the total money paid by Alice, Sam, and Harry in cell **C6** by creating a formula that uses cell addresses.

Figure 2.8   **The completed second worksheet**

```
┌──────────────────────────────────────────────────────────────┐
│ ─                    Microsoft Excel                    ▼ ▲   │
│ File  Edit  Formula  Format  Data  Options  Macro  Window  Help│
│ [▣][▨][▤][▤] Normal  [±][Σ][B][I][A][A] [≡][≡][≡][≡][□][□][□][▣][▣][▨][▨]│
│      C6            =C2+C3+C4                                   │
│ ┌──────────────────────── Sheet2 ─────────────────── ▼ ▲     │
│ │     A     B      C     D     E     F     G     H     I    ▲ │
│ │ 1                                                          │
│ │ 2       Alice   1.25                                       │
│ │ 3       Sam     3.75                                       │
│ │ 4       Harry     2                                        │
│ │ 5                                                          │
│ │ 6                 7                                        │
│ │ 7                                                          │
│ │ 8                                                          │
│ │ 9                                                          │
│ │10                                                          │
│ │11                                                          │
│ │12                                                          │
│ │13                                                          │
│ │14                                                          │
│ │15                                                          │
│ │16                                                          │
│ │17                                                          │
│ │18                                                        ▼ │
│ [←][ ]                                              [→]      │
│ Ready                                                        │
└──────────────────────────────────────────────────────────────┘
```

SAVING A NEW WORKSHEET

Now let's save your new worksheet:

1. Choose **File, Save As**.... Remember, the Save As... command is used to save a worksheet for the first time.

2. Type **myfund** to replace the current file name.

3. Click on **OK** to copy the worksheet in memory to a disk file named MYFUND.XLS.

USING THE KEYBOARD TO CHOOSE MENU COMMANDS

Up to now, we have used the mouse to choose commands from the Excel menu (for example, to choose the File, Save command, you clicked on File and then clicked on Save). You can also use the keyboard to choose menu commands, a very nice feature for those who prefer the keyboard to the mouse. To do this,

• Press the Alt key.

- Type the letter that is underlined in the menu-bar option of your choice (for example, you would type *f* or *F* to choose the File option).

- Type the letter that is underlined in the drop-down menu command of your choice (for example, you would type *s* or *S* to choose the Save).

Let's use the keyboard to close MYFUND.XLS:

1. Press **Alt**.

2. Type **f** to close the File menu option.

3. Type **c** to choose the Close command.

CHAPTER SUMMARY

In this chapter you've learned some fundamental procedures that you'll be using throughout this book, as well as in your day-to-day work with Excel. You've learned how to enter and correct text, numbers, and formulas in a worksheet. You know how to save a worksheet and clear the screen, as well as how to create a new worksheet.

Here is a quick reference guide to the Excel features introduced in this chapter:

Desired Result	How to Do It
Select a cell	Click mouse on cell, or use Arrow keys
Enter text in a cell	Type text. Click mouse on checkmarked **enter box**, or press **Enter**
Enter a formula in a cell	Type = and formula. Click mouse on checkmarked **enter box**, or press **Enter**
Erase a character from a cell	Press **Backspace** during entry
Repeat a character in a cell	Hold down key
Erase entire data entry from a cell	Click mouse on **cancel box**, or press **Escape** key
Drop a menu	Click mouse on menu entry

Desired Result	How to Do It
Choose a menu item	Click mouse on item
Save a file	Choose **File, Save As...** for new or renamed files. Choose **File, Save** to update current file
Close a file	Choose **File, Close**
Create a new worksheet	Choose **File, New**, select **Worksheet**, and click on **OK**
Choose a menu command using the keyboard	Press **Alt,** press underlined letter of desired menu option, press underlined letter of desired command

The next chapter delves deeper into the practical applications of Excel. You will examine worksheets for design and formula construction ideas and be given a chance to alter data and see the results. You will be introduced to such topics as retrieving a file from disk, new movement techniques, worksheet ranges, and the further joys of automatic recalculation.

IF YOU'RE STOPPING HERE

If you need to break off here to start a new program or to turn off your computer, please follow the steps listed in Chapter 1 under "Exiting Excel." If you want to proceed directly to the next chapter, please do so now.

CHAPTER 3: DOING "WHAT IF" ANALYSIS

In the last chapter, you learned the mechanics of creating, modifying, and saving an Excel worksheet. In this chapter, you will improve your worksheet skills while learning the basics of "what if" analysis, a powerful tool for data analysis and financial projection. Traditionally a difficult and time-consuming task, "what if" analysis becomes extremely simple in an Excel electronic worksheet environment.

When you're done working through this chapter, you will know

- How to open a file stored on disk
- How to perform "what if" analysis on your worksheet data
- New ways to move within a worksheet
- More about formula construction
- How to work with ranges
- How to use Excel's on-line Help feature
- How to clear (erase) cells
- How to undo a command

OPENING A FILE

Worksheets are stored as files on disk. Opening a file loads a *copy* of that file from the disk on which it is stored into the memory of your computer. The original file remains intact on disk.

In general, the procedure for opening a file is

- Choose *File, Open...* from the menu.
- If necessary, change the current drive in the Drives list box to the drive containing the file you wish to open.
- If necessary, change the current directory in the Directories list box to the directory containing the file you wish to open.
- Click once on the desired file to select it, then click on OK; or double-click on the desired file. Either of these methods will open the file.

Note: As a file is opening, a running percent count is displayed in the cell-reference area of the formula bar (when it reaches 100 percent, the entire file has been loaded into memory).

Let's open a file stored in your work directory. If you are not currently running Excel, please start it now; for help, see Chapter 1. If there is a worksheet on your screen (Sheet1, or any other), please close it using File, Close. Begin the next procedure with only the Excel application window on the screen:

1. Choose **File, Open...** (click the mouse on **File** to drop the File menu, then click on **Open...**). A dialog box appears. The *.xl*

entry in the File Name text box causes all the Excel files in your current directory to be listed. (An asterisk operates as a *wildcard* which stands for all possible combinations of file name characters.)

2. Note the current drive, displayed in the Drives list box. It is set to drive C, your hard disk. Since the file we are about to open is in your work directory (EX4WORK) on your hard disk, you do not have to change the Drives setting.

3. Note the current directory, displayed in the Directories list box. You must change the current directory to EX4WORK:

   a. Double-click on the **c:** at the top of the Directories box.

   b. Locate **ex4work** in the Directories box. It may be necessary to scroll down through the list.

   c. Double-click on **ex4work**. The current directory should now read c:\ex4work, your work directory (see Figure 3.1).

Figure 3.1   **The Open dialog box**

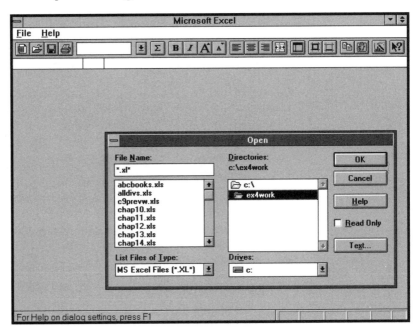

4. Scroll down through the Files list box until **loan.xls** appears.

5. Double-click on **loan.xls** to open the worksheet. (You can also open LOAN.XLS by clicking on it once to select it, then clicking on **OK**. Many people find double-clicking easier.)

Before proceeding, let's *maximize* both the application and document windows. In the upper-right corner of the application window (the window with the title bar Microsoft Excel), you will see a small square button. When this button contains an up arrow, it is called a *Maximize button*, which you use to maximize the size of the window. When the button contains an up and down arrow, it is called a *Restore button*, which you use to restore a maximized window to its original size.

1. If your application window displays a Maximize button (up arrow), click on this button to expand the window to fill the entire screen. If your application window displays a Restore button (up and down arrow), skip to the next step.

2. If your document window (the window entitled LOAN.XLS) displays a Maximize button (up arrow), click on this button to maximize the size of the document display. Note that two Restore buttons are now visible: one for your application window, and one for your document window (see Figure 3.2).

"WHAT IF" ANALYSIS

As you learned in Chapter 2, Excel automatically recalculates every dependent cell whenever you add or modify a numeric entry in a worksheet. You can immediately observe the impact of entering sample numerical values (as opposed to a paper ledger sheet, in which each new value calls for time-consuming manual recalculation and data re-entry).

The technique of modifying values to test the impact of the changes throughout the worksheet is called *"what if" analysis*. You use it to examine the outcomes for a set of sample values. ("What if I increased the retail markup rate by 10, 20, 35, or 50 percent? How would each of these increases affect our projected yearly profit?")

Let's perform some simple "what if" analysis on a loan-amortization worksheet:

1. Observe the worksheet on your screen. It shows a five-year loan-amortization schedule that calculates the monthly payment for a given principal, interest rate, and term, as well as the breakdown into interest and principal payments.

Figure 3.2 **Maximizing the application and document windows**

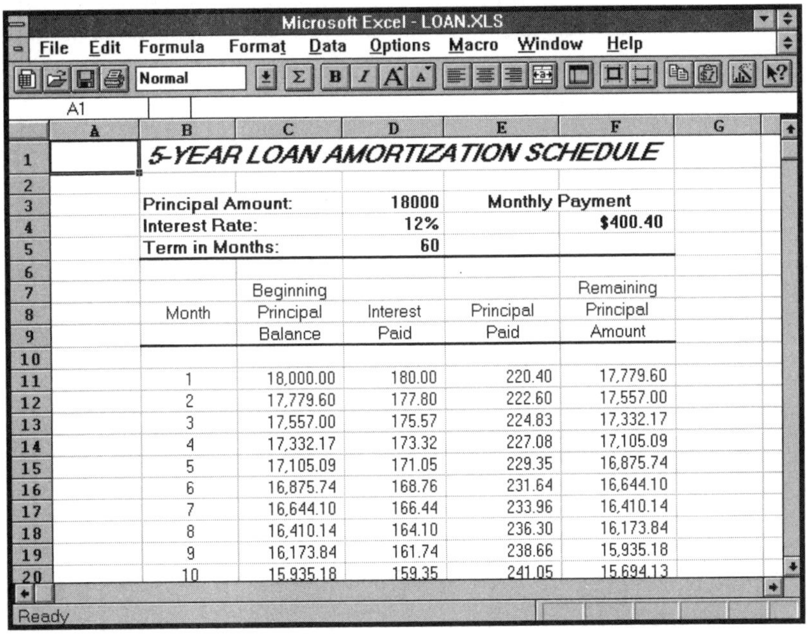

5-YEAR LOAN AMORTIZATION SCHEDULE					
Principal Amount:		18000	Monthly Payment		
Interest Rate:		12%		$400.40	
Term in Months:		60			
Month	Beginning Principal Balance	Interest Paid	Principal Paid	Remaining Principal Amount
1	18,000.00	180.00	220.40	17,779.60
2	17,779.60	177.80	222.60	17,557.00
3	17,557.00	175.57	224.83	17,332.17
4	17,332.17	173.32	227.08	17,105.09
5	17,105.09	171.05	229.35	16,875.74
6	16,875.74	168.76	231.64	16,644.10
7	16,644.10	166.44	233.96	16,410.14
8	16,410.14	164.10	236.30	16,173.84
9	16,173.84	161.74	238.66	15,935.18
10	15,935.18	159.35	241.05	15,694.13

2. Select cell **D3**. The current loan (principal) amount in cell D3 is $18,000 (displayed as 18000). Note the monthly payment of $400.40 in cell F4.

3. In cell D3, type **30000** (do not type $ or ,) to change the loan amount to $30,000. Enter this new value by clicking on the **enter box** or pressing **Enter**.

4. Observe the screen. Many cells contain formulas that depend upon the value in cell D3. When this value is changed, the results of the dependent formulas change as well. Note that the monthly payment has grown from $400.40 to $667.33.

5. In cell D4, type **9%** to change the interest rate for the loan. Enter the data. The new interest rate affects the monthly payment amount ($622.75), along with any other formulas that reference cell address D4. Writing formulas that reference

cells containing variable values effectively accomplishes "what if" analysis.

PRACTICE YOUR SKILLS

Change the principal amount and interest rate in cells D3 and D4. Continue until the monthly payment recalculates between $725.00 and $750.00.

NEW MOVEMENT TECHNIQUES

Given the potential size of an Excel worksheet (over four million cells), it is essential that you know how to move quickly and easily from cell to cell. Excel offers several convenient movement techniques, which are listed below in two groups: the first are for those who prefer to use the mouse, and the second for those who prefer the keyboard.

USING THE MOUSE

With the exception of the final entry (Formula, Goto), all of the following mouse techniques change the displayed area of the worksheet but do not actually select a cell. To select a cell, click the mouse on it. Refer to Figure 3.3 for help with mouse-scrolling terminology.

Technique	Action
Click on the up or down scroll arrow	Moves the screen up or down one row per click
Click on the left or right scroll arrow	Moves the screen left or right one column per click
Click and hold the mouse button on the up or down scroll arrow	Continuously moves the screen up or down one row
Click and hold the mouse button on the left or right scroll arrow	Continuously moves the screen left or right one column
Click within the vertical scroll bar between the vertical scroll box and the up or down scroll arrow	Moves up or down one screen per click

Figure 3.3   Mouse scrolling terminology

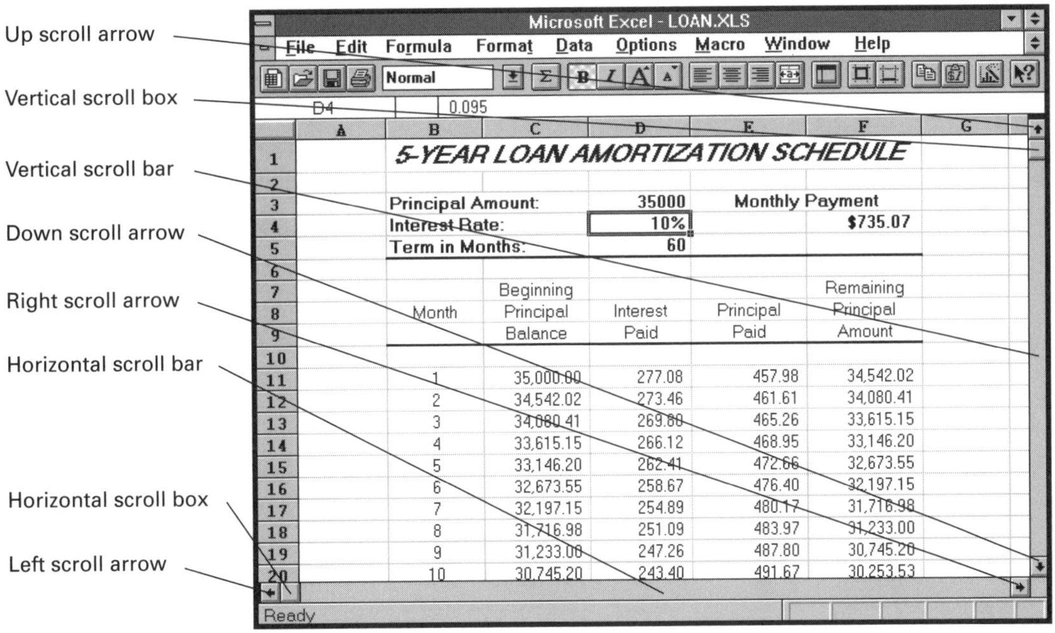

Up scroll arrow

Vertical scroll box

Vertical scroll bar

Down scroll arrow

Right scroll arrow

Horizontal scroll bar

Horizontal scroll box

Left scroll arrow

Technique	Action
Click within the horizontal scroll bar between the horizontal scroll box and the right or left scroll arrow	Moves right or left one screen per click
Drag the scroll boxes	Moves the screen a long distance, vertically or horizontally, through the active worksheet area
Hold the Shift key and drag the scroll box to either end of the scroll bars	Moves rapidly, vertically or horizontally, to the end or beginning of the worksheet
Choose Formula, Goto	Moves to and selects any cell address in the worksheet

Let's practice using the mouse to scroll through the worksheet.

1. Click on the **down scroll arrow** several times to move the worksheet down one row per click.

2. Drag the **vertical scroll box** halfway down the scroll bar (press and hold the mouse button as you move the mouse) to move rapidly to the middle of the worksheet.

3. Drag the **vertical scroll box** back to the top of the scroll bar to move rapidly to the top of the worksheet.

4. Click several times within the **vertical scroll bar** below the scroll box to move down one screen per click.

5. Drag the **vertical scroll box** down as far as it will go to move rapidly to the bottom of the worksheet. Short distances on the scroll bar represent long distances in the worksheet.

6. Drag the **vertical scroll box** to the top of the scroll bar to return to the top of the worksheet.

Note that the active cell does not change when you use any of the above scrolling techniques.

 USING KEYS

The mouse techniques you just learned change the worksheet display but do not change the selected cell. The following keyboard techniques, on the other hand, all select a new cell.

Technique	Action
Press the Left, Right, Up, or Down Arrow key	Moves one cell to the left, right, up, or down
Press Home	Moves to the first column (A) of the current row
Press Ctrl-Home	Moves to cell A1

Technique	Action
Press Ctrl-End	Moves to the intersection of the last active row and the last active column of the worksheet
Press the Page Up key	Moves up one screen
Press the Page Down key	Moves down one screen
Press F5 (*Goto key*)	Moves to any cell address in the worksheet

Now let's practice using the keyboard to navigate through the LOAN.XLS worksheet:

1. Press **Ctrl-End** (hold the Ctrl key down and press End) to move to cell F72, the last active cell of the worksheet.

2. Press **Ctrl-Home** to move to the *home cell*, A1.

3. Choose **Formula, Goto...** from the menu (or press **F5**) to open the Goto dialog box.

4. Type **D3** and click on **OK** to move to cell D3.

5. Choose **Formula, Goto...** (or press **F5**), type **iv16384**, and press **Enter** to move to the last available cell of the worksheet. Whenever a dialog box contains a highlighted (dark-outlined) OK box, you can choose this OK either by clicking on it or simply pressing Enter.

6. Press the **Down Arrow** key; then press the **Right Arrow** key. Note that you cannot move past cell IV16384.

7. Select cell **A1** (press **Ctrl-Home**).

Take a few moments to practice these mouse and keyboard movement techniques. When you are familiar with them, close the file.

1. Press **Alt** and type **f** to choose the menu-bar File option, and then type **c** to choose the Close command. A dialog box appears, showing the prompt:

   ```
   Save changes in 'LOAN.XLS'?
   ```

2. Observe the option buttons at the bottom of this dialog box (Yes, No, Cancel, and Help). Note that the "N" is underlined in the No button. You can choose a dialog-box button (like a menu command) by typing its underlined letter. Type **n** to choose "No" and close the file without saving the changes.

EXAMINING FORMULAS: ORDER OF OPERATIONS

The following formula involves more than one mathematical operation:

```
=B1+B2*B4-B5/B8
```

When creating or examining such a formula, you must know Excel's *order of operations*. Operations are not simply performed left to right through the length of a formula. Certain operations are performed before others. This is the order of operations, from first to last:

Parentheses Calculations enclosed in parentheses are performed first. Calculations in *nested* parentheses (parentheses within parentheses) are performed in order of nesting, deepest first. For example, in the formula

```
=(B1*(B2+B4))
```

B2 and B4 are added first (deepest nesting), then this sum is multiplied by B1.

Exponents Calculations involving exponential numbers are performed next.

Multiplication and Division These operations are performed next. Because they are considered equal in importance, they are performed in the order in which they are encountered (from left to right).

Addition and Subtraction These operations are performed last. They are also performed in the order in which they are encountered (from left to right).

Here's a mnemonic to help you remember the order of operations. **P**lease **E**xcuse **M**y **D**ear **A**unt **S**ally: **P**arentheses, **E**xponents, **M**ultiplication, **D**ivision, **A**ddition, **S**ubtraction (**PEMDAS**).

Let's take a look at a formula calling for several operations:

```
=B1*C5/100-(D6+J8)*J9
```

The order of calculation for this formula is

- Add D6 and J8, and hold the result

- Multiply B1 by C5, and hold the result

- Divide the product of step 2 by 100

- Multiply J9 by the sum of step 1

- Subtract the product of step 4 from the quotient (division result) of step 3

PRACTICE YOUR SKILLS

List the order of calculation for the following formula:

```
=(B1*C5)/((100-D6)+(J8*J9))
```

Note the use of nested parentheses to the right of the division sign (/). Remember that the calculations within the deepest nested parentheses are performed first.

Now let's examine some formulas from a typical worksheet:

1. Open the file named PRICES.XLS. (Choose **File, Open**; make sure that **c:\ex4work** is the current directory; scroll through the Files box to **prices.xls** and click on it; click on **OK**.) This worksheet is used by International Express, Ltd., to determine if their retail selling prices will attain the desired profit margin.

2. If the document window is not already maximized, maximize it now (click on the **Maximize button** in the upper-right corner of the document window). See Figure 3.4.

3. Select cell **C6**. This cell contains the cost of the bonnets.

4. Select cell **D6**. This cell contains the number of bonnets currently in inventory.

Figure 3.4   **The PRICES.XLS worksheet**

	Item	Our Item Cost	Number On Hand	Total Item Cost	Selling Price	Net Profit
6	Bonnets	2.78	26	72.28	3.50	18.72
7	Cases	14.00	350	4,900.00	15.50	525.00
8	Funnels	1.99	1,000	1,990.00	2.50	510.00
9	Paper	0.39	900	351.00	0.95	504.00
10	Reels	25.00	128	3,200.00	26.00	128.00
11	Slides	0.68	2,002	1,361.36	0.95	540.54
12	Tags	0.88	575	506.00	0.95	40.25
13	Trays	39.00	55	2,145.00	41.00	110.00

TOTAL COST: $14,525.64   TOTAL PROFIT AS A

TOTAL PROFIT: $2,376.51   % OF COST: 16%

5. Select cell **E6**. This cell contains a formula that calculates the total item cost by multiplying the bonnet cost in cell C6 by the number of bonnets on hand in cell D6. (To see this formula, observe the formula bar.)

6. Select cell **F6**. This cell contains the retail selling price to be charged for each bonnet.

7. Select cell **G6**. This cell contains a formula that calculates the net profit on bonnets by multiplying the number of bonnets on hand in cell D6 by their possible price in cell F6, and then subtracting the total bonnet cost in cell E6.

WORKING WITH RANGES

You will often want to work with a group of cells, rather than a single cell. For example, if you wanted to clear (erase) the contents of twenty cells, it would be much easier to select all these cells at once, then clear them as a group, rather than clearing each cell, one at a time.

A grouping of two or more contiguous cells (for example, cells A1, A2, B1, and B2) is called a range. Excel uses the format *UL:LR* to define a range, where *UL* stands for the upper-left corner cell and *LR* stands for the lower-right corner cell. For example, the range comprising cells A1, A2, B1, and B2 would be defined as A1:B2.

Let's examine some formulas that make use of ranges:

1. Select cell **D15**. This cell contains a special formula called a *function,* which calculates the total cost of all items by adding the values in the range E6 through E13 (E6:E13).

2. Select cell **D16**. This cell contains a function that calculates the total profit on all items by summing the values in the range G6 through G13.

3. Select cell **G16**. This cell calculates the profit as a percentage of the cost, based on the current retail prices in the range F6 through F13.

Now suppose you wanted to explore the relationship between retail selling price and profit for International Express, Ltd. Follow these steps to perform a "what if" analysis:

1. Note that the total profit (cell D16) is $2,376.51, and the total profit as a percent of cost (cell G16) is 16%.

2. Select cell **F6**. Enter **4.95** (type **4.95**, then press **Enter** or click on the **enter box**) to change the retail price from 3.50 to 4.95. The formulas in cells D16 and G16 have been recalculated:

   • Cell D16 is now $2,414.21

   • Cell G16 is now 17%

PRACTICE YOUR SKILLS

Change the retail selling prices listed for any items in cells F6 through F13. Continue until the total profit as a percent of cost (cell G16) is recalculated to between 33 percent and 35 percent.

SELECTING A RANGE

As mentioned, you will often need to work with a range of cells (A1:B2) rather than a single cell (A1). Use either of the following methods to select a range.

- Drag over the desired cells with the mouse.

- Click the mouse on one corner cell of the range and, while holding down the Shift key, click the diagonally opposite corner cell.

PRACTICE YOUR SKILLS

1. Use the dragging method to select the range A1:A7.

2. Use the click-Shift-click method to select the range A1:D7.

GETTING HELP

Excel provides an extensive on-line Help system that you can use any time you need to get help with Excel commands and dialog-box options. To get help,

- Press *F1* to display a *context-sensitive* Help window, a window containing information relevant to your current Excel activity.

- Click on the *Help tool* in the Standard toolbar. (This is the tool on the far right side of the Standard toolbar; it shows an arrow and a question mark.) The mouse pointer changes to an arrow and a question mark. Click on the Excel command or window element for which you would like help.

- Click on the *Help button* in a dialog box to get information on the options in that dialog box.

- To find pertinent information in a Help window, scroll through the window in the same way you scroll through any other Excel window.

- To close a Help window and return to your work exactly where you left off, choose File, Exit from the Help window menu bar. Do not choose this command from the application window menu bar, as this would cause you to exit Excel.

The next activity includes several hands-on examples of Excel's Help feature.

CLEARING (ERASING) CELLS

To clear, or erase, the contents of a single cell,

- Press Backspace.

- Press Enter.

To clear a range of cells,

- Select the range on the worksheet.

- Choose Edit, Clear from the menu (or press Del).

- Click on one of the four options (All, Formats, Formulas, or Notes). The default option is Formulas, which removes all entered data without affecting cell formats.

- Click on OK.

Let's clear a single cell in the worksheet:

1. Select cell **B1**.

2. Press **Backspace**, then press **Enter** to erase cell B1's contents.

Now let's select and clear a range of cells and, while doing this, use all available methods for getting help on the Clear command:

1. Point to cell **F6** (position the mouse pointer on cell F6).

2. Drag from cell **F6** to cell **F13** (press and hold the mouse button on F6, drag to cell F13, release the mouse button). The range F6 through F13 is now selected (highlighted) and is ready to be cleared. Before doing this, let's use the Help tool to get help on the Clear command.

3. Click on the **Help** tool (the tool in the far right of the Standard toolbar, it shows an arrow and a question mark). Note that the mouse pointer changes to an arrow and a question mark.

4. Click on **Edit** to display the Edit drop-down menu, and then click on **Clear**. A Help window entitled "Clear Command (Edit Window)" appears (see Figure 3.5).

5. From the Help window, choose **File, Exit** to return to your worksheet. (Remember to choose File, Exit from the Help window, not the Excel application window.) Note that your cell range is still selected.

6. Choose **Edit, Clear...** to open the Edit, Clear dialog box in preparation for clearing (deleting) these cells. Before actually clearing, let's use the two remaining methods for getting help on the Clear command.

7. Press **F1** (Help) to display a context-sensitive Help widow on the current Excel topic, the Clear command. A Help window

entitled "Clear Command (Edit Menu for Worksheets)" appears (see Figure 3.6). Note that this Help window differs from the Help window in Figure 3.5. The Help window in Figure 3.5 addresses the Clear command as it applies generally to worksheets, charts, and workbooks. The Help window in Figure 3.6 addresses the Clear command as it applies specifically to worksheets.

Figure 3.5   **Using the Help tool to get help on Clear**

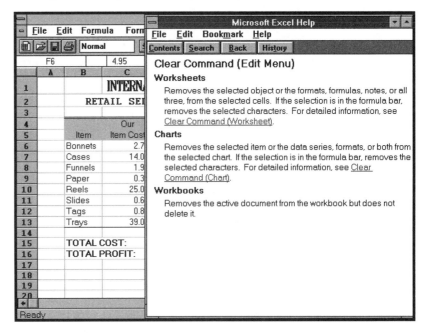

8. From the Help window, choose **File, Exit** to return to the Clear dialog box. Note that *Formulas* is the currently selected option. Let's use the Clear dialog box Help button to find out more about this option.

9. Click on **Help** in the Clear dialog box. A Help window entitled "Clear Command (Edit Menu for Worksheets)" appears; this is the same window that appeared when you pressed F1.

10. Scroll down through the Help window until you reach the heading "Formulas." The Help message reads: "Removes cell contents from selected cells without affecting formats or notes." This means that if you cleared a range of cells with the Formula option selected, any special formats or notes in these cells would *not* be deleted.

Figure 3.6   **Using F1 to get help on Clear**

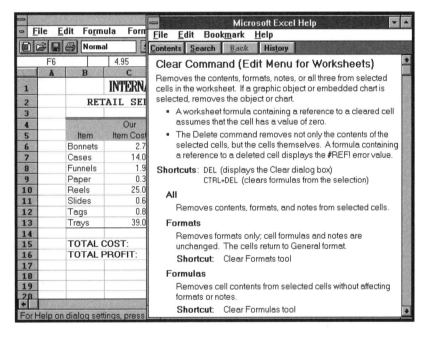

11. From the Help window, choose **File, Exit** to return to the Clear dialog box.

12. Click on **OK** to clear the specified range (F6:F13). As the numbers are deleted, formulas that refer to these cells are automatically recalculated. Note that the resulting negative values (losses) in the Net Profit column are enclosed in parentheses (see Figure 3.7).

Figure 3.7   **PRICES.XLS, after clearing F6:F13**

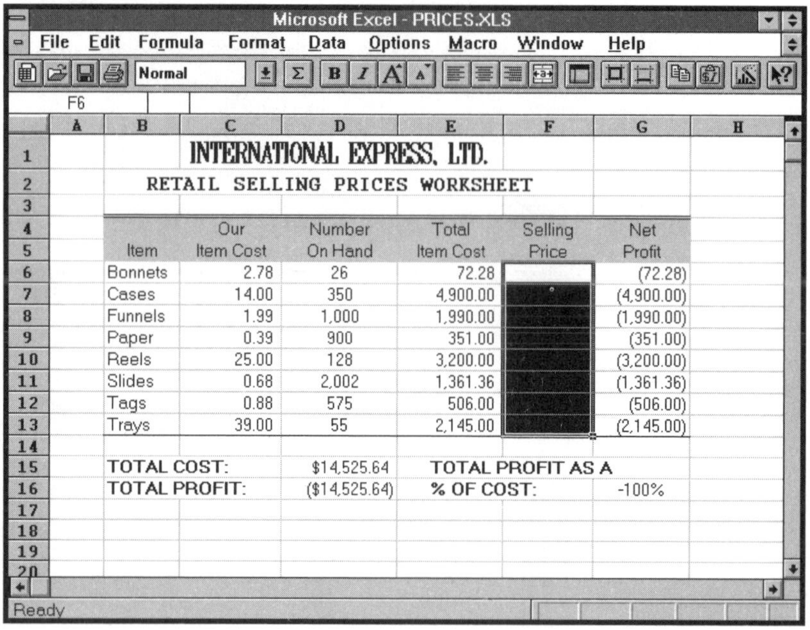

THE UNDO COMMAND

If you change your mind or make a mistake while editing a worksheet, you can—in most cases—choose the Edit, Undo command to reverse any changes you just made to the contents of a cell (for instance, entering $1,000 instead of $10,000). Undo can also reverse any command issued from the Edit menu. Other Excel commands may or may not be reversible with Undo (for example, saving a file is not reversible). If Undo cannot reverse the command you just issued, the screen will display the message "Can't Undo."

Remember, you can only undo the most recently issued command or the last cell entry you typed. For this reason, if you make a mistake, be sure to undo it immediately!

Let's undo your last command (clearing the range of cells in column F):

1. Click on any cell in the worksheet to *deselect* the range F6 through F13. A range does not have to remain selected in order to use Undo.

2. Choose **Edit**. Observe the uppermost item of the drop-down Edit menu: Undo Clear. Note that this item informs you of the command to be undone (Undo *Clear* instead of just Undo). Had Excel not been able to undo your most recent command, the Undo entry would have read "Can't Undo."

3. Choose **Undo Clear**. The worksheet is returned to its prior state.

4. Choose **Edit, Redo [u] Clear**. The cells are cleared once again. Excel allows you to redo a command immediately after you undo it. (Note: the **[u]** in this command indicates that you must type a "u" to issue the command from the keyboard.)

5. Choose **Edit, Undo Clear** to repeat the Undo command issued in step 3 (in other words, to undo the redo). The cell contents reappear.

PRACTICE YOUR SKILLS

1. Select and clear the range D6 through G13.

2. Undo the above clear command.

3. Close the file without saving the changes.

CHAPTER SUMMARY

In this chapter, you've learned the basics of "what if" analysis, a powerful projection and analysis tool. In addition, you've learned how to open a file stored on disk, how to navigate through a worksheet, how to use ranges in formulas, how to clear cells, how to undo a command, and how to get context-sensitive help.

Here is a quick reference guide to the Excel features introduced in this chapter:

Desired Result	How to Do It
Open a file	Choose **File, Open...**
Maximize a window	Click on **Maximize button** (up arrow)
Restore a window	Click on **Restore button** (up and down arrow)

Desired Result	How to Do It
Move screen up/down	Click on **up/down scroll arrows, vertical scroll bar**; drag **vertical scroll box**; or press **Page Up** key or **Page Down** key
Move screen left/right	Click on **left/right scroll arrows, horizontal scroll bar**; or drag **horizontal scroll box**
Move active cell up/down one row	Press **Up/Down Arrow** key
Move active cell left/right one column	Press **Left/Right Arrow** key
Move to a specific cell	Choose **Formula, Goto**; or press **F5**
Move to the home cell	Press **Ctrl-Home**
Move to the last active cell	Press **Ctrl-End**
Move to the first column of the current row	Press **Home**
Select a range	Drag over range; or click on corner cell, press and hold **Shift**, then click on diagonally opposite corner cell (click-Shift-click)
Clear a single cell	Press **Backspace**, then press **Enter**
Clear a range of cells	Choose **Edit, Clear**; or press **Del**
Get Help	Press **F1**, click on **Help tool** and choose the desired command on window element, or click on **Help** in dialog box
Undo the last command	Choose **Edit, Undo**
Redo the command you just undid	Choose **Edit, Redo**

The next chapter completes your training in the nuts-and-bolts mechanics of the Excel worksheet. You will learn the techniques used to develop more advanced formulas and larger, real-world worksheets.

IF YOU'RE STOPPING HERE

If you need to break off here, please exit from Excel. (For help, see "Exiting Excel" in Chapter 1.) If you want to proceed directly to the next chapter, please do so now.

CHAPTER 4: BASIC WORKSHEET DEVELOPMENT

Learning Some New
Data-Entry
Techniques

Using Functions

Copying Cell
Contents with the
Fill, Copy, and
Paste Commands

Up to now, you've learned to create and modify a simple worksheet and to perform elementary "what if" analysis on numerical data. In this chapter, you will learn the basic techniques used to develop a larger worksheet with more advanced formulas and real-world applications.

When you're done working through this chapter, you will know

- How to use new techniques for entering data

- How to use shorthand formulas called *functions*

- How to copy cell contents from one area of the worksheet to another

LEARNING SOME NEW DATA-ENTRY TECHNIQUES

In your day-to-day work with Excel, you will often need to fill a specific range of cells on your worksheet with data. Entering a list of names or several columns of numbers are typical examples. The process of typing data, entering it into a cell, using the mouse or Arrow keys to select the next cell, then repeating this procedure for each cell in your entry range is tedious and time-consuming. Luckily, Excel makes multiple-cell data entry quicker and easier by allowing you to select a range and limit the scope of your active cells to this range.

Within a selected range, use the following keys to change the position of the active cell:

- Pressing Enter (or clicking on the enter box) moves the active cell downward within the selected range. After you reach the bottom cell of a column, Excel activates the top cell of the next column to the right.

- Pressing Tab moves the active cell to the right within the selected range. After you reach the far right cell of a row, Excel activates the far left cell of the next row down.

- When the active cell reaches the lower-right corner of the selected range, pressing Enter or Tab moves the active cell back to the upper-left corner of the range.

- To move backwards within a selected range, press and hold the Shift key, then press Enter to move up or Tab to move to the left.

- Do not use the Arrow keys to activate a cell within a selected range, as this will cause the range to be deselected.

If you are not running Excel, please start it now. If there is a worksheet on your screen, please close it. Your screen should be empty except for a maximized Excel application window. (You learned how to maximize a window in Chapter 3.)

Now, let's see how multiple-cell data entry works by entering data within a selected range:

1. Click on the **Open File** tool (the second tool from the left in the toolbar, it shows a file folder being opened). This is equivalent to choosing File, Open from the Excel menu.

2. Open the file **SALES4.XLS** from your EX4WORK directory. This worksheet currently lists two salespeople and their quarterly sales figures. You will add two new salespeople.

3. If the document window is not already maximized, maximize it (click on the document window's Maximize button). Now press **Ctrl-F10** (hold down the **Ctrl** key and press **F10**). Note that the worksheet is restored to its original size. Press **Ctrl-F10** again. The worksheet is maximized. Ctrl-F10 is the keyboard method of maximizing or restoring an Excel worksheet.

4. Select cell **B7** if it is not already selected.

5. Hold the **Shift** key down and click on cell **F8**. As you learned in Chapter 3, the click-Shift-click method selects the range bound by the active cell and the cell you click on (in this example, B7 through F8).

6. Press **Enter** several times to activate the cell in the next row within the selection. Note that when the bottom cell is reached, pressing Enter activates the top cell of the next column.

7. Press **Tab** several times to activate the cell in the next column within the selection. Note that when the rightmost cell is reached, pressing Tab activates the leftmost cell of the next row.

8. Press **Tab** or **Enter**, as necessary, to select cell **B7**. Do not use the Arrow keys, as this would deselect the range B7:F8.

9. In cell B7, type **Stark**, a new salesperson. Press **Enter** to enter your text and automatically move to cell B8.

10. In cell B8, type **Unger**, another new salesperson. Press **Enter** to enter your text and move to cell C7.

PRACTICE YOUR SKILLS

Using Figure 4.1 or the table below as a guide, enter these numbers in the range C7 through F8:

	C	D	E	F
7	300	180	295	1100
8	220	195	185	1025

Figure 4.1   **The SALES4.XLS worksheet after initial data entry**

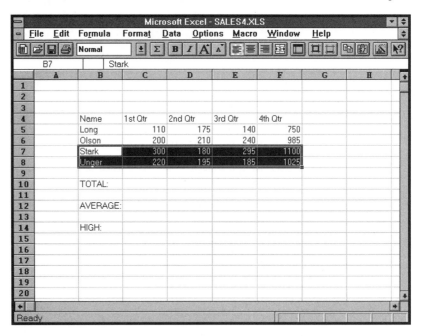

Note: Remember, within a selected range, Tab moves across rows, and Enter moves down columns.

USING FUNCTIONS

Excel 4.0 provides many standard formulas called *functions*, which you use to perform common calculations. These functions are divided into several types (logical, financial, mathematical, statistical, and so on). A function can be used by itself or in combination with other formulas or functions.

THE BASIC STRUCTURE OF A FUNCTION

Functions start with an equal sign (=) and generally have two components:

- The *function name* or an abbreviation of it

- The *argument*, which consists of required data enclosed in parentheses

Here are some examples of typical functions:

=SUM(A4:A10)	SUM is the function name; the range A4:A10 is the argument. This function instructs Excel to add all values in cells A4 through A10.
=AVERAGE(A4:A10)	AVERAGE is the function name; A4:A10 is the argument. This function instructs Excel to average all values in cells A4 through A10.
=MAX(A4:A10)	MAX is the function name; A4:A10 is the argument. This function instructs Excel to find the largest value in cells A4 through A10.

As with a formula, entering a function in a cell causes the numeric result of that function to be displayed. This result is automatically recalculated when the contents of a cell referenced in the function changes.

Let's enter some functions in the worksheet:

1. Select cell **C10**.

2. Enter **=SUM(C5:C8)** to add the designated range (cells C5 through C8, or 1st Qtr.). The cell will display the sum (830).

3. In cell C10, enter **=sum(c5:c8)**. The same result is displayed (830). You can enter functions and formulas in upper- or lowercase letters, whichever you prefer.

4. Select cell **C12**.

5. Enter **=AVERAGE(C5:C8)** The cell will display the average of the designated range (207.5).

PRACTICE YOUR SKILLS

1. Select cell **C14**.

2. Enter the **MAX** function to find the highest value within the range C5:C8 (300).

USING HELP TO EXPLORE AVAILABLE FUNCTIONS

As you learned in the previous chapter, you can get context-sensitive help any time you need it by pressing F1. Let's see how you can use the Help feature to explore an Excel function:

1. Press **F1** to display the main Help window. Note that Help has an index from which you can select the topic appropriate to the situation.

2. Select **Worksheet Functions**. (You will need to click several times on the Help window's **down scroll arrow** to bring Worksheet Functions to your screen. It is under the heading "Reference.")

3. Select **All Worksheet Function (alphabetical list)** to display an alphabetical list of all available worksheet functions.

4. Select **AVERAGE()**. Read through the Help message (see Figure 4.2).

5. Click on the Help window's **Maximize button** to maximize its size. Help windows, like application and document windows, can be maximized and restored.

6. Click on the Help window's **Restore button** to restore the Help window to its original location and size.

7. Press **Ctrl-F10**. Note that the Help window did not maximize. Ctrl-F10 maximizes and restores document windows (worksheets) only. Press **Esc** to deselect the menu-bar File option.

8. From the Help window, choose **File, Exit** to return to the worksheet. (Do not choose File, Exit from the application window or you will exit the program.)

Figure 4.2   **Excel's Help for the AVERAGE function**

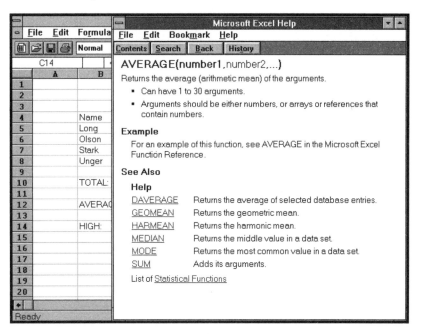

ENTERING A FUNCTION

Functions can be entered in several ways:

- Type the entire function directly into a cell.

- Type the function name with the left parenthesis, select the argument (cell range) with the mouse, then type the right parenthesis.

- Choose Formula, Paste Function to insert the function name with the parentheses, then complete the argument (cell range) by using the mouse or by typing.

Let's use the mouse to enter some function arguments:

1. Begin entering the SUM function by typing **=SUM(** in cell D10.

2. Using the mouse pointer, select the range **D5:D8**. Note the flashing *marquee* (dashed rectangle) around the selected range. Now look at the formula bar. The marqueed range has been automatically inserted into the function after the open parenthesis you typed.

3. Type) to complete the function. Note that the marquee disappears. Excel deselected the range D5:D8 because it was no longer needed for your function.

4. Enter the function. The second-quarter sum (760) is displayed in cell D10.

5. Type **=AVERAGE(** in cell D12.

6. Use the mouse to select the range **D5:D8**. In general, using the mouse allows you to select a range for a function more quickly and accurately than typing it.

7. Enter the function as-is (without the closing parenthesis). Note that the correct second-quarter average is displayed (190). Observe the formula bar. Excel was smart enough to add the closing parenthesis that you left out.

PRACTICE YOUR SKILLS

1. Select cell **D14**.

2. Enter the **MAX** function to find the highest value within the range D5:D8 (210).

USING THE PASTE FUNCTION COMMAND

Now, let's use Formula, Paste Function to insert a function into a formula:

1. Select cell **E10**.

2. Choose **Formula, Paste Function...** to display an alphabetical list of Excel's functions. Note that there are two list boxes in this dialog box. The Function Category box lists subsets of all available functions. The Paste Function box lists all functions specific to whatever Function Category subset is selected. By default, All is the selected subset, meaning that all of Excel's functions are displayed.

3. Type **s** to display function names that begin with the letter *S*. Typing the first letter of a function name is a shortcut to locating the function on the Paste Function list.

4. Select **SUM**. (You will need to scroll.)

5. Uncheck the box **Paste Arguments** so that the SUM function's arguments will not be displayed when the function is pasted into your formula.

6. Click on **OK**. Observe the formula bar. The selected formula, =SUM(), has been inserted. The insertion point is properly positioned within the parentheses, "waiting" for you to specify the argument (the range of cells to be summed).

7. Use the mouse pointer to select the range **E5** through **E8**. The argument E5:E8 is inserted into the function between the parentheses.

8. Enter the function to find the sum of the third quarter (860).

PRACTICE YOUR SKILLS

1. Select cell **E12** and paste the **AVERAGE** function. (Note that the Paste Arguments check box remains unchecked.)

2. Use the mouse pointer to insert the range **E5** through **E8** as the argument. Enter the function.

3. Select cell **E14**, and paste the **MAX** function. (Note that the Paste Arguments check box is still unchecked.)

4. Use the mouse pointer to insert the range **E5** through **E8** as the argument. Enter the function. Your worksheet should now match Figure 4.3.

COPYING CELL CONTENTS WITH THE FILL, COPY, AND PASTE COMMANDS

One of the most powerful and timesaving features of Excel is its ability to copy the contents of cells from one worksheet location to another. Three commands can achieve this: *Fill*, *Copy*, and *Paste*. Fill is used to reproduce data or functions within a selected range; Copy and Paste are used to reproduce them anywhere in the worksheet. Choose Fill (rather than Copy and Paste) as a shortcut to quickly reproduce an item in a range of adjacent cells (for example, to copy a SUM function to every cell in a totals row).

Figure 4.3   **SALES4.XLS with functions**

	A	B	C	D	E	F	G	H
1								
2								
3								
4		Name	1st Qtr	2nd Qtr	3rd Qtr	4th Qtr		
5		Long	110	175	140	750		
6		Olson	200	210	240	985		
7		Stark	300	180	295	1100		
8		Unger	220	195	185	1025		
9								
10		TOTAL:	830	760	860			
11								
12		AVERAGE:	207.5	190	215			
13								
14		HIGH:	300	210	295			
15								
16								
17								
18								
19								
20								

Microsoft Excel - SALES4.XLS

File   Edit   Formula   Format   Data   Options   Macro   Window   Help

Normal

E14   =MAX(E5:E8)

Ready

THE FILL COMMAND

The *Fill Right* and *Fill Down* commands copy the contents of cells from either the leftmost column or top row of a selected range into the remaining columns or rows of that range.

To copy cell contents using the Fill command,

- Select a range that includes *both* the cells you want to copy from *and* the cells you want to fill.

- Choose Edit, Fill Right to copy the contents of the cells in the leftmost column of a selected range into the remaining columns of that range.

- Choose Edit, Fill Down to copy the contents of the cells in the top row of a selected range into the remaining rows of that range.

- Pressing and holding down Shift when clicking on the Edit menu changes the Fill choices to *Fill Left* and *Fill Up*.

Let's use Fill Right to copy formulas within a range:

1. Select the range **E10** through **F10**. This range includes the cell you want to copy from (E10), as well as the cell you want to fill (F10).

2. Choose **Edit, Fill Right** to copy the formula from cell E10 to the right (cell F10).

ADJUSTMENT OF CELL REFERENCES DURING COPYING

When Excel copies a formula to a new location, it automatically adjusts any cell references within this formula, relative to the new location. For example, if the formula =SUM(A1:A7) were copied from cell A10 to cell B10, Excel would adjust the copied formula in B10 to read =SUM(B1:B7).

Cell references that change when copied are called *relative references*. Constant values—both numbers and text—do not change when copied to another location.

Let's look at how Excel adjusted the cell references in the Fill Right copying command that you just issued:

1. Select cell **E10**. Observe the formula =SUM(E5:E8) in the formula bar. The cell references in the argument range E5:E8 are relative references; they will change when copied.

2. Select cell **F10**. Observe the formula =SUM(F5:F8). Note that the argument references were automatically changed from E5:E8 (cell E10) to F5:F8 (cell F10). The original formula =SUM(E5:E8) was copied one column to the right, so Excel adjusted its references by adding one to the original column (column E plus one equals column F).

3. Select the range **E12:F14**. (Drag across the cells in the range, or use the click-Shift-click technique.)

4. Choose **Edit, Fill Right** to copy the formulas from column E to the selected column on the right (column F). Your worksheet should now match Figure 4.4.

Now let's practice using the Fill Down command:

1. Select cell **G4** and enter the column heading **Yr. Total**.

2. Select cell **G5**. Choose **Formula, Paste Function…** .

Figure 4.4   **SALES4.XLS, after filling right**

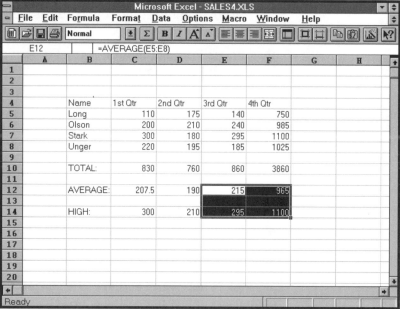

3. Paste the **SUM** function. (Scroll to display **SUM**, select it, then click on **OK** to paste it into the formula bar.)

4. Select the range **C5:F5** with the mouse. Note that this range is automatically inserted within the parentheses of the SUM function. Enter the function to complete the formula and insert it in the active cell (G5).

5. Select the range **G5:G8**.

6. Choose **Edit, Fill Down** to copy the function through the remainder of the range. Your worksheet should now match Figure 4.5.

 LONG TEXT

When dealing with longer text entries, such as headings and titles, Excel distinguishes between what a cell contains and what is actually displayed in that cell. Standard worksheet cells are approximately eight characters wide. Each cell can, however, contain up to 255 characters.

If the text is longer than the space allotted to a cell on screen, the extra characters will spill into the adjacent cell(s) to its right, providing these cell(s) are empty. If any cell does contain information, the text display will be truncated at its border.

Figure 4.5   **SALES4.XLS after using the Edit, Fill commands**

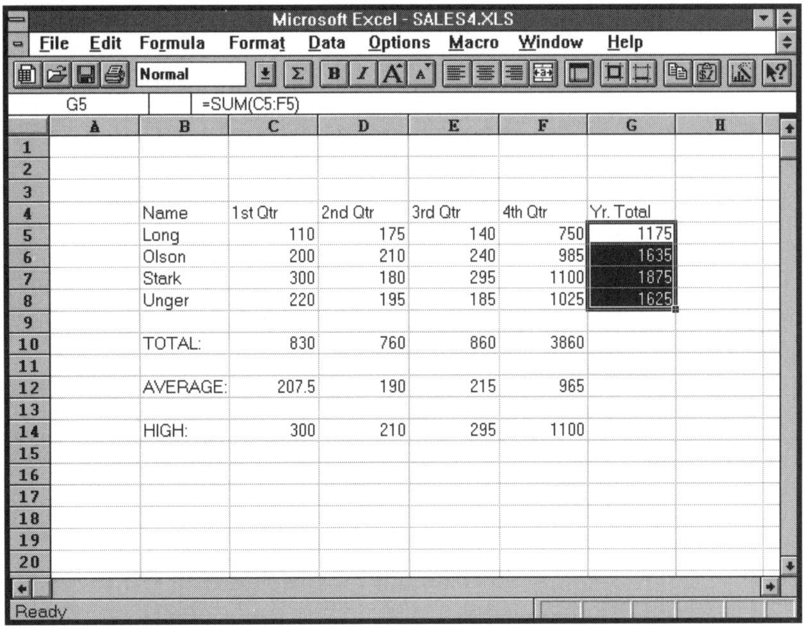

	A	B	C	D	E	F	G	H
		Name	1st Qtr	2nd Qtr	3rd Qtr	4th Qtr	Yr. Total	
		Long	110	175	140	750	1175	
		Olson	200	210	240	985	1635	
		Stark	300	180	295	1100	1875	
		Unger	220	195	185	1025	1625	
		TOTAL:	830	760	860	3860		
		AVERAGE:	207.5	190	215	965		
		HIGH:	300	210	295	1100		

G5 = =SUM(C5:F5)

Let's enter a title longer than the standard cell width:

1. Select cell **C2**.

2. Type **European Division** and enter the text. The text display spills over into the adjacent cell, D2.

3. Select cell **D2**. Note that the formula bar is empty.

4. Enter **5**. The text display is now truncated, because cell D2 is no longer empty.

5. Select cell **C2**. Note that the full text appears in the formula bar ("European Division"). Cell C2 contains the full text, even though it appears truncated on the screen.

6. Select cell **D2**.

7. Press **Backspace**, then press **Enter** to clear the number 5 from cell D2. The full text from cell C2 is once again displayed.

THE COPY AND PASTE COMMANDS

The Copy command enables you to duplicate the contents of one range of cells to another range. The general procedure for this technique is

- Select the range that you want to copy from
- Choose Edit, Copy
- Select the range that you want to copy to
- Choose Edit, Paste

After you issue an Edit, Copy command, Excel encloses the selected area with a marquee. As long as this marquee is displayed, you can paste the marqueed range to any number of locations. Remember, however, that pasting the marqueed range by pressing the Enter key will cause the marquee to disappear from the screen. Pressing the Esc key also clears the marquee.

Let's explore how to use the Copy and Paste commands:

1. Select cell **C18**. (You may need to scroll the worksheet.)

2. Enter **Australian Division**.

3. Select the range **B4:G4**.

4. Choose **Edit, Copy**. Note the marquee indicating that the enclosed data can be pasted to another location.

5. Observe the status bar message at the bottom of your screen:

    Select destination and press ENTER or choose Paste

    Excel is waiting for you to select a location to copy the cells to.

6. Select cell **B20**. Note that this is only a single cell. You need to specify only the first (upper-left corner) cell of the copy destination range.

7. Choose **Edit, Paste** to paste the marqueed range to the selected destination area.

8. Observe cell range **B4:G4**. As long as the marquee remains on screen, the marqueed range can be copied to additional locations. Note that the status-bar message remains active, reminding you that you can still copy. (Had you copied the marqueed range by pressing Enter in step 7 rather than

choosing Edit, Paste, both the marquee and the message would have been cleared from the screen.)

9. Press the **Esc** key to clear the marquee and message. Your worksheet should now match Figure 4.6.

Figure 4.6 **SALES4.XLS, after using Copy and Paste**

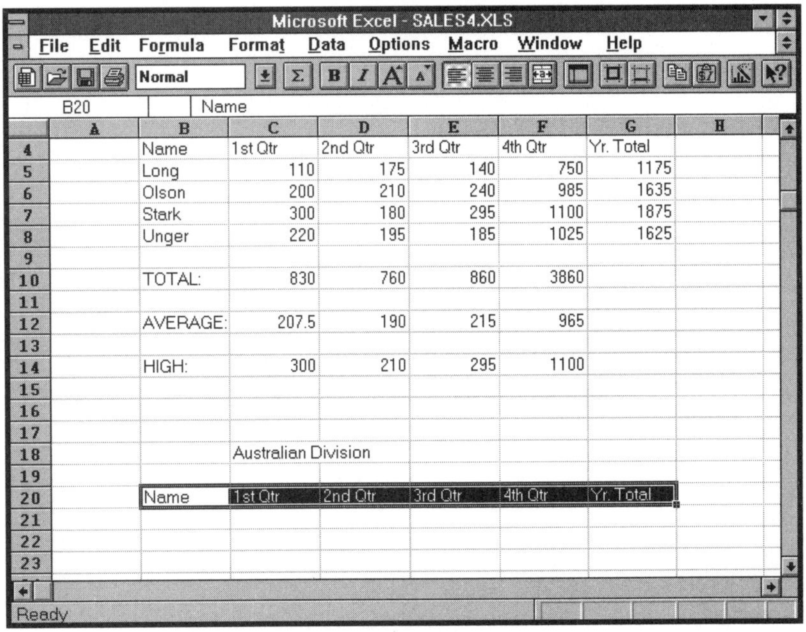

10. Save this worksheet as MYSALES. (Choose **File, Save As...**, type **mysales**, make sure the current drive/directory is **c:\ex4-work**, then click on **OK**.)

11. Close the file.

PRACTICE YOUR SKILLS

You've learned a great deal in the first four chapters of this book: how to create, modify, save, and open an Excel worksheet; how to move around within a worksheet; how to build a formula, select a range, and paste a function; how to perform "what if" analysis;

how to copy and paste a range of cells. The following activity is designed to increase your fluency with these techniques.

Other "Practice Your Skills" activities will appear at key points throughout the course of this book. Please don't think of these activities as tests, but rather as opportunities to hone your Excel skills. Only through repetition will you internalize the techniques you've learned. In case you need help, you'll find the relevant chapter numbers in parentheses after each activity step.

In the following activity, you will edit the worksheet file PRU4.XLS to match Figure 4.7.

Figure 4.7   **The completed worksheet MYPRU4.XLS**

	A	B	C	D	E	F	G	H	I
1			EXMAC CORPORATION						
2			Regional Sales Data						
3			(Current Year)						
4									
5		PERIOD 1	PERIOD 2	PERIOD 3	PERIOD 4	YR TOTALS			
6	Atlanta	22345	25663	24100	25666	97774			
7	Rochester	12567	13444	14536	15328	55875			
8	Boston	34622	35332	36411	37621	143986			
9	New York	32886	36731	37614	39954	147185			
10	Chicago	45321	40120	43987	45354	174782			
11	Denver	23114	24117	25119	26432	98782			
12	San Diego	23176	20432	24776	26998	95382			
13	Seattle	19887	18334	17338	16333	71892			
14									
15	Totals:	213918	214173	223881	233686	885658			
16	Averages:	26739.75	26771.625	27985.125	29210.75	110707.25			
17									
18									
19									
20									

1. Open **PRU4.XLS** (Chapter 3).

2. Maximize the document window, if it is not already maximized (Chapter 3).

3. In cell **F6**, enter a function to sum the range **B6:E6** (Chapter 4).

4. Duplicate the formula in cell **F6** into the range **F7:F13** (Chapter 4).

5. In cell **B15**, enter a function to sum the range **B6:B13** (Chapter 4).

6. Duplicate the formula in cell **B15** into the range **C15:F15** (Chapter 4).

7. In cell **B16**, paste in a function to average all cities for Period 1 (Chapter 4).

8. Duplicate the formula in cell **B16** into the range **C16:F16** (Chapter 4).

9. Compare your worksheet to Figure 4.7.

10. Save your file as **MYPRU4.XLS** in your EX4WORK directory (Chapter 2).

11. Close the file (Chapter 2).

The following activity is designed to further increase your Excel fluency. Perform these steps to edit the worksheet file OPT4.XLS to match Figure 4.8.

Figure 4.8   **The completed worksheet MYOPT4.XLS**

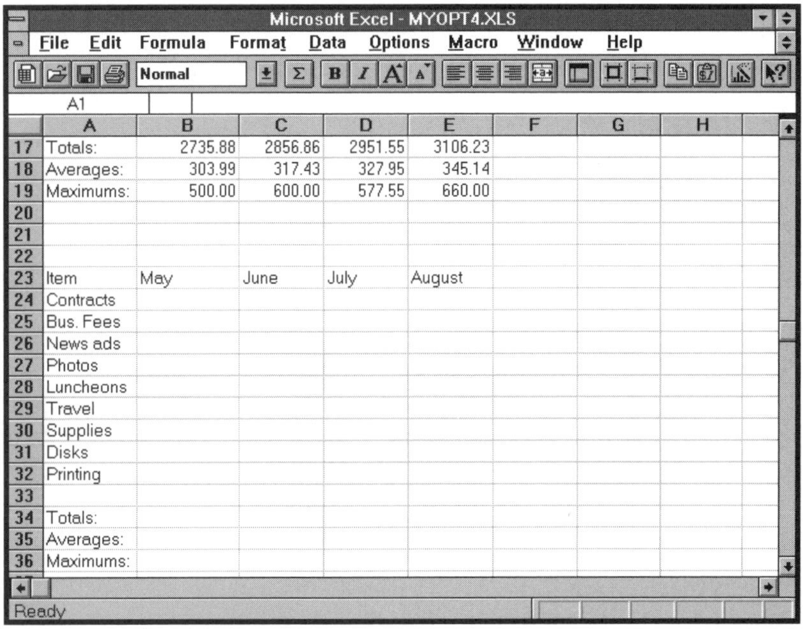

1. Open **OPT4.XLS** (Chapter 3).

2. Maximize the document window, if necessary (Chapter 3).

3. Clear the range **F7:F15** (Chapter 3).

4. In cells **B17**, **B18**, and **B19**, enter functions to determine the total, average, and highest values in the Jan. column (Chapter 4).

5. Duplicate the formulas in the range B17:B19 so that they apply to the remaining three columns, February through April (Chapter 4).

6. Copy the range **A6:A19** (Chapter 4).

7. Paste the copied range into cell **A23** (Chapter 4).

8. Enter the following text (Chapter 4):

In cell B23	**May**
In cell C23	**June**
In cell D23	**July**
In cell E23	**August**

9. Compare your worksheet to Figure 4.8. (You will have to scroll your worksheet to match the figure.)

10. Save your file as **MYOPT4.XLS** in your EX4WORK directory (Chapter 2).

11. Close the file (Chapter 2).

CHAPTER SUMMARY

In this chapter, you've learned the basics of creating a larger, more involved worksheet. You've explored new data-entry techniques; Excel functions; and the Fill, Copy, and Paste commands. Your knowledge of basic Excel skills will prove to be a strong foundation for the following chapters.

Here is a quick reference guide to the Excel features introduced in this chapter:

Desired Result	How to Do It
Move active cell right or left within a selected range	Press **Tab** (right), or press **Shift-Tab** (left)
Move active cell down or up within a selected range	Press **Enter** (down), click on **enter box** (down); or press **Shift-Enter** (up)
Maximize/restore the document window	Click on **Maximize/Restore buttons** or press **Ctrl-F10**
Enter a function	Type entire function; or type function name, type (, select argument, then type); or choose **Formula, Paste Function...** to paste function name, complete with (), then select argument
Enter a function argument range	Type range, or use mouse to select range
Sum a range	Use **SUM** function
Average a range	Use **AVERAGE** function
Find the maximum within a range	Use **MAX** function
Fill selected columns to the right or left	Choose **Edit, Fill Right**; or hold down **Shift** key, then choose **Edit, Fill Left**
Fill selected rows down or up	Choose **Edit, Fill Down**; or hold down **Shift** key, then choose **Edit, Fill Up**
Copy a cell(s)	Select cell(s) to copy from, choose **Edit, Copy**, select cell(s) to copy to, choose **Edit, Paste** (for additional copying) or press **Enter** (no additional copying)

The next chapter concentrates on advanced techniques that you can use to enhance the structure and appearance of your Excel worksheets. In addition, you'll learn more about formulas and cell editing.

IF YOU'RE STOPPING HERE

If you need to break off here, please exit from Excel. If you want to proceed directly to the next chapter, please do so now.

CHAPTER 5:
EDITING AND
FORMATTING YOUR
WORKSHEETS

Editing a Cell

Absolute References

Inserting and Deleting Cells, Columns, and Rows

Using Cut and Paste to Move a Range of Cells

Formatting

Copying Specific Attributes of a Cell

A properly formatted, smoothly laid-out worksheet is not only attractive to the eye, but vital for an accurate portrayal of your data. This chapter teaches you how to *format* a worksheet: how to customize the appearance of its cell contents and page layout to your individual needs. You'll also learn how to edit a cell (change its contents without having to retype the entire entry) and how to create more sophisticated formulas.

When you're done working through this chapter, you will know

- How to edit the contents of a cell
- How to use absolute, rather than relative, cell references in formulas
- How to insert and delete cells, columns, and rows
- How to use the Cut and Paste commands to move data within the worksheet
- How to change the format of worksheet numbers and text
- How to use the Paste Special command to copy specific attributes of cells (formulas, values, formats, etc.)

A special note for this chapter: As mentioned in the Introduction, we recommend that you allot enough time to work through a chapter without interruption. However, because this chapter is so long, you may want to split it into two work sessions. About halfway through (immediately before the section entitled "Formatting"), a note has been added instructing you how to do this.

EDITING A CELL

Excel's *editing* feature allows you to change the contents of a cell without retyping the entire entry. Editing is particularly useful for longer entries. For example, if you wanted to change a single cell reference in the middle of a long, involved formula, you could simply edit this reference instead of retyping the entire formula.

You can edit a cell by using either the mouse or the *Edit* key (F2) in conjunction with the arrow keys.

USING THE EDIT KEY TO EDIT A CELL

To edit using F2 and the arrow keys,

- Select the cell you wish to edit.
- Press the Edit key (F2).
- Use the Left or Right Arrow keys to position the insertion point (flashing vertical line) at the desired location.
- Press Backspace or Delete (Del) to erase any undesired text.

- Type any corrections or insertions.

- Enter the revised data.

If you are not running Excel, please start it now. If there is a work-sheet on your screen, please close it. Your screen should be empty except for a maximized Excel application window.

Now let's use the Edit key to alter some text in a worksheet cell:

1. Open the file **SALES5.XLS** (remember to select your EX4WORK directory).

2. Maximize the document window, if necessary. (Use the mouse, or press **Ctrl-F10**.) Your screen should now match Figure 5.1.

Figure 5.1   **The maximized SALES5.XLS worksheet**

Microsoft Excel - SALES5.XLS

File   Edit   Formula   Format   Data   Options   Macro   Window   Help

Normal

A1

	A	B	C	D	E	F	G	H
1			Eurpeanes Sales				Comm Rate	0.15
2								
3		Name	1st Qtr	2nd Qtr	3rd Qtr	4th Qtr	Totals	Commissions
4		Long	110	175	140	750	1175	
5		Olson	200	210	240	985	1635	
6		Stark	300	180	295	1100	1875	
7		Unger	220	195	185	1025	1625	
8								
9		TOTALS:	830	760	860	3860	6310	
10								
11		AVERAGES:	207.5	190	215	965	1577.5	
12								
13		HIGH:	300	210	295	1100	1875	
14			Australian Division					
15								
16		Name	1st Qtr	2nd Qtr	3rd Qtr	4th Qtr	Totals	Commissions
17		Kraft	305.5	195	203	232	935.5	
18		Oakes	219	147	136.7	205	707.7	
19		Rider	104	230	185	245.1	764.1	
20		Sweet	125.2	99.5	206	201	631.7	
21		Wilson	320	255	235	145	955	

Ready

3. Select cell **C1**.

4. Press **F2** (for Edit). Note that the insertion point (flashing verti-cal line) is positioned at the end of the contents in the formula

bar. The word "Eurpeanes" in the formula bar is incorrect; it should be "European."

5. Press the **Left Arrow** key several times to position the insertion point between the "r" and the "p" of "Eurpeanes."

6. Type **o** to insert an *o* between the "r" and "p".

7. Enter the partially corrected text in cell C1. The cell now reads "Europeanes Sales."

USING THE MOUSE TO EDIT A CELL

To edit using the mouse,

• Select the cell you wish to edit.

• Move the mouse pointer over the cell contents in the formula bar (the pointer becomes an *I-beam*).

• Position this I-beam at the point where you want to make an insertion or deletion.

• Revise the data, using one of the following techniques:

  • To *insert* data, click the mouse to create an insertion point. Type the new data. Characters will be inserted to the left of the insertion point as you type them.

  • To *delete* data, drag the I-beam to select the data you wish to delete. Press Delete (Del) to erase the selection.

  • To *overwrite* data, drag the I-beam to select the data you wish to overwrite (replace). Type the new data. Excel replaces the selection with the new data.

Note: To select an entire word for deletion or overwriting, simply position the I-beam on the word and double-click.

Let's use the mouse to finish editing cell C1:

1. Select cell **C1**, if necessary.

2. Move the mouse pointer to the formula bar. Position the I-beam anywhere within the word "Sales."

3. Double-click to select the entire word. Note that the highlight extends to the end of the formula bar.

4. Type **Division** to replace the selected text with the revised text.

5. Drag the I-beam across the final **es** of "Europeanes."

6. Press **Delete** (**Del**) to erase these two letters.

7. Enter the revised text in cell C1. Note that the cell now reads "European Division" (see Figure 5.2).

Figure 5.2   **SALES5.XLS, worksheet after editing cell C1**

	A	B	C	D	E	F	G	H
			European Division					
1			European Division				Comm Rate	0.15
2								
3		Name	1st Qtr	2nd Qtr	3rd Qtr	4th Qtr	Totals	Commissions
4		Long	110	175	140	750	1175	
5		Olson	200	210	240	985	1635	
6		Stark	300	180	295	1100	1875	
7		Unger	220	195	185	1025	1625	
8								
9		TOTALS:	830	760	860	3860	6310	
10								
11		AVERAGES:	207.5	190	215	965	1577.5	
12								
13		HIGH:	300	210	295	1100	1875	
14			Australian Division					
15								
16		Name	1st Qtr	2nd Qtr	3rd Qtr	4th Qtr	Totals	Commissions
17		Kraft	305.5	195	203	232	935.5	
18		Oakes	219	147	136.7	205	707.7	
19		Rider	104	230	185	245.1	764.1	
20		Sweet	125.2	99.5	206	201	631.7	
21		Wilson	320	255	235	145	955	

ABSOLUTE REFERENCES

As you learned in Chapter 4, when you copy a cell containing a formula, Excel automatically adjusts the cell references relative to the formula's new location (for example, the formula =A1+A2 copied one column to the right becomes =B1+B2). There are times, however, when you will want to copy a formula *without* having all of its references adjusted.

Let's look at a situation in which reference adjustment is not desirable:

1. Select cell **H4**.

2. Enter the formula **=G4*H1** (commission rate multiplied by total sales) to calculate the sales commission for salesperson Long (176.25).

3. Select the range **H4:H7**.

4. Choose **Edit, Fill Down** to copy the formula in cell H4 to cells H5, H6, and H7. Note the erroneous results in these cells.

5. Examine the formulas in cells H4, H5, H6, and H7.

When the original formula in cell H4 was copied, its references were changed relative to their new locations: the reference "H1" in the original formula changed to "H2" in cell H5, "H3" in cell H6, and "H4" in cell H7. In this example, however, the commission rate—a fixed value used by all the copied formulas—resides *only* in cell H1. We need all references to cell H1 to remain the same.

To prevent a cell reference from being adjusted when you copy the formula containing it, you must create an *absolute*, rather than a relative, reference. To create an absolute cell reference, simply insert a dollar sign ($) before both the column and row of the reference (for example, F22 is relative and $F$22 is absolute). To prevent either the column or the row (but not both) of a cell reference from being adjusted, you must create a *mixed reference* ($F22 or F$22). Study the following examples to understand what happens when relative, absolute, and mixed references are copied:

Type	Reference	Copied One Row Down and One Column to the Right
Relative	A1	B2
Absolute	$A$1	$A$1
Mixed	A$1	B$1
Mixed	$A1	$A2

ABSOLUTE REFERENCING WITH THE FILL COMMAND

Let's redo the last copy operation using absolute referencing:

1. Select cell **H4**. The formula in this cell must be modified to prevent errors from occurring when you copy it.

2. Press **F2** (for Edit) to begin editing.

3. Press the **Left Arrow** key twice to move the insertion point to the left of the *H* of cell reference "H1."

4. Type **$** to insert a $ character before the *H*.

5. Press the **Right Arrow** key to move the insertion point between the *H* and *1* of "H1."

6. Type **$**. The cell reference should now read $H$1. This is an absolute reference.

7. Enter the revised formula.

8. Select the range **H4:H7**.

9. Choose **Edit, Fill Down**. Note the correct results (see Figure 5.3). Because you fixed the reference to the commission rate cell as an absolute ($H$1), it did not change when copied.

Figure 5.3   **SALES5.XLS, with absolute references**

	Microsoft Excel - SALES5.XLS							
File	Edit	Formula	Format	Data	Options	Macro	Window	Help

H4   =G4*$H$1

	A	B	C	D	E	F	G	H	
1			European Division				Comm Rate	0.15	
2									
3		Name	1st Qtr	2nd Qtr	3rd Qtr	4th Qtr	Totals	Commissions	
4		Long	110	175	140	750	1175	176.25	
5		Olson	200	210	240	985	1635	245.25	
6		Stark	300	180	295	1100	1875	281.25	
7		Unger	220	195	185	1025	1625	243.75	
8									
9		TOTALS:	830	760	860	3860	6310		
10									
11		AVERAGES:	207.5	190	215	965	1577.5		
12									
13		HIGH:	300	210	295	1100	1875		
14			Australian Division						
15									
16		Name	1st Qtr	2nd Qtr	3rd Qtr	4th Qtr	Totals	Commissions	
17		Kraft	305.5	195	203	232	935.5		
18		Oakes	219	147	136.7	205	707.7		
19		Rider	104	230	185	245.1	764.1		
20		Sweet	125.2	99.5	206	201	631.7		
21		Wilson	320	255	235	145	955		

Ready

10. Select cell **H4**. The formula reads =G4*$H$1.

11. Select cell H5. The formula reads =G5*$H$1. When you copied the formula from cell H4, the reference to G4 was automatically updated to "G5." However, the absolute reference "$H$1" remained the same.

12. Examine cells H6 and H7. Note the changes analogous to those in cell H5.

ABSOLUTE REFERENCING WITH THE COPY COMMAND

Now let's learn to copy an absolute reference using the Copy, instead of the Fill, command (Fill is used to copy within a selected range; Copy is used to copy anywhere on the worksheet):

1. Select cell **H4**.

2. Choose **Edit, Copy**.

3. Select the range **H17:H21**.

4. Choose **Edit, Paste** to copy the formula from cell H4 to the range H17:H21.

5. Examine the contents of cells H17:H21. The formulas all correctly refer to the commission rate in cell H1 ($H$1).

Finally, let's save this revised SALES5.XLS worksheet under a new file name:

1. Choose **File, Save As...** to begin the procedure of saving under a new file name. Had you wanted to save the revised worksheet under the same name (SALES5.XLS), you would have chosen File, Save. However, this would have erased the previous version of SALES5.XLS (the one you opened at the beginning of this chapter) and replaced it with your current, revised version. Remember to use Save *only* when you can afford to lose the previous version of the worksheet you are saving.

2. Check to make sure your **EX4WORK** directory is selected.

3. Type **mysales** in the Save Worksheet box. Click on **OK**. The *alert box* shown in Figure 5.4 appears, informing you that a file named MYSALES.XLS already exists in your work directory. (You created it in Chapter 4.) Saving the worksheet currently on screen as MYSALES.XLS will replace (erase) the previous version of MYSALES.XLS. Since we do not need the old MYSALES.XLS, it is okay to do this.

Figure 5.4   **The Replace Existing File alert box**

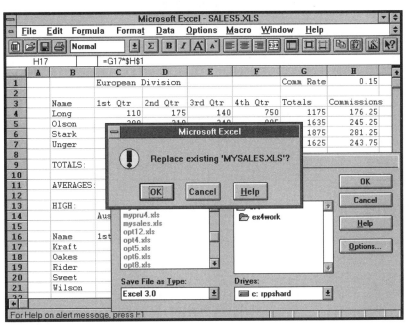

4. Click on **OK** to replace the old MYSALES.XLS with your new (on-screen) version.

A word of caution: Replacing a file *permanently* erases it from your disk. Do not, therefore, replace a file if you want to keep a disk copy (rather than only a paper copy) of it. To preserve different versions of the same worksheet, you would use File, Save As to save them under slightly different names (MYSALES1.XLS, MYSALES2.XLS, etc.).

INSERTING AND DELETING CELLS, COLUMNS, AND ROWS

Inserting or deleting a cell, column, or row in a paper spreadsheet can be a formidable task. Large chunks of data may have to be erased and re-entered, and the overall page layout may have to be changed. Excel simplifies the tasks of insertion and deletion.

To insert columns or rows,

- Use the mouse (click or drag) to select one or more columns or rows at the point where you want the insertion to occur.

- Choose *Edit, Insert...* to insert the same number of columns or rows you just selected. Columns are inserted to the left of the selection; rows are inserted above the selection.

To insert a range of cells,

- Select a range of cells at the point at which you want the insertion to occur.

- Choose Edit, Insert... .

- Select Shift Cells Down or Shift Cells Right to shift the selected range of cells down or to the right. Shifting the selected cells prevents any worksheet data from being lost (overwritten). For this reason, inserting ranges is often preferable to cutting and pasting.

- Click on OK to insert a cell range the same size as the range you selected at the beginning of this procedure.

To delete cells, columns, or rows,

- Select the cells, columns, or rows to be deleted.

- Choose the *Edit, Delete...* command.

Take care to distinguish between deleting and clearing. Deleting (using Edit, Delete) both erases the contents of and removes the space taken up by the selected cells, columns, or rows. Clearing (using Edit, Clear or the Delete key) erases the contents of the selected area without removing the space it takes up in the worksheet.

Let's insert some rows in your worksheet:

1. Place the mouse pointer on the row heading labeled "1."

2. Select rows **1, 2**, and **3** (click and drag the pointer down). To select a single column or row, click on its heading; to select two or more columns or rows, drag across their headings.

3. Click the mouse pointer repeatedly on the **right scroll arrow**. Note that rows 1, 2, and 3 remain selected no matter how far you scroll. When you select a row or column, the selection extends across or down the entire worksheet.

4. Use the **left scroll arrow** to return to the beginning of your worksheet. Rows 1, 2, and 3 should still be selected.

5. Choose **Edit, Insert**... to insert three blank rows above this selection. Note that no dialog box appears; the insertion was automatic.

Now let's take a look at a common insertion error:

1. Click on the **right scroll arrow** several times to view the Sales Inventory data in the range J6:N22. Note that from row 8 down, no blank rows appear in the inventory list.

2. Press **Ctrl-Home** to return to cell **A1**.

3. Select row **10** (click on the row heading labeled "10").

4. Choose **Edit, Insert**... to insert a new row across the entire worksheet.

5. Click on the **right scroll arrow** several times. Note that your newly inserted row left a gap in the Sales Inventory area (see Figure 5.5).

Figure 5.5   **Gap in the worksheet layout due to row insertion**

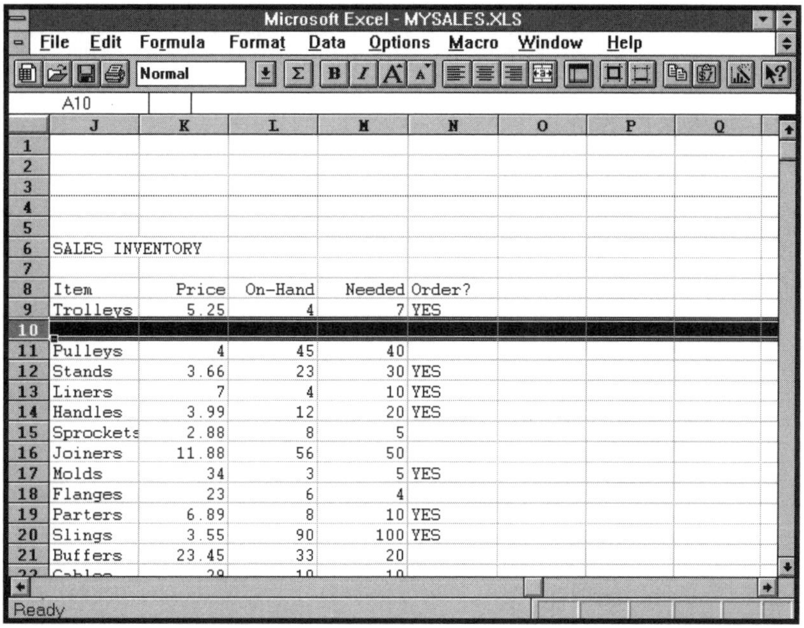

6. Choose **Edit, Undo Insert** to undo the row insertion.

Let's see how to insert a row of cells that does not cut all the way across the worksheet:

1. Select cell **C12**. The formula sums C7:C10.

2. Select the range **B10:H10**.

3. Choose **Edit, Insert...** . Note the Insert dialog box that appears when you issue an Insert command after having selected a range.

4. If necessary, select **Shift Cells Down**.

5. Click on **OK**. The cells in the selected range (B10:H10) are shifted down to make room for a single blank row of cells that covers only the width of the range (from columns B to H).

6. Select cell **C13**. The formula has correctly adjusted its cell references by one row and now sums the range C7:C11 (instead of C7:C10 as in step 1).

7. Click on the **right scroll arrow** several times.

8. Note that the Sales Inventory data have not been split. By selecting a range of cells before issuing the Insert command, you limited the width of the inserted row to that of the selected range.

PRACTICE YOUR SKILLS

1. In the first five cells of the inserted range, type the following data:

	B	C	D	E	F
10	Todd	150	200	125	185

2. Select the range **G9:H10**.

3. Use the **Fill Down** command to copy the formulas from the range G9:H9 to G10:H10. Your worksheet should now match Figure 5.6.

4. Note that the absolute reference to the commission rate cell—now $H$4 instead of $H$1, because three rows were inserted at the top of the worksheet—remained intact in the formula copied to cell H10.

Figure 5.6   **MYSALES.XLS, after inserting a new row of data**

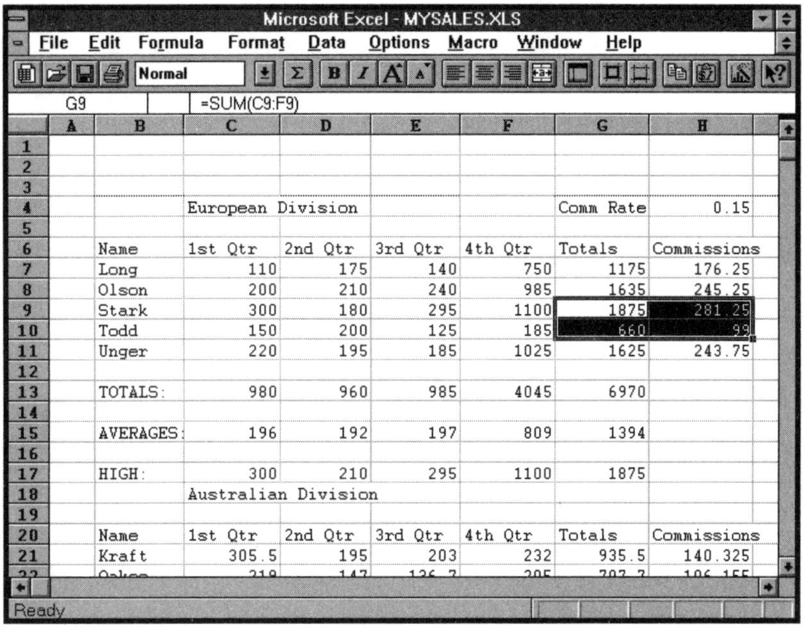

USING CUT AND PASTE TO MOVE A RANGE OF CELLS

In Chapter 4, you learned how to copy a selected range of cells from one location to another using the Copy and Paste commands. Excel also allows you to *move* a selected range. The two features differ in that copying leaves you with two copies of the selected range (the original and the copy), whereas moving erases the original, leaving only the moved range.

To move a range of cells,

- Select the range that you wish to move.

- Choose Edit, Cut.

- Select the upper-left corner of the destination range.

- Choose Edit, Paste.

Be forewarned that when data is pasted into a worksheet, it replaces (erases) any previously existing data it lands upon. For this reason, make sure to paste data into an empty worksheet area or an area containing data you can afford to lose.

Let's use the Cut and Paste commands to move a single cell:

1. Select cell **C4**.

2. Choose **Edit, Cut**. Note the marquee surrounding cell C4—though it appears otherwise, the entire label "European Division" is contained in this cell—and the status bar message at the bottom of the screen:

   ```
   Select destination and press ENTER or choose Paste
   ```

3. Select cell **C2**.

4. Choose **Edit, Paste** to move the contents of cell C4 to C2.

Now let's move a selected range of cells:

1. Enter your initials in cell **B33**. They will serve as a marker.

2. Select **B18:H31**. This is the range to be moved.

3. Choose **Edit, Cut** to cut the information from cells B18:H31.

4. Select cell **B20**. Remember, you need to specify only the upper-left corner of the destination paste range.

5. Choose **Edit, Paste** to complete the move operation.

6. Select cell **B33**. Your initials are no longer here. As mentioned above, when data is pasted, it replaces (erases) any previously existing data it covers.

7. Scroll the worksheet to the right. The Sales Inventory data have not been split. Cut and Paste moves only the specified range of cells.

You could have retained your initials without creating a gap in the Sales Inventory data by selecting cell B33 and using Edit, Insert to shift the item down past the bottom of the range which you were about to move.

 FOR THOSE WHO WANT TO STOP HERE

As mentioned earlier, you may want to work through this chapter in two sessions. To do this:

1. Choose **File, Save** to save the current version of MYSALES.XLS.

2. Close the file and exit from Excel.

3. When you are ready to continue, start Excel, close **Sheet1**, open **MYSALES.XLS** from your work directory, maximize the document window, and begin with the following section entitled "Formatting."

If you don't want to stop, please proceed directly to "Formatting."

FORMATTING

Formatting changes the way that the contents of a worksheet cell are displayed. For example: the number ten could be displayed as 10, 10.00, $10, or $10.00; the word "Totals" could be displayed as Totals, **Totals**, or *Totals*; and so on. Proper cell formatting is vital to producing an effective representation of your worksheet data.

Formatting changes a cell's appearance (how it is displayed on your screen or printed out on paper), not its contents. No matter how the cell containing the number ten in the above example were formatted, the cell would still contain the number ten.

NUMBER FORMATS

Unless you specify otherwise, all worksheet cells use Excel's *general* number format: no commas (1250), a minus sign to denote a negative number (-250), and as many decimals as will fit in the cell (.666667).

To choose a different number format,

- Select the range of cells to be formatted.

- Choose *Format, Number...* .

- Select the desired format type (All, Number, Currency, Date, and so on) in the *Category* list box.

- Select the desired format in the *Format Codes* list box.

- Click on OK.

The following shows how number formats affect the display of numeric cell contents:

Number format	Cell contents	Cell display
0	1234.567	1235
0.00	1234.567	1234.57
#,##0	1234.567	1,235
$#,##0_);($#,##0)	1234.567	$1,235
0.000	1.25	1.250
#.###	1.25	1.25

Zeros (0) and pound signs (#) are used as digit placeholders in number formats. A zero forces Excel to display either a digit or zero (for example, entering the number 2 in a cell formatted as 0.000 would be displayed as 2.000). A # cancels the display of unnecessary zeros (for example, a 2 entered in a cell formatted as #.### would be displayed as 2).

Some of Excel's format definitions are composed of two parts separated by a semicolon (;). The first part defines the format for positive numbers; the second part defines the format for negative numbers. If you entered 10 in a cell formatted as $#,##0_);($#,##0), it would be displayed as $10; if you entered -10, it would be displayed as ($10).

Let's apply a new number format to the entire worksheet:

1. Select cell **A1** (press **Ctrl-Home**) to reorient your screen.

2. Move the mouse pointer to the empty box directly above the "1" of row 1 and to the left of the "A" of column A.

3. Click the mouse button. Note that the entire worksheet (every cell) was selected.

4. Choose **Format, Number...** to display the Number Format dialog box. Note that All is selected as the category and General is selected as the format. Spend a moment browsing through the categories and formats on this list.

5. Select the **Currency** category. Select the format **$#,##0_);($#,##0)**. Click on **OK** to format all the numbers in

your worksheet as currency (that is, preceded with a $) with zero decimal places.

6. Press **Ctrl-Home** to select cell **A1** and deselect the entire worksheet (see Figure 5.7).

Figure 5.7   **MYSALES.XLS, after formatting numbers to currency**

	A	B	C	D	E	F	G	H

Microsoft Excel - MYSALES.XLS

File   Edit   Formula   Format   Data   Options   Macro   Window   Help

A1

	A	B	C	D	E	F	G	H
1								
2			European Division					
3								
4							Comm Rate	$0
5								
6		Name	1st Qtr	2nd Qtr	3rd Qtr	4th Qtr	Totals	Commissions
7		Long	$110	$175	$140	$750	$1,175	$176
8		Olson	$200	$210	$240	$985	$1,635	$245
9		Stark	$300	$180	$295	$1,100	$1,875	$281
10		Todd	$150	$200	$125	$185	$660	$99
11		Unger	$220	$195	$185	$1,025	$1,625	$244
12								
13		TOTALS:	$980	$960	$985	$4,045	$6,970	
14								
15		AVERAGES:	$196	$192	$197	$809	$1,394	
16								
17		HIGH:	$300	$210	$295	$1,100	$1,875	
18								
19								
20			Australian Division					
21								
22		Name	1st Qtr	2nd Qtr	3rd Qtr	4th Qtr	Totals	Commissions

Ready

7. In cell **A1**, enter **20**. The number is displayed with a dollar sign and no decimals ($20).

8. Clear cell **A1** (select **A1**, press **Backspace**, then **Enter**).

OVERFLOW MARKERS

Applying a number format to a cell may cause additional characters to be displayed in this cell. For instance, applying the format $##,##0.00 to a cell which contained the number 6789 would cause $6,789.00 to be displayed. When the total number of characters displayed in a numeric cell is greater than the cell's width, overflow markers (######) will appear.

These markers serve to inform you that the entire contents of the cell did not fit within the current cell width. A partially visible display without overflow markers could cause serious confusion; imagine what could happen if $14,791,000 were truncated to be displayed as $14,791. Bear in mind that overflow markers only affect the cell display, not its actual numeric contents. A cell displaying overflow markers will still deliver its correct numeric value to a formula in which it is referenced.

To remove overflow markers from a cell and allow its full contents to be displayed, simply widen the column in which the cell is located (see below, "Changing Column Width").

Let's force Excel to generate some overflow markers:

1. Select the range **C13:G17**.

2. Choose **Format, Number...** to display the list of number formats. Note that Currency is still selected.

3. Select **$#,##0.00_);($#,##0.00)**. Click on **OK** to display the numbers as dollar amounts with two decimal places.

4. Note the overflow markers (######) in columns F and G. These markers appear when numeric data exceed a cell's width.

PRACTICE YOUR SKILLS

1. Select cell **H4**. Note the discrepancy between the actual value in the formula bar (0.15) and the screen display ($0).

2. Change the number format of cell **H4** to **0%**. (Hint: Select the **Percentage** category.)

3. Note that the screen display changed to 15%, but the actual value stayed the same (0.15).

CHANGING COLUMN WIDTH

To change the width of a worksheet column, use any of the following three methods:

• Place the mouse pointer on the dividing line to the right of the column heading, and drag this line to the right (to widen the column) or to the left (to narrow the column).

- Select a cell in the column whose width you wish to change; choose *Format, Column Width...*; type the new width (in characters); and click on OK.

- Select the entire column; choose Format, Column Width...; then select *Best Fit*. The Best Fit option forces Excel to automatically calculate the column width needed to accommodate the longest entry in the column.

Let's practice the first of these three methods—dragging the dividing line to change column width:

1. Place the mouse pointer on the dividing line between the F and G column headings. Note that the mouse pointer changes from an open plus sign to a cross with horizontal arrows.

2. Drag the dividing line to the right to widen column F and display the missing numbers.

Now let's change column width using the Format menu:

1. Select cell **G4**. (You can select any cell in a column you wish to widen. You need not select the entire column.)

2. Choose **Format, Column Width...**.

3. Type **10**. Click on **OK** to change the width of the selected column to ten characters. Note that the missing numbers are now displayed.

Finally, let's try out the Best Fit option:

1. Choose **Edit, Undo Column Width** to undo step 3 above. The overflow markers reappear.

2. Select the entire column **G** (click on the column heading).

3. Choose **Format, Column Width...** .

4. Select **Best Fit**. Excel has chosen the minimum width that will allow all of column G's data to be displayed.

ALIGNING THE CONTENTS OF A CELL

Excel gives you full control over the *alignment* (positioning) of data within a cell. Cell contents can be *left-aligned*, *right-aligned*, *centered*, *general-aligned* (text is left-aligned, numbers are right-aligned), or *filled* (the entry is repeated as many times as needed to fill the cell). Figure 5.8 shows the effect of each of these alignments on text, numbers, and symbols.

Figure 5.8 **Alignment of cell contents**

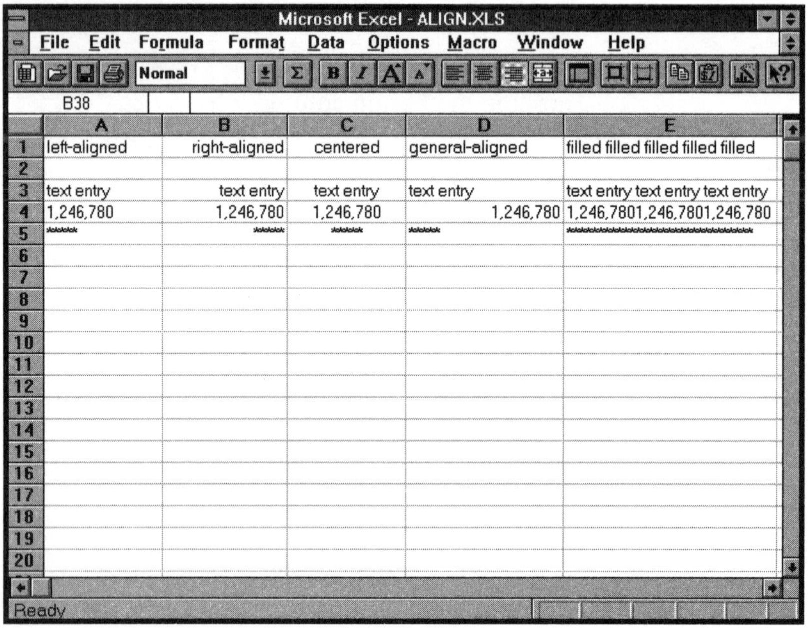

To change the alignment of text or numbers in a cell,

- Select the range to be aligned.
- Choose *Format, Alignment...* .
- Select the desired alignment.
- Click on OK.

Let's experiment with alignment:

1. Select the range **C6:G6**.

2. Choose **Format, Alignment...** to open the Format, Alignment dialog box.

3. In the Horizontal box, select **Right**. Click on **OK** to push the text within the selected range against the right cell borders.

4. Select cell **C2**.

5. Choose **Format, Alignment...** .

6. In the Horizontal box, select **Center**. Click on **OK**. The text in cell C2 is centered over the range B2:D2, although the text is actually contained only within cell C2. When a long text label is centered, the middle of the text is displayed in the original cell, while the remaining text spills out to either side.

7. Examine cells B2 and D2 to confirm that "European Division" is contained wholly in cell C2.

PRACTICE YOUR SKILLS

Center the contents of the cells in the range **G4:H4**.

CHANGING FONTS

With the *Format, Font* command, you can change the typeface, size, style, and color of any data in a cell. To do so,

- Select the range to be formatted.

- Choose *Format, Font...* .

- Select the desired font in the *Font* list box.

- Select the desired font size in the *Size* list box.

- Select the desired style in the *Font Style* box.

- Select (check) the desired effects in the *Effects* box.

- Select the desired color in the *Color* list box.

- Click on OK.

Be aware that the Format, Font command affects the entire contents of a cell. You cannot, for example, underline just one word in a cell that contains several words.

Let's change the font of a cell:

1. Select cell **C2**.

2. Choose **Format, Font...** to open the Font dialog box. Observe the sample box. This box shows you a sample of the selected font (Courier).

3. Select **Helv** (Helvetica) in the Font list box. Note the change in the Sample box.

4. Select **14** in the Size list box. Note the change in the Sample box.

5. Select **Bold Italic** in the Font Style list box. Note the changes.

6. Click on **OK**.

The font of the active cell changed to your new selection (Helvetica, 14 point, bold italic). Note also that the height of row 2 was increased to accommodate the larger font. When you choose a font whose characters are higher than the row in which they appear, Excel automatically adjusts the height of this row.

PRACTICE YOUR SKILLS

Format the range **B6:H6** to **Helv**, **10**, **Italic**. Your worksheet should now match Figure 5.9.

Figure 5.9   **MYSALES.XLS, after changing the font format**

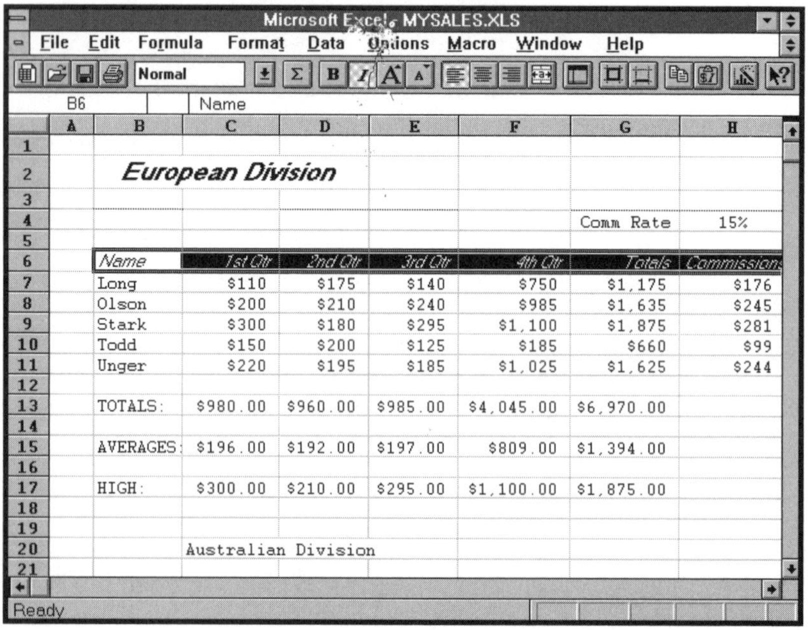

CREATING BORDERS AND SHADING

Excel allows you to visually emphasize cells by adding borders and shading to them. To do this,

- Select the range to be bordered or shaded.

- Choose *Format, Border...* .

- Select the desired location of your border in the *Border* box. You can place a border on the left, right, top, or bottom edge of every cell in the selected range, or around the outer edge (outline) of the entire selection.

- Select the desired style of border in the *Style* box. The choices include hairline, thin, medium, thick, double, dotted, and dashed.

- Select *Shade*, if shading is desired.

- Click on OK.

Let's add borders and shading to emphasize the totals, averages, and high data of MYSALES.XLS:

1. Select the range **B13:G17**.

2. Choose **Format, Border**... to open the Border dialog box.

3. Select **Outline** in the Border box. The Outline option places a border around the outer edge of the selected range.

4. Select the heaviest line in the Style box.

5. Check the **Shade** box.

6. Click on **OK**.

7. Click on cell **A8** to deselect the formatted range. The border and shading are now clearly visible, as shown in Figure 5.10.

COPYING SPECIFIC ATTRIBUTES OF A CELL

When you copy a cell to a new location by using the Edit, Paste command, Excel copies every *attribute* of the cell: its text, formulas, numeric values, and formats. However, you may want to copy just one of these attributes (for instance, the cell's format but not its contents). The *Edit, Paste Special* command allows you to accomplish this.

To copy specific attributes of one or more cells,

- Select the desired cell range.

Figure 5.10   **The bordered and shaded section of MYSALES.XLS**

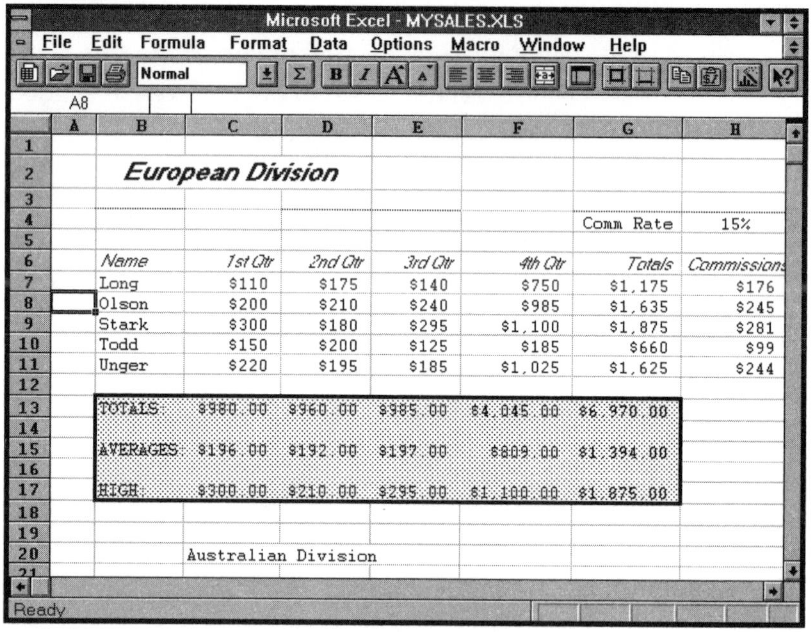

- Choose Edit, Copy.
- Select the upper-left corner of the destination range.
- Choose Edit, Paste Special... .
- Select the desired Paste Special options.
- Click on OK.

Let's use Paste Special to copy the format, but not the contents, of a single cell:

1. Select cell **C2**.

2. Choose **Edit, Copy** to copy cell C2.

3. Select cell **C20** as the destination cell.

4. Choose **Edit, Paste Special...** to open the Paste Special dialog box.

5. Select **Formats** in the Paste box.

6. Click on **OK** to copy the formats (alignment, font, and so on) from the original cell (C2) to the destination cell (C20).

7. Note that cell C2 is still marqueed and that the status-bar copy message is still active. Excel allows you to repeat copy operations.

Now let's use Paste Special on a range of cells:

1. Select the range **B6:H17**.

2. Choose **Edit, Copy** to copy the range B6:H17. Note that cell C2 is no longer marqueed, because a new copy range was selected.

3. Select cell **B22**, the upper-left corner of the destination range.

4. Choose **Edit, Paste Special...** to open the Paste Special dialog box.

5. Select **Formats** in the Paste box.

6. Click on **OK** to copy the formats (alignment, font, borders, number formats, and so on) from the original cells to the destination range. Note that the marquee is still active, as is the status-bar message.

7. Scroll down until all the Australian Division data is displayed. If necessary, widen column **C** until the value in cell C29 is fully displayed. (Drag the column dividing line, or use the **Format, Column Width** command.)

8. Update and close **MYSALES.XLS**. (Choose **File, Save**, then **File, Close**.)

PRACTICE YOUR SKILLS

The following activity is designed to sharpen the Excel formatting skills you acquired in this chapter. Perform these steps to edit the worksheet file PRU5.XLS to match Figure 5.11:

1. Open **PRU5.XLS** (Chapter 3).

2. Maximize the document window (Chapter 3).

3. Clear cell **D2** to allow the long label in cell C2 to be displayed completely (Chapter 4).

4. Select row **4**. Insert one row.

Figure 5.11   **The completed worksheet MYPRU5.XLS**

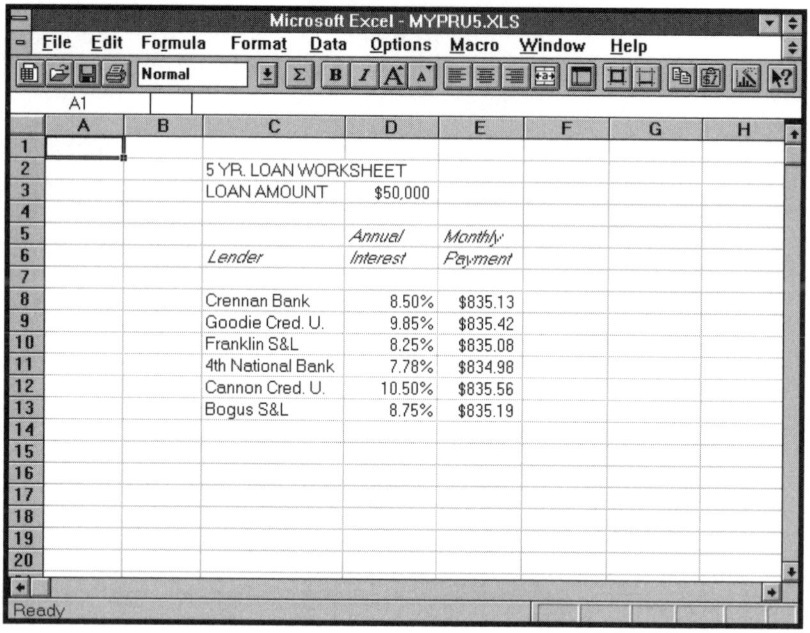

5. Format the range **C5:E6** to **Italic**.

6. Format cell **D3** to currency with no decimal point.

7. Format the range **D8:D13** to percent with two decimal places.

8. Format the range **E8:E13** to currency with two decimal places.

9. Widen column **C** until all the labels are completely displayed.

10. Save your worksheet as **MYPRU5.XLS** (Chapter 2).

11. Compare your worksheet to Figure 5.11.

12. Close the file (Chapter 2).

The following activity is designed to further sharpen your formatting skills. Perform these steps to edit the file OPT5.XLS to match Figure 5.12:

1. Open **OPT5.XLS** (Chapter 3).

2. Maximize the document window (Chapter 3).

3. Insert one row at row **3**.

Figure 5.12   The completed MYOPT5.XLS worksheet

	A	B	C	D	E	F	G	H	I
1			EXMAC CORPORATION						
2			Personnel Accounts Worksheet						
3									
4			*Pay*	*Regular*	*Overtime*	*Overtime*	*Weekly*		
5	*Emp#*	*Employee*	*Rate*	*Pay*	*Hours*	*Pay*	*Salary*		
6									
7	1	Arbuckle, F.	$5.00	$200	10	$75.00	$275		
8	2	Barnum, P.	$5.00	$200	0	$0.00	$200		
9	3	Cranston, L.	$6.50	$260	0	$0.00	$260		
10	4	Doro, S.	$6.00	$240	5	$45.00	$285		
11	5	Eastwood, C.	$7.75	$310	13	$151.13	$461		
12	6	Fargo, W.	$8.25	$330	3	$37.13	$367		
13	7	Grant, U.	$8.00	$320	6	$72.00	$392		
14	8	Hoover, H.	$9.00	$360	0	$0.00	$360		
15	9	Ignatowski, J.	$7.35	$294	12	$132.30	$426		
16	10	Jolson, A.	$5.85	$234	4	$35.10	$269		
17									
18									
19									
20									

4. Insert cells through the range **A4:A17**, shifting the remainder of those rows to the right.

5. In cell **A5**, enter the text **Emp#** (Chapter 2).

6. In column **A**, number the employees **1** through **10** (Chapter 4).

7. Delete row **6** (using the **Edit, Delete** command).

8. Format cell **A1** to **Bold**.

9. Format the range **A4:G5** to **Italic**.

10. Format the range **C7:C16** to currency with two decimal places.

11. Format the range **D7:D16** to currency with no decimal places.

12. Copy the formats from the range **C7:D16** to the range **F7:G16**.

13. Move the range **A1:B2** to the range **C1:D2**.

14. Reduce the width of column **A** to slightly wider than the text in cell A5.

15. Center the contents of column **A**.

16. Widen column **B** to exactly twelve characters.

17. Center the contents of the range **C4:G16**.

18. Save your worksheet as **MYOPT5.XLS** (Chapter 2).

19. Compare your worksheet to Figure 5.12.

20. Close the file (Chapter 2).

CHAPTER SUMMARY

In this chapter, you learned the fundamentals of worksheet formatting: how to change column width, align the contents of a cell, change fonts, and create borders and shading. You also learned how to edit a cell; how to create a formula using absolute references; how to insert and delete cells, columns, and rows; how to insert, cut, and paste data; and how to use the Paste Special command to copy specific cell attributes.

Here is a quick reference guide to the Excel features introduced in this chapter:

Desired Result	How to Do It
Edit a cell	Use **F2** (for Edit) and arrow keys, or use mouse
Create an absolute reference	Type **$** before row and column references (for example, $B$2)
Create a mixed reference	Type **$** before row or column reference (for example, $A1)
Insert one or more columns/rows	Select one or more columns/rows, choose **Edit, Insert...**
Select one or more columns/rows	Click on (drag over) one or more column/row headings
Insert cells into a range	Select range, choose **Edit, Insert...**, select **Shift Cells Down** or **Shift Cells Right**, click on **OK**
Move a cell or cells	Select cell(s) to move, choose **Edit, Cut**, select destination, choose **Edit, Paste**

Desired Result	How to Do It
Change number format	Select cell(s) to be formatted, choose **Format, Number...**, select desired category and format, click on **OK**
Change column width	Drag column dividing line; or select cell in column, choose **Format, Column Width...**, type new width, click on **OK**; or select entire column, choose **Format, Column Width...**, select **Best Fit**
Change alignment	Select cell(s) to be aligned, choose **Format, Alignment...**, select desired alignment, click on **OK**
Change font, size, style, effects, color	Select cell(s) to be formatted, choose **Format, Font...**, select desired font, size, style, effects, and color, click on **OK**
Create a border/ shading	Select cell(s) to be bordered/shaded, choose **Format, Border...**, select desired border/-shading, click on **OK**
Copy specific cell attributes	Select cell(s) to copy from, choose **Edit, Copy**, select cell(s) to copy to, choose **Edit, Paste Special...**, select attributes to copy, click on **OK**

In the next chapter, you will complete your foundation in formatting techniques. You'll learn how to use Excel's toolbar to apply formats quickly and easily, how to spell-check the contents of a worksheet's cells, and how to preview and print your worksheet.

IF YOU'RE STOPPING HERE

If you need to break off here, please exit from Excel. If you want to proceed directly to the next chapter, please do so now.

CHAPTER 6: ADVANCED ENHANCEMENT TECHNIQUES

More on Formatting: The Standard Toolbar

Spell-Checking a Worksheet

Printing a Worksheet

Previewing the Printout

This chapter introduces several advanced techniques for enhancing the appearance of a worksheet. In the first half, we'll show you how to use the Standard toolbar to format cells quickly and how to use the Spelling feature to spell-check the text in your worksheets. In the second half, we'll show you how to use Excel's page-setup options to create professional-looking printouts and how to preview a printed worksheet on your screen before actually printing it out.

When you're done working through this chapter, you will know

- How to use the Standard toolbar to format text
- How to sum a range automatically
- How to spell-check a worksheet
- How to print a worksheet
- How to preview a printout on your screen

MORE ON FORMATTING: THE STANDARD TOOLBAR

The Excel 4.0 Standard toolbar allows you to quickly format a cell without having to choose a command from the Format menu. Toolbar formatting options include bold and italic font styles, cell-contents alignment (left, centered, and right), and a Center Across Columns tool. The Standard toolbar also contains several other tools that greatly extend the power and versatility of Excel (see Figure 6.1).

Figure 6.1   **The Standard toolbar, with tools labeled**

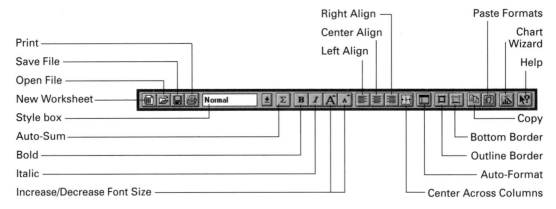

USING THE STANDARD TOOLBAR TO FORMAT TEXT

If you are not running Excel, please start it now. If there is a worksheet on your screen, please close it. Your screen should be empty except for a maximized Excel application window.

Let's use the Standard toolbar to format text contained in a single cell:

1. Open the file **INVENT.XLS** from your EX4WORK directory. This is a sales inventory worksheet.

2. Maximize the document window, if necessary.

3. Select cell **C1**. Note that the Bold, Italic, and Center Alignment buttons are selected on the toolbar, reflecting the format of the text in C1.

4. Select cell **A2**.

5. Click on the toolbar's **Bold button** to bold the contents of cell A2.

6. Click on the **Bold button** again to remove the bold formatting. Clicking on a toolbar format button both selects and deselects the formatting option.

7. Click on the **Bold button** once again to rebold the contents of cell A2.

8. Select the range **A2:E2**. Click on the Standard toolbar's **Center Across Columns button** (see Figure 6.1) to center the contents of cell A2 ("SALES INVENTORY") over columns A through E (see Figure 6.2). The Center Across Columns button centers text over several columns. To center text within a single cell (as for "INTERNATIONAL EXPRESS, LTD."), use the Center Align button.

Now let's use the toolbar to format a range of cells:

1. Select the range **A4:E4**.

2. Click on the toolbar's **Italic button** to italicize the selected range.

3. Click on the **Center Align button** (*not* the Center Across Columns button) to center the contents of each cell in the selected range.

PRACTICE YOUR SKILLS

1. Select the range **C5:E14**.

2. Center the cells in the selected range (see Figure 6.3).

Figure 6.2   **Centering text across columns**

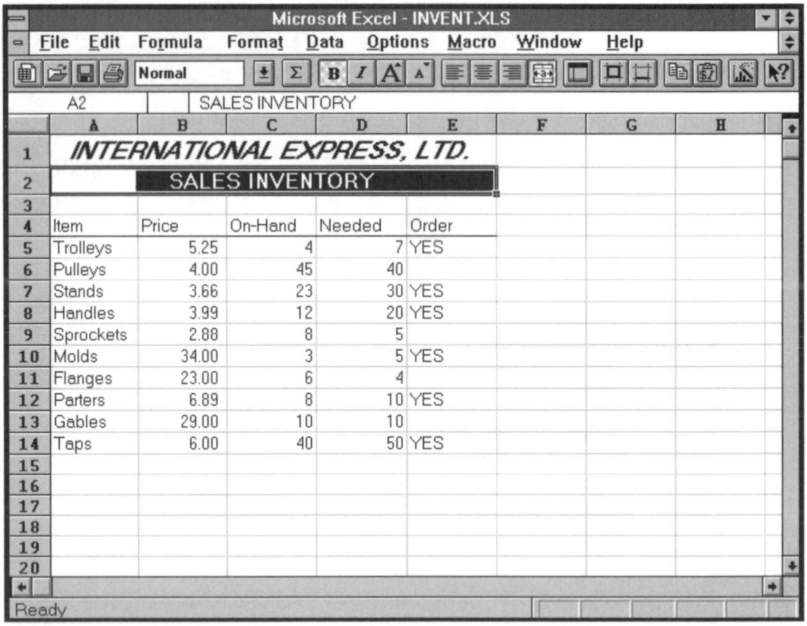

Figure 6.3   **INVENT.XLS, after formatting with the Standard toolbar**

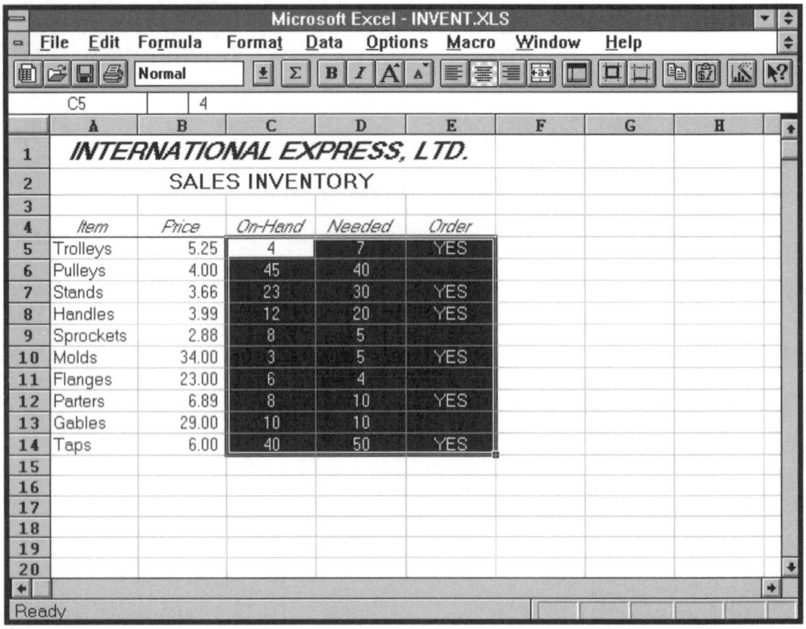

SUMMING A RANGE AUTOMATICALLY

The toolbar contains an *Auto-Sum button* that you use to automatically sum a range of numbers. To do so,

- Select the cell in which you want the sum to appear. This cell must be directly *beneath* a column of numbers to be summed or directly *to the right* of a row of numbers to be summed.

- Click on the Auto-Sum button. Excel enters a SUM formula in the selected cell, choosing as its SUM argument the contiguous range of cells in either the same column above or the same row to the left of the selected cell.

- Enter the SUM formula into the cell.

Let's use the Auto-Sum button to sum a range automatically:

1. Select cell **C15** and observe the toolbar. This cell has already been centered.

2. Click on the toolbar's **Auto-Sum button** (the button to the left of bold, containing the mathematical symbol for summation, Σ). Observe your screen.

3. Note the formula that Excel has automatically created in the formula bar, =SUM(C5:C14), and the marquee enclosing the range of cells that make up this formula's argument (C5:C14). Excel chose as its SUM argument the contiguous range of cells in the column above the selected cell.

4. Enter the formula and observe the result (159).

Now let's see what happens if you try to auto-sum a column containing text, rather than numbers:

1. Select **A15**.

2. Click on the toolbar's **Auto-Sum button**. Note that the formula bar now contains the formula =SUM() and that no marquee has appeared (see Figure 6.4). Excel chose not to enter a SUM argument, because it saw that the proposed auto-sum cells contained text rather than numbers ("Trolleys," "Pulleys," etc.).

3. Click on the **cancel box** (or press **Esc**) to cancel the auto-sum procedure.

4. Use **File, Save As...** to save the file as MYINVENT.XLS.

5. Close the file.

Figure 6.4   **Trying to use Σ to sum text**

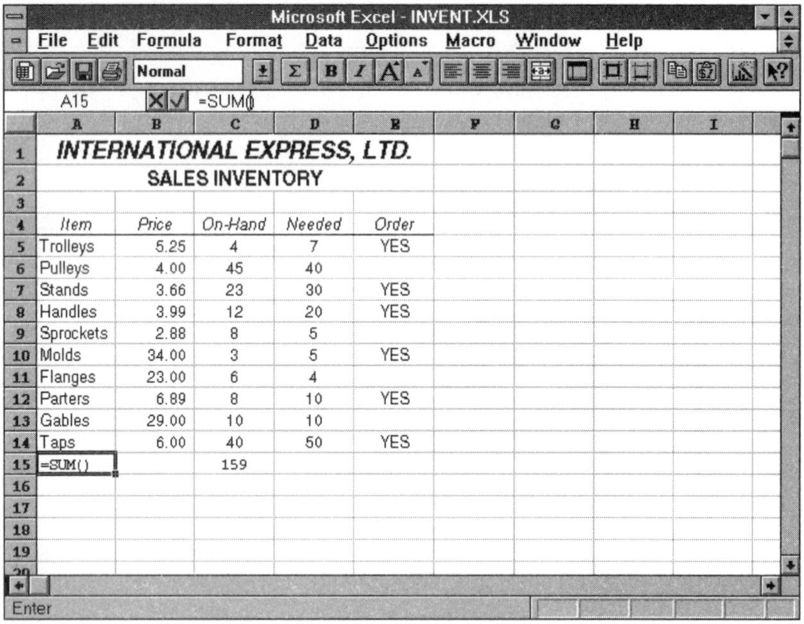

SPELL-CHECKING A WORKSHEET

Excel 4.0 provides a *Spelling* feature that allows you to spell-check the text contained in the cells of a worksheet. You can spell-check an entire worksheet or a selected range of cells, as outlined in the following procedures.

To spell-check an entire worksheet,

- Press Ctrl-Home to select cell A1.

- Choose *Options, Spelling* to open the Spelling dialog box and begin the spell-checking procedure (see Figure 6.5). If Excel finds a word that is not in its internal dictionary, it pauses to display this word along with a group of alternative spellings in the *Change To* and *Suggestions* boxes. (In Figure 6.5, Excel found the misspelled word "Interntional" and offered the suggestions "Intentional," "Intentionally," "Intentionality," "International," and so on.) At this point, you can choose any of the following options:

Figure 6.5   **The Spelling dialog box**

- To accept the alternative spelling in the Change To box, click on *Change*; the original (misspelled) word will be replaced with the alternative (correctly spelled) word, and the spell check will resume. Or, click on *Change All* to replace all instances of the original word in the worksheet with the alternative word.

- To accept one of the alternative spellings in the Suggestions box, click on the desired spelling to move it to the Change To box, and then click on Change; the original (misspelled) word will be replaced with the alternative (correctly spelled) word, and the spell check will resume. Or, click on Change All to replace all instances of the original word with the alternative word in the Change To box.

- To skip a word that Excel has found, click on *Ignore*; the word will remain as is, and the spell check will resume. Or, click on *Ignore All* to skip all instances of the found word.

- To add a found word to a custom dictionary (so that this word will not be considered misspelled in subsequent spell checks), click on *Add*; the dictionary currently selected in the *Add Words To* list box will be modified and the spell check will resume. The Add option is particularly useful for unusual proper names and acronyms.

- To specify an alternative spelling not displayed in the Change To and Suggestions boxes, select the word in the Change To box, type in your desired alternative spelling, and then click on Change or Change All.

- To specify an alternative spelling if Excel offers no suggestions, select the Change To text box, type in your desired alternative spelling, and then click on Change or Change All.

- When the entire document has been spell-checked, a dialog box appears informing you of this fact. Click on OK to remove this dialog box and return to your document.

To spell-check a range of cells in a worksheet,

- Select the desired range of cells.

- Choose Options, Spelling and follow the spell-check procedure outlined above.

Let's spell-check a selected range of cells from a new worksheet:

1. Open the file **SALES6.XLS** from your EX4WORK directory.

2. Maximize the document window, if necessary.

3. Observe the worksheet; press **PgDn** to view the bottom half. Note that there are several spelling errors.

4. Select the range **C1:C2**. These are the cells that contain the first two lines of text. (The contents of both these cells are centered over columns C through F.)

5. Choose **Options, Spelling** to spell-check the contents of C1:C2. The Spelling dialog box opens and the spell-checker finds the misspelled word "Interntional." We want to change this to "International." Observe the Change To box: it contains "Intentional," not the alternative we want. Now observe the Suggestions box: the fourth entry is "International," our desired alternative. Before clicking on Change, we must move this alternative to the Change To box.

6. Click once on **International** to move it to the Change To box. Click on **Change** to change "Interntional" to "International" in the worksheet and to resume the spell check. Note the corrected spelling in the worksheet.

7. The next word that the spell-checker finds is "Ltd." We want to keep this word as is, because it is an acceptable business

abbreviation for "Limited." Since "Ltd." is quite common and may appear in several worksheets, let's add this word to the selected custom dictionary, CUSTOM.DIC (shown in the Add Words To list box).

8. Click on **Add** to add "Ltd." to CUSTOM.DIC. The next word that the spell-checker finds is "Amercan," a misspelling of "American." Since the proper spelling is not in the Change To box, we'll have to move it there from the Suggestions box.

9. Click on **American** in the Suggestions box, and then click on **Change** to change the word in the worksheet and resume the spell check. A dialog box appears, informing you that your requested spell checking is complete (in this case, you only requested that cells C1:C2 be checked).

10. Click on **OK** to remove this box and return to the worksheet. Note the corrected spellings of "International" and "American."

Now let's spell-check the entire worksheet:

1. Press **Ctrl-Home** to select cell **A1**.

2. Choose **Options, Spelling**. The Spelling dialog box opens, and the word "Qtr" is found (see Figure 6.6). (Note that "Ltd." was not found this time, because we added it to our custom dictionary.) We'll leave "Qtr" as is, because it is an acceptable abbreviation for "Quarter," and add it to our CUSTOM.DIC custom dictionary.

3. Click on **Add**. The spell-checker resumes operation and finds "Qt," another abbreviation for "Quarter." Let's be consistent and only use the "Qtr" abbreviation. To do this, we'll have to change all occurrences of "Qt" to "Qtr." Note that "Qtr" appears in the Suggestions box, because you just added it to the custom dictionary.

4. Click on **Qtr** to move it to the Change To box, and then click on **Change All** to change all occurrences of "Qt" to "Qtr." The spell-checker finds "Mott," a proper name that we don't want to change.

5. Click on **Ignore** to leave "Mott" as is. (If "Mott" or any other proper name appeared regularly in your worksheets, you'd probably want to add it to your custom dictionary.) The spell-checker finds "Abel," another proper name.

Figure 6.6   **Spell-checking the entire SALES6.XLS worksheet**

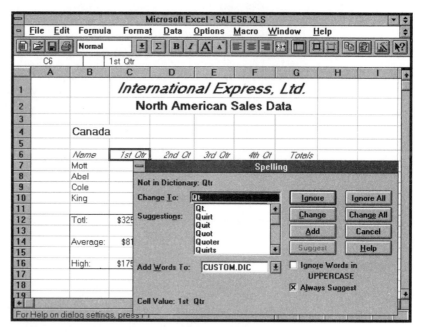

6. Click on **Ignore** to leave "Abel" as is. The spell-checker finds "Cole," another proper name.

7. Click on **Ignore** to leave "Cole" as is. The spell-checker next finds "Totl," a misspelling of "Total." (Note that the proper name "King" was not found, because "king" is a standard English word.) "Total," our desired alternative spelling, is not in the Change To box, so we need to search for it in the Suggestions box.

8. Scroll down through the Suggestions box until "Total" is displayed, and then click on **Total** to move it to the Change To box.

9. Click on **Change** to change "Totl" to "Total." The spell-checker finds "USA." Let's keep this as is and add it to our custom dictionary.

10. Click on **Add**. Next, the spell-checker finds the proper name "Kane." (Note that it did not find the names "Wolf," "Hart," or "Adams." The words "wolf" and "hart" are standard English, and "Adams" is a common enough surname that Excel included it in its internal dictionary.)

11. Click on **Ignore** to keep "Kane" as is. The spell-checker finds "Sbrtshr," a bizarre misspelling of "Average" caused by the typist's hands being positioned one key too far to the right on the keyboard. Note that the correct alternative does not appear in the Suggestions box. We'll have to enter the proper spelling manually.

12. Select **Sbrtshr** in the Change To box, if it is not already selected. Type **Average**.

13. Click on **Change** to change "Sbrtshr" to "Average." The spell-checker finds "Hiigh." Since the correct alternative spelling is already in the Change To box ("High"), you can simply click on Change.

14. Click on **Change** to change "Hiigh" to "High." A dialog box appears, informing you that the spell check is complete.

15. Click on **OK** to remove this box and return to your worksheet. Scroll through and observe the spelling changes.

16. Save the worksheet as **MYSALES6.XLS**.

PRINTING A WORKSHEET

To print a worksheet, use the *File, Print* command. Unless otherwise directed, Excel will print the entire *active area* of a worksheet (that is, the area bound by cell A1 and the most distant active cell, found by pressing Ctrl-End). The File, Print dialog box allows you to specify the number of copies and range of pages to print, the print quality (standard or draft), the print contents (worksheet, notes, or both), and whether to print on paper or on your screen (print preview).

To print a worksheet,

* Choose File, Print... .

* Change any desired Print dialog box settings.

* Click on OK.

Let's print out the MYSALES6.XLS worksheet:

1. Press **Ctrl-Home** to select cell **A1**.

2. Choose **File, Print...** and click on **OK** to print the entire worksheet using the current Print dialog box settings.

3. Compare your printout to Figure 6.7. Depending on the printer you are using, your printout may vary slightly from the one depicted here.

4. If your worksheet failed to print, make sure your printer is on line, then repeat step 2. If it still won't print, please refer to Appendix A for help with selecting your printer.

SETTING THE PRINT AREA

At times, you may want to print a limited area of your worksheet. Excel allows you to specify the area you wish to print by using the *Set Print Area* command.

To print a part of the worksheet,

- Select the area (cell range) you want to print.

- Choose Options, Set Print Area.

- Choose File, Print... .

- Change any desired Print dialog box settings.

- Click on OK.

Let's use Set Print Area to specify a limited area of MYSALES6.XLS to print:

1. Select the range **B1:G16** (the Canadian sales data). This is the area we will specify to print.

2. Choose **Options, Set Print Area** to set the print area to the selected range.

3. Select any cell to deselect the range. Note Excel's use of a dashed border to visually define the print area.

SETTING UP THE PAGE: HEADERS AND FOOTERS

As mentioned above, the File, Print command allows you to set various print options (number of copies, range of pages, print quality, and so on). To further control your printout, use the *File, Page Setup* command.

File, Page Setup allows you to define a header and footer (text that repeats on the top or bottom of every worksheet page); set margins, paper size, print reduction/enlargement, and page orientation

Figure 6.7   **The printed MYSALES6.XLS worksheet**

MYSALES6.XLS

	A	B	C	D	E	F	G
1			International Express, Ltd.				
2			North American Sales Data				
3							
4		Canada					
5							
6		Name	1st Qtr	2nd Qtr	3rd Qtr	4th Qtr	Totals
7		Mott	175	500	200	20	$895.00
8		Abel	50	225	245	99	$619.00
9		Cole	20	275	104	30	$429.00
10		King	80	100	211	54	$445.00
11							
12		Total:	$325.00	$1,100.00	$760.00	$203.00	$2,388.00
13							
14		Average:	$81.25	$275.00	$190.00	$50.75	$597.00
15							
16		High:	$175.00	$500.00	$245.00	$99.00	$895.00
17							
18							
19							
20							
21		USA					
22							
23		Name	1st Qtr	2nd Qtr	3rd Qtr	4th Qtr	Totals
24		Wolf	55	285	234	350	$924.00
25		Hart	75	200	376	488	$1,139.00
26		Adams	80	190	264	833	$1,367.00
27		Kane	116	175	95	275	$661.00
28							
29		Total:	$326.00	$850.00	$969.00	$1,946.00	$4,091.00
30							
31		Average:	$81.50	$212.50	$242.25	$486.50	$1,022.75
32							
33		High:	$116.00	$285.00	$376.00	$833.00	$1,367.00

Page 1

(portrait or landscape); and specify whether to print cell gridlines and row/column headings.

Unless you tell Excel to do otherwise, a default header and footer will be printed with your worksheet. The default header consists of the document name, centered at the top of every page; the default footer consists of the word "Page," followed by the page number, centered at the bottom of every page.

Excel allows you to change the following attributes of a header or footer: page number, total number of pages, date, time, document name, or any other typed text; left, centered, or right alignment; font typeface (Helvetica, Courier, and so on), font size (10 point, 12 point, and so on), and font style (normal, bold, or Italic); and general layout.

The following six tools are available in both the Header and Footer dialog boxes (see Figure 6.8):

Tool	Code	Click on This Button to
Font		Specify font typeface, size, and style of selected header/footer text
Page Number	&P	Insert active page number
Total Pages	&N	Insert total number of pages in worksheet
Date	&D	Insert current date
Time	&T	Insert current time
File Name	&F	Insert file name of active worksheet

Figure 6.8   **Header and Footer dialog-box tools**

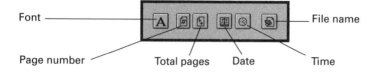

Font —   — File name

Page number   Total pages   Date   Time

Note that each of these tools (except for the Font tool) has a corresponding text code (&P, &N, and so on). In the next activity, you'll see how these codes are used.

Let's use File, Page Setup to modify the standard Excel header and footer for your worksheet:

1. Choose **File, Page Setup...** to open the Page Setup dialog box (see Figure 6.9). Take a moment to observe the many options presented here. You use this dialog box to modify all aspects of a worksheet's page layout.

Figure 6.9   **The Page Setup dialog box**

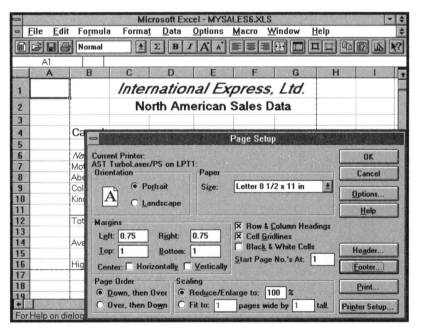

2. Click on the **Header button** (on the right) to open the Header dialog box. Note the six tool buttons, as depicted in Figure 6.8. Note also the division into three text-entry boxes—Left, Center, and Right—allowing you to enter left-, center-, and right-aligned text.

3. Double-click on the **&f** code (in the Center section) to select it. As mentioned earlier, this code causes the file name of the

active worksheet (MYSALES6.XLS) to be displayed in the header. (Capitalization is insignificant; *&f* is equivalent to *&F.*)

4. Type ***your name*'s Report** (for example, Bill's Report or Virginia's Report) to replace the file name code.

5. Press **Tab** to select the Right section text box. Click on the **Date button** (see Figure 6.8) to enter the date code, &D. The current date will now appear, right-aligned, in the worksheet's header.

6. Click on **OK** to accept your modified header and return to the Page Setup dialog box.

7. Click on the **Footer button** to open the Footer dialog box. Note that it is identical to the Header dialog box.

8. Use the mouse to highlight **Page &p** in the Center section text box. The &P code displays the active page number. The entire entry causes "Page *N*" to be displayed in the footer, where *N* is the active page number (1, 2, and so on).

9. Press **Del** to delete the Center section entry.

10. Press **Shift-Tab** to select the Left section text box. Type **Page**, press **Spacebar**, and then click on the **Page Number button**. Your entry should now read "Page &P," exactly as it originally read in the Center section box. All we've done is change the position of "Page &P" from center- to left-aligned.

11. Click on **OK** to accept your modified footer and return to the Page Setup dialog box.

Now let's change some settings in the Page Setup box:

1. Use your mouse to select the **0.75** in the Margins, Left text box.

2. Type **.5** to change the left margin from .75 inches to .5 inches.

3. Uncheck the boxes **Row & Column Headings** and **Cell Gridlines** to suppress the printout of row/column headings and gridlines.

4. Click on **OK** to return to your worksheet. Note that its appearance has not changed. In order to view the Page Setup modifications you just made, you must preview the printout, which we'll do in the next activity.

PREVIEWING THE PRINTOUT

Excel allows you to *preview* your printout: to view each page on your screen exactly as it will be printed. To do this, use the *File, Print Preview* command. The preview appears in a *preview window*. The buttons at the top of this window allow you to magnify or reduce the preview display, print the document, open the Page Setup dialog box to change any desired settings, display and change current margins, or return to the worksheet.

Let's preview the printout of your worksheet:

1. Choose **File, Print Preview** to display your printout preview (see Figure 6.10). Note that only that portion of the worksheet you set in a previous activity as the print area is shown.

2. Position the mouse pointer over the worksheet area of the preview. The pointer changes to a magnifying glass.

Figure 6.10   **Previewing the printout of MYSALES6.XLS**

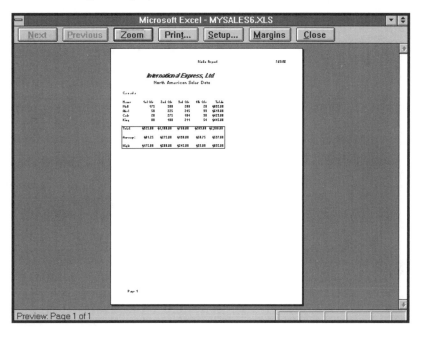

3. Click the mouse button to magnify the document to *actual-size view*. The mouse pointer now appears as an arrow.

4. Scroll vertically and horizontally to view the header and footer.

5. Click the mouse button anywhere over the text to reverse the magnification to *full-page view*.

6. Click on **Zoom** to magnify the view; click on **Zoom** again to reduce it. Clicking on Zoom is equivalent to using the magnifying-glass tool for magnification/reduction.

Now let's use the preview window's *Setup* command to change margins and view the results:

1. Click on **Margins** to display the previewed document's margins.

2. Click on **Setup...** to open the same Page Setup dialog box you previously opened by choosing File, Page Setup. Note the current settings.

3. Change the left-margin setting to **1**.

4. Click on **OK** to return to your preview. Note the new, one-inch left margin.

5. Drag the top margin down approximately one inch from its current position. (Place the mouse pointer anywhere on the dashed horizontal line and drag down.) You can change a margin either by using the Setup command or by dragging the margin line on the preview screen.

6. Click on **Margins** to turn off the margin-line display (see Figure 6.11).

7. Choose **Close** to return to the worksheet.

8. Use **File, Save As** to save the file as **MYPRINT1.XLS**. Your customized print settings will be saved along with the worksheet.

REMOVING THE PRINT AREA

After having used the Set Print Area command to choose a limited print area, if you decide you want to print your entire worksheet, you must first use the Remove Print Area command to remove this print area. To do this,

• Select the entire worksheet.

Figure 6.11   **Preview of MYSALES6.XLS, after changing the margins**

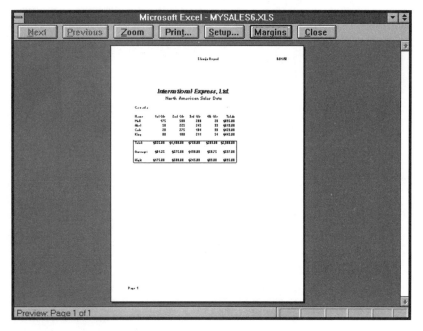

- Choose *Options, Remove Print Area*.

Let's remove the print area from MYPRINT1.XLS and preview the modified printout:

1. Select the entire worksheet. (Click on the empty box above row 1 and to the left of column A.)

2. Choose **Options, Remove Print Area**.

3. Select any cell to deselect the worksheet.

4. Choose **File, Print Preview**. Note that the printout once again includes the entire active area of the worksheet (A1:G33). Note, also, that your customized print options have remained intact (see Figure 6.12).

5. Click on **Close** to return to the worksheet.

6. Save the file as **MYPRINT2.XLS**.

7. Close the file.

Figure 6.12 **Preview of MYPRINT1.XLS, after removing the print area**

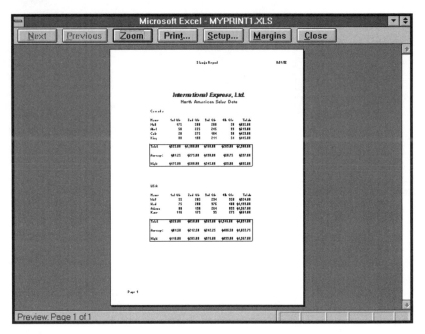

PRACTICE YOUR SKILLS

The following activity is designed to sharpen your Excel formatting and printing skills. Perform these steps to edit the worksheet file PRU6.XLS to match Figure 6.13:

1. Open **PRU6.XLS** (Chapter 3).

2. Maximize the document window (Chapter 3).

3. In cell **D2**, change the font to **Tms Rmn, 14** (Chapter 5).

4. In cell **D3**, change the font to **Tms Rmn, 12** (Chapter 5).

5. Center the contents of cells **D2** and **D3**.

6. Make the contents of cell **D2** bold.

7. Italicize the contents of cell **D3**.

8. Center the contents of cells **D6:D16**. (Be sure to include the empty cell D16.)

Figure 6.13   **MYPRU6.XLS as printed**

		EXMAC CORPORATION			
		CURRENT TOTAL BUDGET ALLOCATION BY CATEGORY			
Salaries		$433,100			
Utilities		$14,150			
Office supplies		$2,480			
Travel		$13,650			
Lunches		$1,675			
Phone		$5,100			
Training		$49,000			
Advertising		$265,000			
Rent		$629,000			
Investments		$58,000			
	TOTALS:	$1,471,155			

9. In cell **D16**, have Excel sum the numbers automatically.

10. Save the file as **MYPRU6.XLS** (Chapter 2).

11. Print the entire worksheet using all the current settings.

12. Compare your printout to Figure 6.13. Depending on the printer you are using, your printout may vary slightly from the one depicted here.

13. Close the file (Chapter 2).

The following activity is designed to further sharpen your formatting and printing skills. Perform these steps to edit the file OPT6.XLS to match Figure 6.14.

1. Open **OPT6.XLS** (Chapter 3).

2. Maximize the document window (Chapter 3).

3. Set the range **B6:D16** as the print area.

4. Set the following Page Setup options:

   • Center the header **BUDGET FIGURES**.

   • Change the left margin to **2.75**.

   • Turn off the **Cell Gridlines**.

5. Preview the document.

Figure 6.14   **OPT6.XLS as shown in Print Preview**

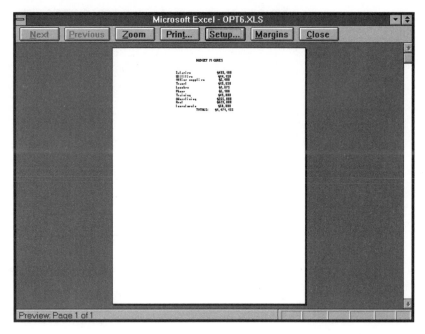

6. From the Print Preview window, add a footer specifying a center-aligned page number without the word "Page" preceding it.

7. Compare your print preview to Figure 6.14.

8. Save the file as **MYOPT6.XLS** (Chapter 2).

9. Close the file (Chapter 2).

CHAPTER SUMMARY

In this chapter, you finished acquiring your foundation of Excel formatting techniques begun in Chapter 5. You learned how to use the Standard toolbar to format text and sum a range automatically, and how to use the Spelling command to spell-check the text contents of a worksheet. You also learned the basics of printing: how to set the desired print options and print area, and then print out your worksheet, on either paper or the screen.

Here is a quick reference guide to the Excel features introduced in this chapter:

Desired Result	How to Do It
Bold a cell	Click on toolbar's **Bold button**
Italicize a cell	Click on toolbar's **Italic button**
Align a cell	Click on toolbar's **Left-Align**, **Center**, or **Right-Align button**
Auto-sum a column/ row of numbers	Select cell below column, or to right of row, click on toolbar's **Auto-Sum button**
Spell-check an entire worksheet	Press **Ctrl-Home** to select cell A1, choose **Options, Spelling**, follow Spelling dialog box prompts
Spell-check a range of cells	Select desired cells, choose **Options, Spelling**, follow Spelling dialog box prompts
Print a worksheet	Choose **File, Print...**, set options, click on **OK**
Set a print area	Select area, choose **Options, Set Print Area**
Remove a print area	Choose **Options, Remove Print Area**
Set print options	Choose **File, Print...**, set options; or choose **File, Page Setup...**, set options; or choose **File, Print Preview**, click on **Setup...**, set options
Set header or footer	Choose **File, Page Setup...**, Click on **Header** or **Footer**; or choose **File, Print Preview**, click on **Setup...**, fill in desired dialog box settings
Preview a printout	Choose **File, Print Preview**; or choose **File, Print...**, check **Preview**, click on **OK**
Magnify/reduce a previewed printout	Click on previewed printout, or click on **Zoom**

Desired Result	**How to Do It**
Set margins	Choose **File, Page Setup...**, set margins; choose **File, Print Preview**, click on **Setup...**, set margins; or choose **File, Print Preview**, click on **Margins**, drag margins
Return from preview window to worksheet	Click on **Close** in preview window

The next chapter introduces selected advanced Excel topics, including non-Standard toolbars, new techniques for selecting and formatting cell ranges, working with multiple document windows, and linking worksheet files.

IF YOU'RE STOPPING HERE

If you need to break off here, please exit from Excel. If you want to proceed directly to the next chapter, please do so now.

CHAPTER 7: ADVANCED WORKSHEET TOPICS

Displaying
Specialized
Toolbars

Selecting a
Noncontiguous
Range of Cells

Creating a Number
Format

Working with
Defined Names

Opening Multiple
Worksheet
Windows

Linking Worksheets

Using Macros to
Automate Tasks

This chapter introduces you to an assortment of advanced Excel worksheet topics. We'll begin by showing you how to display toolbars other than the Standard toolbar, and how to use new options for selecting, formatting, and naming cell ranges. Then we'll show you how to work with two or more worksheets at the same time, and how to link worksheets so that formulas in one worksheet are dependent on the data in another worksheet. We'll end the chapter with a brief look at automating Excel tasks using macros.

This chapter completes your foundation in Excel's electronic accounting skills. In further chapters, you will explore Excel's extensive database management and charting capabilities.

When you're done working through this chapter, you will know

- How to display and use specialized toolbars
- How to select a noncontiguous range
- How to create a number format
- How to work with defined names
- How to open multiple worksheet windows
- How to link worksheets
- How to use macros to automate tasks

DISPLAYING SPECIALIZED TOOLBARS

By default, Excel 4.0 displays the Standard toolbar, which provides a wide variety of Excel options (filing, formatting, copying, help, and so on). You can also display and use the following more specialized toolbars:

- The *Formatting toolbar* provides frequently used formatting options.

- The *Utility toolbar* provides frequently used Excel utilities (spell checking, database sorting, and so on).

- The *Chart toolbar* provides options used in creating and modifying charts.

- The *Drawing toolbar* provides options used in drawing on-screen graphics.

- The *Microsoft Excel 3.0 toolbar* provides the same options contained in the Excel 3.0 toolbar.

- The *Macro, Stop Recording,* and *Macro Paused toolbars* provide options used in creating, modifying, and running macros.

You can choose to display one or more of these toolbars at a time, and you can move your toolbar(s) to any desired position on the screen. Excel remembers the position and shape of all displayed toolbars when you exit and restores this setup when you restart.

To display a toolbar,

- Choose *Options, Toolbars.*
- Select the desired toolbar in the *Show Toolbars* list box.

- Click on *Show*.

To hide a toolbar,

- Choose Options, Toolbars.
- Select the desired toolbar in the Show Toolbars list box.
- Click on *Hide*.

To move a toolbar,

- Press and hold the mouse button on the desired toolbar to select it. When selected, an outline appears around the toolbar.
- Drag the selected toolbar to a new location. Depending upon where you are moving from/to, the shape of the toolbar may change.

If you are not running Excel, please start it now. If there is a worksheet on your screen, please close it. Your screen should be empty except for a maximized Excel application window. Let's use the Toolbars' dialog box to display a non-Standard toolbar:

1. Open **PROJECT.XLS** from your EX4WORK directory. Maximize the document window, if necessary.

2. Choose **Options, Toolbars...** to open the Toolbars' dialog box. Observe that there are a total of nine available toolbars.

3. In the Show Toolbars list box, select the **Standard toolbar** (if it is not already selected). Note that the button at the top right of the dialog box reads "Hide." This is the *Hide/Show button*. If the selected toolbar is currently shown on screen (as is the Standard toolbar), this button displays the Hide option. If the selected toolbar is hidden, this button displays the Show option.

4. Select (click once on) the **Formatting toolbar**. Note that the Hide/Show button now displays the Show option, because the Formatting toolbar is currently hidden (not shown on screen).

5. Select the **Utility toolbar**. Note that the Hide/Show button again displays the Show option, because the Utility toolbar is also hidden.

6. Select the **Formatting toolbar** and click on **Show**. The Formatting toolbar appears on screen in the upper-left quadrant of the document window (see Figure 7.1). Let's move this toolbar to the top of the screen, where it will not block our view of the

worksheet. (If your Formatting toolbar is already at the top of the document window, please skip steps 7 and 8.)

Figure 7.1 **The Formatting toolbar, when first shown**

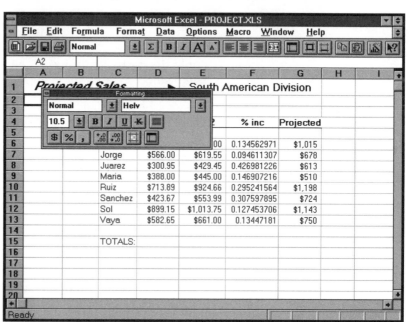

7. Point the mouse to the title bar of the Formatting toolbar. Press and hold the mouse button to select the toolbar; note the dashed outline. Drag slowly upward, until the toolbar outline changes to a long, narrow rectangle.

8. Release the mouse button. The Formatting toolbar appears directly beneath the Standard toolbar, with the same shape as the Standard toolbar (see Figure 7.2). As mentioned, toolbars may change shape, depending upon where you are moving them.

Now let's use the Formatting toolbar to format a range of numbers:

1. Select the range **G6:G13**. This range is formatted to display currency with no decimal places.

Figure 7.2   **The Formatting toolbar, moved to the top**

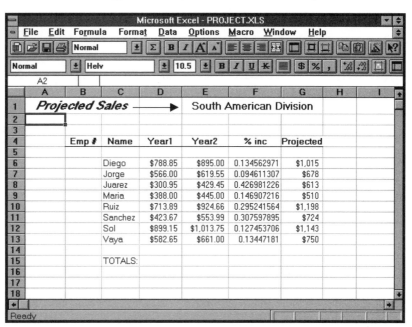

2. In the Formatting toolbar, click on the **Currency Style button** (the seventh button from the right, it shows a dollar sign, $). This tool formats the selected range to currency with two decimal places.

3. Select the range **F6:F13**. This range is formatted to display up to eight decimal places.

4. In the Formatting toolbar, click on the **Percent Style button** (the sixth button from the right, it shows a percent sign, %). This tool formats the selected range to percent with no decimal places.

5. In the Formatting toolbar, click on the **Increase Decimal button** (the fourth button from the right, it shows one decimal place being expanded to two). This tool adds a decimal place to the numbers in the selected range. The range is now formatted to show percent with one decimal place.

6. Click again on the **Increase Decimal button** to add a second decimal place to the selected range.

7. Choose **Format, Column Width**, type **8**, and click on **OK** to change the "% inc" column width to fit your modified numeric display. Your screen should now match Figure 7.3.

Figure 7.3   **PROJECT.XLS, after reformatting**

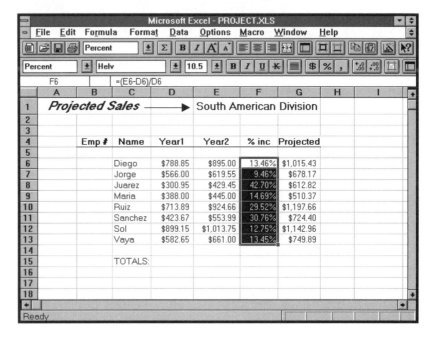

PRACTICE YOUR SKILLS

1. Hide the **Formatting toolbar**. (Hint: Use the **Options, Toolbars…** command.)

2. Save the worksheet to your EX4WORK directory as **MYPROJ.XLS**.

SELECTING A NONCONTIGUOUS RANGE OF CELLS

Until now, whenever you selected a range of cells, these cells were contiguous (adjacent to one another). Sometimes, however, you will want to select a noncontiguous range. In the next activity, you'll select three noncontiguous cells (G6, G10, and G12) and shade them for emphasis.

To select a noncontiguous range of cells,

- Hold down the Ctrl key.

- Click or drag the mouse as many times as required to select the desired noncontiguous cells.

- Release the Ctrl key when your selection is complete. Excel maintains your noncontiguous selection until you select a new cell.

Let's practice selecting a noncontiguous range:

1. Observe cells G6, G10, and G12. These values are the highest projected sales.

2. Select cell **G6**.

3. Hold down the **Ctrl** key and click on cells **G10** and **G12**. Note that these cells have been added to the current selection (see Figure 7.4).

Now let's apply a format to cells G6, G10, and G12:

1. Choose **Format, Border...** to open the Border dialog box.

2. Check **Shade** to turn on shading.

3. Click on **OK** to shade the noncontiguous selected range.

4. Press **Ctrl-Home** to deselect the range and get a better view of the shading.

CREATING A NUMBER FORMAT

As you learned in Chapter 5, the Format, Number dialog box provides you with a large selection of standard number formats (0.00%, #, ##0, and so on). Occasionally, however, none of these formats will fit your particular needs. For this reason, Excel allows you to create your own customized number formats.

To create a number format,

- Select the cell(s) you wish to format.

- Choose Format, Number....

- Select the current format in the *Code* text box.

- Type your new number format.
- Click on OK. Your new format will be added to the list of available formats, allowing you to use it again at a later date.

Figure 7.4 **PROJECT.XLS, with noncontiguous cells selected**

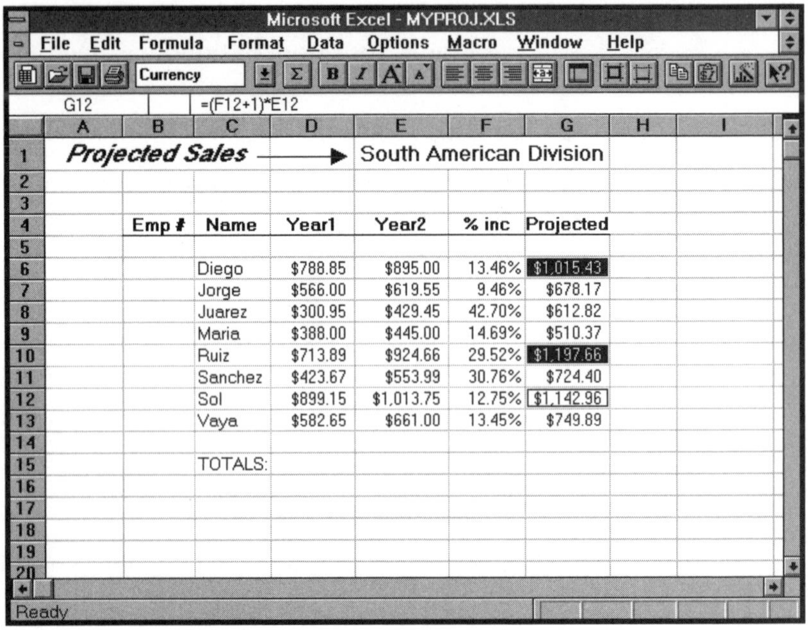

In creating a number format, you can use standard digit holders (0 forces Excel to display a digit or a zero, # cancels the display of unnecessary zeros), a decimal point, and Excel's date and time characters. For example:

Number Format	Entry	Display
0.0000	8.2	8.2000
$###,###,##0	1245	$1,245
(000)-000-0000	7165551212	(716)-555-1212

Number Format	Entry	Display
mm/dd/yy	7/25	07/25/91
hh:mm (AM/PM)	1:2 pm	01:02 (PM)

Let's create a simple number format:

1. Select the range **F6:F13**. These cells display two decimal places. Let's expand this to three.

2. Choose **Format, Number...** .

3. Note that the number format of the selected cells appears in the Format Codes text box (0.00%). Change this format to **0.000%**. (To do this, select the current format in the Code text box, then type **0.000%**.)

4. Click on **OK** to apply your new three-decimal format to the values in the selection.

5. Choose **Format, Number...** . Note that your new format (0.000%) has been added to the list of percentage formats. It is now available for future use with this worksheet. (It is not available for use in any other worksheet; you must recreate it within each worksheet where you want to use it.)

6. Click on **Cancel** to exit the Number Format dialog box.

ADDING TEXT TO A NUMBER FORMAT

Excel allows you to include text in a number format. Simply surround the text with quotation marks ("). For example, if you entered 5 in a cell formatted as "Department 00", Department 05 would be displayed. (The quotation marks do not appear in the screen display.)

Let's create a number format that includes text:

1. Select the range **B6:B13**.

2. Choose **Format, Number...** .

3. Select the current entry in the Code text box (**General**). Type **"EN"00**. The abbreviation EN stands for Employee Number. Remember that text included in a number format must be enclosed by quotation marks.

4. Click on **OK** to apply this new format to the selected cells. Since nothing has yet been entered in these cells, they remain blank.

5. In cell **B6**, enter **2**. Note that this entry is displayed as EN02; the quotation marks around the EN do not appear. The format you created precedes the entered number with EN and forces this number to take at least two digits (02 instead of just 2).

6. In cell **B7**, enter **15**. EN15 is displayed.

7. In cell **B8**, enter **100**. EN100 is displayed. The 00 in your customized format ("EN"00) are only placeholders. If you enter a number containing more than two digits, the format automatically adjusts to display the entire number.

PRACTICE YOUR SKILLS

1. Enter the following numbers into the indicated cells:

	B
9	7
10	9
11	46
12	133
13	58

2. If necessary, select the range **B6:B13**. Click on the Standard toolbar's **Left-Align button**. Compare your worksheet with Figure 7.5.

WORKING WITH DEFINED NAMES

An Excel *defined name* is a descriptive label that refers to a single cell or a cell range. Names are used for clarity and convenience. For example, in a large, multiscreen worksheet, you might want to define names for several data areas, then use Goto to move quickly to these areas by name (for instance, Totals), instead of by range (D15:G15). Names also help to simplify formulas, as they allow descriptive text labels to take the place of unwieldy ranges; for example, =SUM(Totals) instead of =SUM(D15:G15).

Figure 7.5   **PROJECT.XLS, with customized number formats**

	Microsoft Excel - MYPROJ.XLS								
	File Edit Formula Format Data Options Macro Window Help								
	Normal								
B6	2								

	A	B	C	D	E	F	G	H	I
1	*Projected Sales* ——▶			South American Division					
2									
3									
4		Emp #	Name	Year1	Year2	% inc	Projected		
5									
6		EN02	Diego	$788.85	$895.00	13.456%	$1,015.43		
7		EN15	Jorge	$566.00	$619.55	9.461%	$678.17		
8		EN100	Juarez	$300.95	$429.45	42.698%	$612.82		
9		EN07	Maria	$388.00	$445.00	14.691%	$510.37		
10		EN09	Ruiz	$713.89	$924.66	29.524%	$1,197.86		
11		EN46	Sanchez	$423.67	$553.99	30.760%	$724.40		
12		EN133	Sol	$899.15	$1,013.75	12.745%	$1,142.96		
13		EN58	Vaya	$582.65	$661.00	13.447%	$749.89		
14									
15			TOTALS:						
16									
17									
18									
19									
20									

Ready

To define a name,

- Select the cell(s) you wish to name.

- Choose Formula, Define Name... .

- Type a name or use the name Excel proposes in the Name text box. Follow these guidelines when defining a name:

  - The first character of the name must be a letter.

  - After the first letter, you can use letters, numbers, periods (.), and underscores (_).

  - Spaces are not allowed in the name. ("August Totals" is invalid; "August_Totals" is valid.)

  - The name cannot resemble a cell reference or range. (A1, B12, D100, E14:E18 are all invalid names.)

  - The name can contain up to 255 characters.

  - Capitalization is disregarded. (TOTALS, Totals, and totals are all interpreted as the same name.)

- Click on OK.

Let's see how Excel defines names automatically:

1. Select the range **C4:E15**.

2. Choose **Options, Set Print Area** to define a print area.

3. Select any cell to deselect the print area.

4. Choose **Formula, Define Name…** . Observe the Names In Sheet list box. Issuing a Set Print Area command caused Excel to create a range named "Print_Area."

5. Select **Print_Area**. Observe the Name text box and the Refers To box. Note that the name "Print_Area" refers to the absolute range $C$4:$E$15 (you selected this range in step 1).

6. Click on **Close** to return to the worksheet.

Now let's define a name for a range of cells:

1. Select the range **D6:D13**.

2. Choose **Formula, Define Name…** . Observe the Name text box. It is empty, except for a flashing insertion point prompting you to enter a name. Observe the Refers To box. It contains the absolute range $D$6:$D$13 (the one you just selected).

3. Type **Year1** and click on **OK**. You've just defined the selected range as "Year1," an appropriate choice as it mirrors the column heading.

USING A DEFINED NAME IN A FORMULA

As mentioned above, you can use defined names to take the place of hard-to-read cell references in formulas. Let's substitute a defined name for a range in a formula:

1. Select cell **D15** and enter **=SUM(D6:D13)**, a formula to sum the value in cells D6:D13. Note the result ($4,663.16).

2. Select cell **D15** again and enter the formula **=SUM(year1)**. The result is the same as in step 2 ($4,663.16). The defined name "Year1" took the place of the range D6:D13, making a tidier, more readable formula.

PRACTICE YOUR SKILLS

1. Define the name **Year2** for the range **E6:E13**.

2. Select cell **E15**.

3. Enter a formula that uses the name "Year2" to sum the values in cells E6:E13 ($5,542.40).

USING A DEFINED NAME WITH *GOTO*

As mentioned above, a defined name can be used with Goto to select a cell range quickly and easily. Let's try it:

1. Choose **Formula, Goto...** (or press **F5**).

2. Select **Year1** in the Goto box and click on **OK**. Note that the cells that make up Year1 (D6:D13) are selected (see Figure 7.6).

3. Go to the range named **Print_Area**. (Follow the procedure laid out in steps 1 and 2 above.)

4. Choose **File, Save** to update the file.

5. Close the file by double-clicking on the document **Control Menu button**, the small box in the upper-left corner of the document window, next to the word "File" in the menu bar. (Don't click on the application window Control Menu button, or you will exit from Excel.) Files can be closed either by choosing File, Close or by double-clicking on the file's Control Menu button.

OPENING MULTIPLE WORKSHEET WINDOWS

Until now, you have always opened one worksheet at a time. When you were finished with a worksheet, you closed it before opening another. At times, however, you may find it fruitful to work on two or more worksheets at the same time (one such instance would be copying the contents of a range of cells from one worksheet to another).

Excel allows you to open several worksheet windows at the same time. Each window can display the same section of the same worksheet, a different section of the same worksheet, or a different worksheet altogether. Data (text, numbers, formulas, and so on) can be entered into each window, and each window can be scrolled independently. Each window can be displayed separately as a full screen, or all of the windows can be sized and displayed together on one screen.

Figure 7.6   **Using a defined name with Goto**

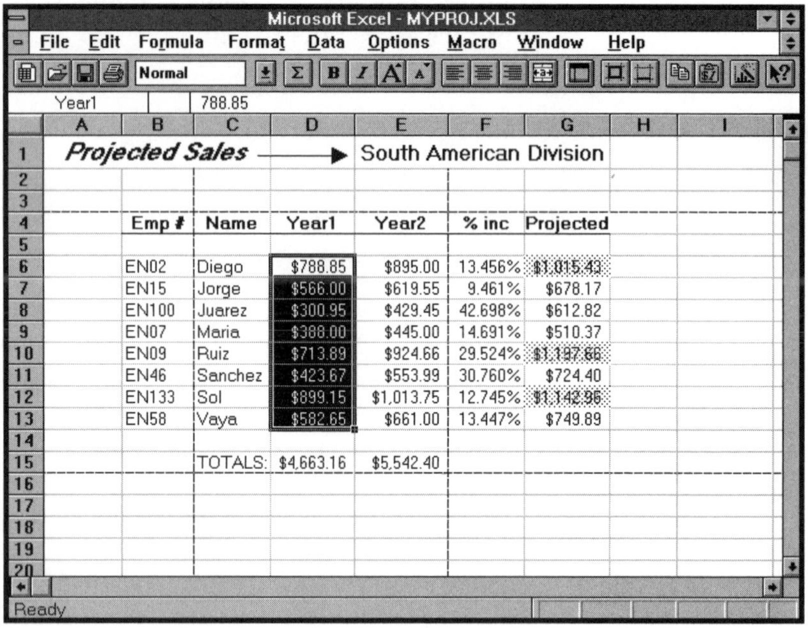

To open multiple worksheet windows,

- Choose File, Open.

- Select (click once on) the name of the first file that you want to open.

- If the other files that you want to open are listed adjacent to the first file, press and hold Shift, click on the last file name, then release Shift.

- If the other files that you want to open are not listed adjacent to the first file, press and hold Ctrl, click on each of the other file names, then release Ctrl.

- Click on OK.

Let's open four adjacently listed worksheet files:

1. Click on the **Open File tool** (second from the left in the Standard toolbar) to display the Open dialog box.

2. In the File Name list box, select (click once on) **DIV1.XLS**.

3. Press and hold **Shift**, select **DIV4.XLS**, and then release **Shift**. Note that all four adjacently listed files, DIV1.XLS through DIV4.XLS, are selected.

4. Click on **OK** to open these four files. Note that the worksheet windows overlap, so that DIV4.XLS is the only visible worksheet.

ACTIVATING A WORKSHEET WINDOW

When two or more worksheet windows are open, only one of these windows is *active* (selected) at any given time. The active window can be identified by its scroll bars, Maximize or Restore button (upper-right corner), and Control Menu button (upper-left corner); the inactive windows do not display these items.

Note: The active window may lie on top of other, inactive, windows, in some cases completely obscuring these windows (as in the four worksheets you just opened).

To activate a window,

- Either click on the window's title bar, or

- Choose Window and click on the name of the window you want to activate

Let's practice activating windows:

1. Choose **Window**. Note that the four worksheets you just opened are listed. The check next to DIV4.XLS marks it as the active worksheet.

2. Click on **DIV2.XLS**. Check the document title bar ("DIV2.XLS"). Note the appearance of scroll bars, a Maximize button, and a Control Menu button. DIV2.XLS is now the active worksheet.

3. Choose **Window**. Note that DIV2.XLS is checked.

4. Click on **DIV1.XLS**. DIV1.XLS is now the active worksheet.

ARRANGING MULTIPLE WINDOWS

When working with multiple windows, you may find your screen cluttered with overlapping worksheets. The *Window, Arrange...* command will arrange all your open windows to fit evenly on the screen without overlaps. To do this,

- Choose Window, Arrange... to open the *Arrange Windows* dialog box.

- Select one of the following Arrange options:
  - *Tiled* arranges windows in an even, tile-like pattern.
  - *Horizontal* stacks windows evenly from top to bottom.
  - *Vertical* arranges windows evenly from left to right.

- Click on OK.

Let's try these Arrange options on our four open worksheets:

1. Choose **Window, Arrange...** to open the Arrange Windows dialog box.

2. Select the **Horizontal** option and click on **OK**. Observe the results.

3. Repeat steps 1 and 2, this time selecting the **Vertical** option.

4. Repeat steps 1 and 2, this time selecting the **Tiled** option. Your screen should now match Figure 7.7.

Figure 7.7   **DIV1.XLS through DIV4.XLS, windows tiled**

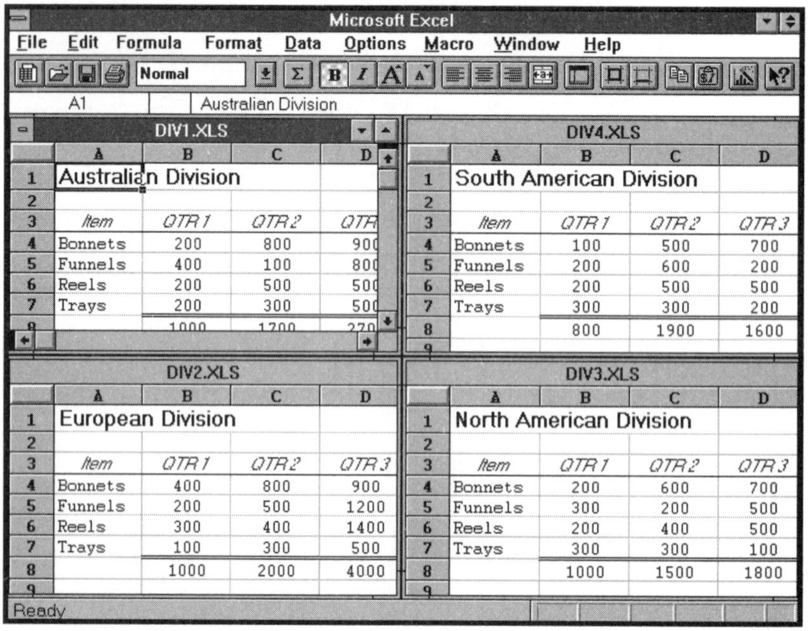

5. Note the arrangement of the windows: proceeding column-wise, we have DIV1.XLS, DIV2.XLS, then DIV4.XLS *before* DIV3.XLS. The Window, Arrange... command causes Excel to arrange windows columnwise in the order they were last selected (the most recently selected window appears at the top of the leftmost column). Tracing back through the last two activities, the order of selection was DIV1.XLS, DIV2.XLS, DIV4.XLS, and then DIV3.XLS.

6. Click on the **DIV3.XLS** title bar to select it as the active window. Note the scroll bars.

CLOSING MULTIPLE WINDOWS SIMULTANEOUSLY

You can close all of your windows in one step by holding down Shift and choosing *File, Close All*. (Please do *not* do this now.) Before closing a file you have modified, Excel will ask you whether you wish to save the changes.

LINKING WORKSHEETS

Excel allows you to link separate worksheets by writing a formula in one that refers to a cell in another. If the cell to which your formula refers is changed, the formula is updated automatically.

Linking allows you to consolidate data from two or more worksheets into a single document. You can break large, complicated worksheets into smaller documents that are faster to open, calculate, and save.

Let's examine and update a linked formula:

1. Open **ALLDIVS.XLS**.

2. Choose **Window, Arrange...**, select tiled, and click on OK to view all five open worksheets. ALLDIVS.XLS is active.

3. Note that the ordering of the windows on the screen reflects the sequence in which these windows were last selected: ALLDIVS.XLS, DIV3.XLS, DIV1.XLS, DIV2.XLS, DIV4.XLS.

4. In ALLDIVS.XLS, select cell **B4** and note its value (900). This cell contains a linked formula that sums bonnet sales for all four divisions for the first quarter (see the formula bar in Figure 7.8).

Figure 7.8   **Examining a linked formula**

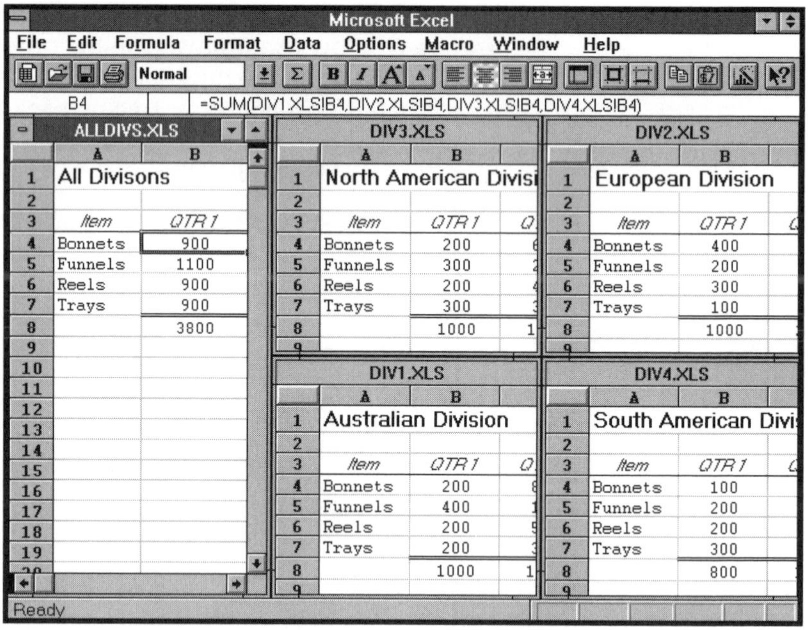

5. Observe the argument of the SUM function. Instead of cell references alone, this argument contains file/cell references (DIV1.XLS!B4 refers to cell B4 of file DIV1.XLS). A file/cell reference includes the file name, an exclamation point (!), and finally the cell address (with *no* spaces). Commas are used to separate cell references.

6. Activate **DIV1.XLS** by clicking on its title bar.

7. Select cell **B4**.

8. Enter **500** to change the number of bonnets in the Australian Division for the first quarter from 200 to 500.

9. Observe cell B4 in ALLDIVS.XLS. Note that its value has changed from 900 (in step 4) to 1200. The formula in this cell is linked to the value in cell B4 of DIV1.XLS, so changing the value in DIV1.XLS caused Excel to automatically recalculate the value in ALLDIVS.XLS.

10. Hold down **Shift** and choose **File, Close All** to close all open worksheets simultaneously. Do not save changes to any file.

USING MACROS TO AUTOMATE TASKS

A *macro* is a set of actions that Excel automatically performs. For example, the macro we'll be running in the following activity automatically inserts a four-row header in a worksheet, types and formats a heading, and then alphabetically sorts the worksheet data. Macros are used to automate complex or repetitive tasks; instead of performing these tasks yourself, you can simply run the macro and let it do all the work for you.

To run a macro,

- Open the macro sheet that contains the macro program. Macro sheets always end with the extension .XLM.

- Open the worksheet in which you want to run the macro.

- Activate the worksheet, if necessary.

- Choose *Macro, Run*. Or, if the macro has a shortcut key, press and hold Ctrl, and then press the shortcut key. (See below for instructions on how to find out if a macro has a shortcut key.) Capitalization is significant; if the assigned shortcut key is h, pressing Ctrl-h would run the macro, but pressing Ctrl-H would not.

To see if a macro has a shortcut key,

- Activate the macro sheet.

- Choose *Formula, Define Name*.

- Select the desired macro in the Names In Sheet list box.

- Observe the *Key* box. If there is a shortcut key assigned to the macro, it is shown here.

- Click on Close to remove the Define Name dialog box.

Let's use this procedure to run a simple macro:

1. Open the macro sheet **HEADER.XLM**. (To do this, use **File, Open** exactly as if your were opening a worksheet.)

2. Open the worksheet **INVENTRY.XLS**.

3. Choose **Window, Arrange...**, select **Horizontal**, and click on **OK** to arrange the windows horizontally. Note that the worksheet window (INVENTRY.XLS) contains inventory data, and the macro sheet window (HEADER.XLM) contains commands.

4. Click on the title bar of the macro sheet window to activate it. Choose **Formula, Define Name** and select **Header** in the Names In Sheet list box. Observe the Key box; this macro has been assigned the shortcut key "h." Click on **Close** to remove the Define Name dialog box.

5. Press the shortcut key combination **Ctrl-h** to run the macro. After a moment, the macro stops and a *Macro Error box* appears. Why? As mentioned above, you must activate the worksheet in which the macro will run *before* running the macro. Click on **Halt** to remove the Macro Error box. Let's try again.

6. Activate and maximize the **INVENTRY.XLS** worksheet window. Note that the worksheet contains no header, and that the items in column B are not alphabetically arranged.

7. Press **Ctrl-h** and observe your screen. This time, the macro runs properly. (If the macro had no shortcut key, you could have chosen Macro, Run to run it.)

8. Observe the changes in the worksheet (see Figure 7.9). The HEADER.XLM macro automatically inserted four rows in the worksheet, typed and formatted a heading, and sorted the data, saving you the time and tedium involved in doing this.

9. Hold down **Shift** and choose **File, Close All** to close the macro sheet and worksheet. Do not save the changes.

Note: This section was meant to give you a taste of Excel's powerful and extensive macro capabilities. Further discussion of macros (in particular, their creation and modification) is beyond the scope of this book. Interested readers are encouraged to refer to their Excel 4.0 User's Guides.

PRACTICE YOUR SKILLS

The following activity is designed to review the major topics covered in the electronic accounting section of this book, Chapters 1 through 7. Perform these steps to edit and print the file PRACEXER.XLS to match Figure 7.10:

1. Open **PRACEXER.XLS** (Chapter 3).

2. Maximize the document window, if necessary (Chapter 3).

Figure 7.9   **INVENTRY.XLS, after running the HEADER.XLM macro**

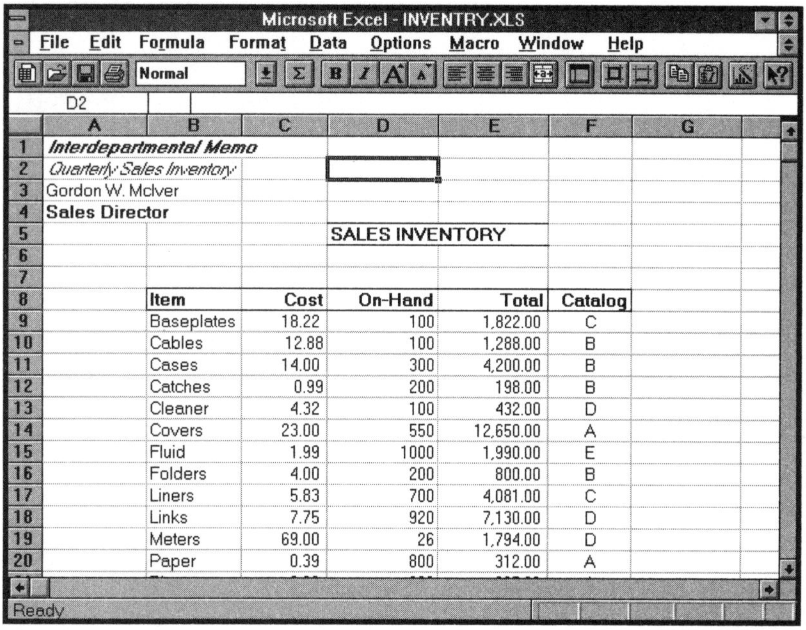

3. In cell **C13**, enter a function that will sum the range **C6:C11** (Chapter 4).

4. In cell **C14**, paste a function to average the range **C6:C11** (Chapter 4). (Hint: Remember to uncheck **Paste Arguments** before pasting.)

5. Duplicate the formula in cell **G6** to the range **G7:G11** (Chapter 4).

6. Duplicate the formulas in the range **C13:C14** to the range **D13:D14** (Chapter 4).

7. Clear the contents of cell **D13** (Chapter 3).

8. Copy the formulas in the range **C13:C14** to the range **G13:G14** (Chapter 5).

9. Select row **3**. Insert one row (Chapter 5).

10. Delete column **E** (Chapter 6).

11. Format the range **A4:F5** to **Italic** (Chapter 6).

Figure 7.10   **The printed worksheet MYPRACEX.XLS**

	A	B	C	D	E	F
1			EXMAC CORPORATION			
2			LOAN WORKSHEET			
3						
4		Used		Annual	Monthly	Monthly
5	Lender	For	Principal	Interest	Term	Payment
6						
7	Chase M.	Computer	$3,000	17.50%	24	$125.23
8	Cred. U.	Printers	$800	18.75%	12	$66.73
9	S&L	Building	$8,500	12.65%	36	$236.57
10	Chase M.	Expansion	$3,000	12.50%	24	$125.16
11	Cred. U.	Hardware	$1,000	13.75%	12	$83.40
12	S&L	Building	$2,000	14.00%	24	$83.45
13						
14	TOTALS:		$18,300			$720.55
15	AVERAGES:		$3,050	14.86%		$120.09

12. Format the range **C7:C15** to display currency with no decimal points (Chapter 5).

13. Format the range **D7:D15** to 0.00% (Chapter 5).

14. Format the range **F7:F15** to display currency with two decimal points (Chapter 5).

15. Adjust the widths of columns **C**, **D**, and **E** to display the longest text in each column (Chapter 5).

16. Center the contents of the range **E7:E12** (Chapter 6).

17. Format the range **A1:A2** to **Bold** (Chapter 6).

18. Center the range **A1:A2** over columns **A** through **F** (Chapter 6).

19. Save your file as **MYPRACEX.XLS** (Chapter 2).

20. Print the document using all current settings (Chapter 6).

21. Compare your printout to Figure 7.10.

22. Close the file (Chapter 2).

The following activity is designed to further review your Excel accounting skills. Perform these steps to edit and print the file OPTEXER.XLS to match Figure 7.11:

1. Open **OPTEXER.XLS** (Chapter 3).

2. Maximize the document window, if necessary (Chapter 3).

3. In cell **D9**, enter a formula that subtracts the value in cell **B9** from cell **C9**, then divides the result by **C9**. Use parentheses in the formula (Chapter 3).

4. In cell **E9**, enter a formula that calculates the projected sales for the third year. To do so, multiply the percentage increase by the second year's sales, and add that result to the second year's sales (Chapter 3).

5. In cell **F9**, calculate the projected commissions for the third year. You will be copying it in step 6, so use an absolute reference (Chapter 5).

6. Fill the range **D9:F9** to the range **D10:F16** (Chapter 4).

7. Copy the formulas in the range **D9:F16** to the range **D23:F30** (Chapter 5).

8. Edit the text in cell **A2** by inserting **rd** after "3" (Chapter 5).

9. Move the range **A1:A2** to the range **D1:D2** (Chapter 5).

10. Copy the contents of cell **D2** to cell **D22** (Chapter 4).

11. Select rows **23:27** and insert five rows (Chapter 5).

12. Copy the range **A6:F8** to the range **A25:F27** (Chapter 4).

13. Calculate totals by entering or copying SUM functions into the following cells (Chapter 4):

    B18

    C18

    E18

    F18

    B37

    C37

    E37

    F37

Figure 7.11   **The printed worksheet MYOPTEX.XLS**

MYOPTEX.XLS

Southern Division
2 Year Sales Report and 3rd Year Projections

Name	Sales 1st Year	Sales 2nd Year	Percentage Increase	Sales Projection 3rd Year	Projected Commissions 3rd Year
Binga, A.	$345.80	$567.80	39.0983%	$789.80	$59.24
Califano	$1,010.76	$1,212.56	16.6425%	$1,414.36	$106.08
Chen	$789.67	$950.00	16.8768%	$1,110.33	$83.27
Pedro	$567.27	$489.00	-16.0061%	$410.73	$30.80
Roland	$874.90	$998.89	12.4128%	$1,122.88	$84.22
Binga, S.	$560.00	$760.89	26.4020%	$961.78	$72.13
Tranler	$990.00	$1,100.56	10.0458%	$1,211.12	$90.83
Biron	$1,080.45	$1,020.67	-5.8569%	$960.89	$72.07
TOTALS:	$6,218.85	$7,100.37	0.996150692	$7,981.89	$598.64

Page 1

14. Align the contents of the range **B6:F8** to the right (Chapter 6).

15. Format the range **A6:F8** to be **Italic** (Chapter 6).

16. Select the ranges **D1:D2** and **D21:D22** together. Center the contents of the cells (Chapter 6).

17. Together, format the ranges **D1:D2** and **D21:D22** to be **Bold** (Chapters 6 and 7).

18. Format both ranges **B9:C18** and **E9:F18** together to display currency to two decimal places (Chapters 5 and 7).

19. Create a format for both cell **C4** and range **D9:D16** that displays percentages to four decimal places.

20. Copy only the formats from the range **A6:F18** to the range **A25:F37** (Chapter 5).

21. Adjust column widths as necessary to show all text and numbers (Chapter 5).

22. Save the file as **MYOPTEX.XLS** (Chapter 2).

23. Print only the range **A21:F37** without cell gridlines, or row or column headings (Chapter 6). Do not change any of the other current settings.

24. Compare your printout to Figure 7.11.

25. Update **MYOPTEX.XLS** (Chapter 2).

26. Close the file (Chapter 2).

CHAPTER SUMMARY

In this chapter, you were introduced to several advanced Excel worksheet topics. You learned to use non-Standard toolbars, to select a noncontiguous range, to define a name, and to create a customized number format. You also experimented with opening and linking multiple worksheets and running macros.

With this chapter, your foundation in Excel electronic accounting techniques is complete. Congratulations! You now possess the skills to create sophisticated, full-featured worksheets.

Here is a quick reference guide to the Excel features introduced in this chapter:

Desired Result	How to Do It
Display a toolbar	Choose **Options, Toolbars**, select desired toolbar in the Show Toolbars list box, click on **Show**
Hide a toolbar	Choose **Options, Toolbars**, select desired toolbar in the Show Toolbars list box, click on **Hide**
Move a toolbar	Press and hold mouse button on desired toolbar to select it (outline appears), drag selected toolbar to new location
Select a noncontiguous range	Hold **Ctrl**, select noncontiguous cells, release **Ctrl**
Create a number format	Select cell(s) to format, choose **Format, Number...**, type format in Code text box, click on **OK**
Include text in a number format	Surround text with quotation marks (")
Define a name	Select cell(s) to name, choose **Formula, Define Name...**, type name, click on **OK**
Use a name in a formula	Replace formula range with name
Go to a name	Choose **Formula, Goto...** (or **F5**), select name, click on **OK**
Close a file	Choose **Close, File**, or double-click on file's **Control Menu button**

Desired Result	How to Do It
Open multiple worksheet windows	Choose **File, Open**, select name of first file to open. If other files to open are listed adjacent to first file, press and hold **Shift**, click on last file name, then release **Shift**; if other files to open are not listed adjacent to first file, press and hold **Ctrl**, click on each file name, then release **Ctrl**. Click on **OK**
Activate a worksheet window	Click on window title bar, or choose **Window**, click on worksheet name
Arrange multiple windows on screen	Choose **Window, Arrange...**, select desired Arrange option (**Tiled**, **Horizontal**, or **Vertical**), click on **OK**
Close multiple windows simultaneously	Hold **Shift**, choose **File, Close All**
Create a linked formula cell reference	Type file name, followed by !, followed by cell address (for example, DIV1.XLS!B4)
Run a macro	Open macro sheet containing macro program, open worksheet in which to run macro, activate worksheet if necessary. Choose **Macro, Run**; or, if macro has shortcut key, press and hold **Ctrl**, then press shortcut key (capitalization is significant)
Find out if a macro has a shortcut key	Activate macro sheet, choose **Formula, Define Name**, select macro in Names In Sheet box, observe Key box, click on **Close** to remove dialog box

The next chapter begins the section of this manual devoted to Excel's database-management system (Chapters 8 through 11). You will learn to create and modify an Excel database and to sort (rearrange) the information contained within such a database.

IF YOU'RE STOPPING HERE

If you need to break off here, please exit from Excel. If you want to proceed directly to the next chapter, please do so now.

CHAPTER 8: SORTING DATABASE RECORDS

Database
Management

Performing a
One-Key Sort

Numbering
Records with the
Data, Series
Command

Performing a
Multiple-key Sort

Database Design
Considerations

This chapter introduces our second major topic: *database manage ment.* Along with its electronic accounting abilities, Excel can help you manage (edit, sort, customize, and analyze) a complex body of data—for example, a collection of personnel records containing the vital statistics for every employee in a large company.

After a short synopsis of database-management terminology, you will learn to create and modify an Excel database, and to rearrange (sort) the information in such a database using the *Data, Sort* command.

When you're done working through this chapter, you will know

- How to perform one-key and multiple-key sorts
- How to undo and redo a sort
- How to number database records
- What to consider when designing a database

DATABASE MANAGEMENT

Database management is the systematic arrangement of information (data) so that it can easily be searched, extracted, and rearranged. Given a database (body of data) consisting of personnel information, typical database-management tasks might be

- Extracting a list of employees and salaries from one department
- Listing employees according to hire date
- Realphabetizing a list of employees by first, rather than last, names (useful for in-house telephone listings)

The benefits of an *electronic* database-management system are the great quantities of data that you can store and the speed with which you can extract or rearrange this data.

The following are the terms that describe the primary parts of a database (see Figure 8.1):

Database	A collection of related data. Common examples of databases include phone books, mailing lists, inventory lists, and address books.
Record	A single row of data in a database. Figure 8.1 contains six records: Abel, Binga, Califano, Culbert, Halal, and Harper.
Field	A single column of data in a database. Figure 8.1 contains four fields: last name, first name, address, and phone number.
Field Name	A name that identifies the data stored in a field. In Figure 8.1, the field names are "Last," "First," "Address," and "Phone."

Note: An Excel database is stored as a worksheet file in the same form as the ones presented in the first seven chapters of this book. This allows you to perform both accounting and database-management operations on the same file.

Figure 8.1 **Primary parts of a database**

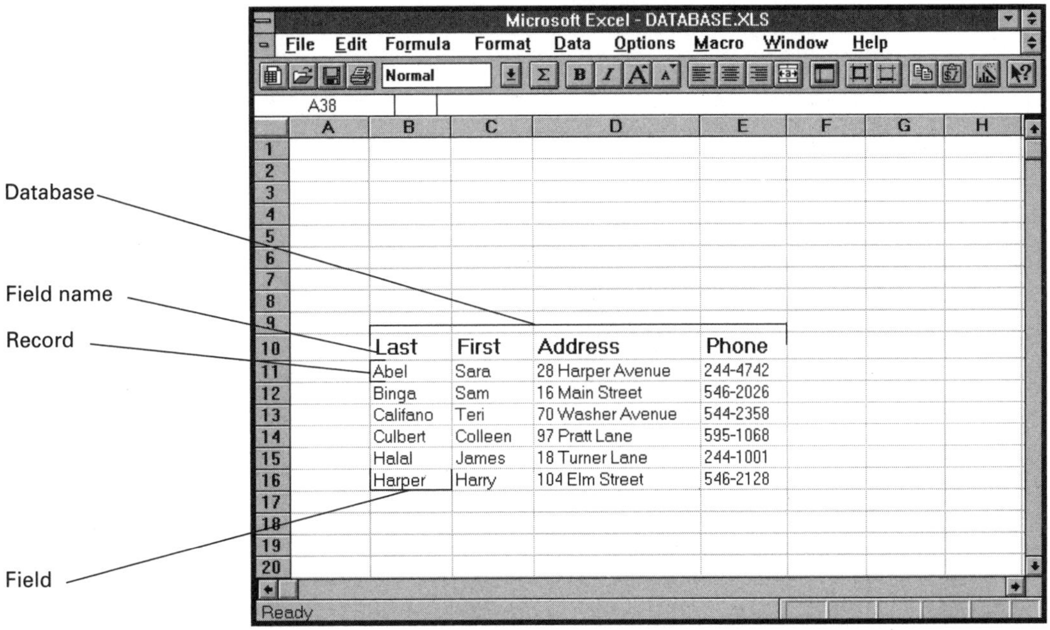

If you are not running Excel, please start it now. If there is a worksheet on your screen, please close it. Your screen should be empty except for a maximized Excel application window.

Let's take a look at a worksheet containing a typical payroll database:

1. Open **CHAP8.XLS** from the EX4WORK directory.

2. Maximize the document window if necessary. This file tracks payroll information for the ABC Company (see Figure 8.2). Your current date (in cell H1) will differ from the date shown in the figure. Your Years Employed data (cells F5:F19) will also differ from those in the figure, because the number of years employed is dependent upon the current date.

Figure 8.2   **The CHAP8.XLS worksheet**

	A	B	C	D	E	F	G	H	I
1			***The ABC COMPANY PAYROLL for the Period Ending-->					28-Jul-92	
2									
3					DATE of	YEARS		HRLY	GROSS
4		FIRST	LAST	EMP#	HIRE	EMPLOYED	HRS	RATE	PAY
5		James	Halal	MPS45	5-Jun-82	10.15	35	$24.00	$840.00
6		Sara	Abel	CCE29	24-Dec-81	10.60	35.5	$12.50	$443.75
7		Sam	Binga	MPS09	5-Jul-80	12.07	35.5	$13.30	$472.15
8		Harry	Harper	CES25	30-Dec-85	6.58	40	$21.50	$860.00
9		Colleen	Culbert	CCE58	26-Jul-85	7.01	42	$16.75	$703.50
10		Teri	Califano	EEE55	7-Jun-83	9.15	40	$8.75	$350.00
11		Frank	Bally	MMS07	12-Jul-78	14.06	40	$12.60	$504.00
12		Theresa	Binga	MSS19	26-Feb-84	8.43	35.5	$13.30	$472.15
13		Barry	Keen	CES04	15-Apr-78	14.30	40	$21.50	$860.00
14		Sam	Freshita	MSS26	1-Feb-85	7.49	35.5	$13.30	$472.15
15		Shing	Chen	MPS05	8-Aug-79	12.98	35.5	$13.30	$472.15
16		Alice	Binga	MMS76	5-Apr-85	7.32	32	$5.50	$176.00
17		Bob	Abel	CCE14	25-Jan-80	12.52	35.5	$12.50	$443.75
18		Chris	Hall	MMS59	12-May-83	9.22	40	$7.22	$288.80
19			AVG. YRS/HRS/RATE			10.13	37.29	$14.00	
20			TOTAL GROSS PAYROLL						$7,358.40

3. Select cell **B4**. Note the contents in the formula bar (FIRST). Cells B4 through I4 contain text rather than numbers or formulas.

4. Observe the contents of cells D5 through D18. They contain text representing unique five-character employee identification codes.

5. Observe the content of cells E5 through E18. They contain dates in *d-mmm-yy* format.

6. Select cell **H1** and observe its contents. It contains the formula =NOW(). NOW is a function that automatically enters the current date in a worksheet. As mentioned above, your current date will differ from the date in the figure.

7. Observe the contents of cells H5 through H18. They each contain a constant value representing an hourly wage. These cells have been formatted to display a dollar sign and two digits to the right of the decimal point.

8. Observe the contents of cells I5 through I18. They each contain a formula that calculates gross pay (hours multiplied by

hourly wage). These cells have also been formatted to display a dollar sign and two decimal digits. (Remember that only the results of a calculated formula are displayed, not the formulas themselves.)

9. Observe the contents of cells H19 and I20. These cells contain, respectively, the AVERAGE and SUM functions. H19 calculates the average hourly rate; I20 calculates the company's total gross payroll.

PERFORMING A ONE-KEY SORT

At times, you may need to rearrange the order of records in a database. For example, you might need to change a list of employees from alphabetical order to gross-pay order (highest to lowest gross pay or vice versa). Excel allows you to rearrange (sort) data by using the Data, Sort command.

In sorting a database, you must specify one or more *sort keys*, which identify the data fields you would like Excel to base its sort on. For example, if you would like to sort by last names, you would choose the column containing the last name field as your sort key. You can display database records in alphabetical, numeric, or date order.

To perform a one-key sort,

- Select the range of cells (records) to be sorted.
- Choose Data, Sort….
- To rearrange rows, select Rows (under *Sort by*); to rearrange columns, select Columns.
- Under *1st Key*, enter a cell in the column or row by which you would like to sort.
- Select the sort order: ascending or descending.
- Click on OK.

Let's perform a simple one-key sort:

1. Observe the data structure of CHAP8.XLS. The rows (records) are not arranged in any particular order (neither alphabetically, by employee number, nor by date of hire).

2. Select cells **B5:I18** to specify the records to be sorted. Note that the title, headings, and totals rows (1 through 4, 19 and

20) were not included in this selection; we want these rows to remain fixed in their current locations, *not* to be sorted. When preparing to sort, make sure to select only the information you would like rearranged.

3. Choose **Data, Sort...** to open the Sort dialog box.

4. If necessary, drag the dialog box down by its title bar until you can see the column headings for the list ("FIRST," "LAST," etc.). This makes it easier to identify the column by which you would like to sort.

5. Select **Rows** in the Sort By box. You can sort by rows or columns. In this case, you will be rearranging rows (records) of data.

6. Select the **$B$5** entry in the 1st Key box. Excel automatically entered $B$5 in this box because it assumed you wanted to sort by the column of the currently active cell (B5). However, we want to sort on a different column.

7. Click anywhere within column **F** ("YEARS EMPLOYED"). When choosing a sort-key column or row, you can click anywhere within this column or row.

8. Select **Descending** in the 1st Key box to tell Excel to sort by years employed in descending order (that is, the more years employed, the higher up on the list).

9. Click on **OK** to sort the selected records and return to the worksheet. Examine the new database order. All records have been rearranged by their Years Employed data (see Figure 8.3).

PRACTICE YOUR SKILLS

Sort the selected records (B5:I18) again by the field in column F ("YEARS EMPLOYED"), but this time in ascending order.

 ### UNDOING AND REDOING A SORT

After performing a sort, you may decide you do not want to keep the new arrangement of records. If you realize this immediately (before you perform another Excel action), you can simply undo the sort by choosing *Edit, Undo Sort*. To redo a sort you just undid, choose *Edit, Redo [u] Sort*.

Figure 8.3   **CHAP8.XLS, after sorting on years employed**

	A	B	C	D	E	F	G	H	I
1			***The ABC COMPANY PAYROLL for the Period Ending-->					28-Jul-92	
2									
3					DATE of	YEARS		HRLY	GROSS
4		FIRST	LAST	EMP#	HIRE	EMPLOYED	HRS	RATE	PAY
5		Barry	Keen	CES04	15-Apr-78	14.30	40	$21.50	$860.00
6		Frank	Bally	MMS07	12-Jul-78	14.06	40	$12.60	$504.00
7		Shing	Chen	MPS05	8-Aug-79	12.98	35.5	$13.30	$472.15
8		Bob	Abel	CCE14	25-Jan-80	12.52	35.5	$12.50	$443.75
9		Sam	Binga	MPS09	5-Jul-80	12.07	35.5	$13.30	$472.15
10		Sara	Abel	CCE29	24-Dec-81	10.60	35.5	$12.50	$443.75
11		James	Halal	MPS45	5-Jun-82	10.15	35	$24.00	$840.00
12		Chris	Hall	MMS59	12-May-83	9.22	40	$7.22	$288.80
13		Teri	Califano	EEE55	7-Jun-83	9.15	40	$8.75	$350.00
14		Theresa	Binga	MSS19	26-Feb-84	8.43	35.5	$13.30	$472.15
15		Sam	Freshita	MSS26	1-Feb-85	7.49	35.5	$13.30	$472.15
16		Alice	Binga	MMS76	5-Apr-85	7.32	32	$5.50	$176.00
17		Colleen	Culbert	CCE58	26-Jul-85	7.01	42	$16.75	$703.50
18		Harry	Harper	CES25	30-Dec-85	6.58	40	$21.50	$860.00
19			AVG. YRS/HRS/RATE			10.13	37.29	$14.00	
20			TOTAL GROSS PAYROLL						$7,358.40

Let's undo, then redo, the sort operation you just performed in the above Practice Your Skills activity:

1. Choose **Edit, Undo Sort** to undo the previous sort. The records are returned to their former order (years employed in descending order).

2. Choose **Edit, Redo [u] Sort** to redo the ascending sort. The records are returned to their final order (years employed in ascending order).

NUMBERING RECORDS WITH THE DATA, SERIES COMMAND

Excel allows you to number the individual records in your database automatically. The *Data, Series* command numbers a list of records, based on the sequence of these records when the command is issued. Record numbering is especially useful if your records are in no particular order (as was the case when you first opened CHAP8.XLS), and you wish to assign numeric labels to them.

Note: Bear in mind that your record numbers may be moved out of sequence if you sort the records.

To number a series of records,

- Enter the starting number in the appropriate cell.

- Select the range of cells to contain the record numbers (this range must contain the starting-number cell).

- Choose Data, Series....

- Select Rows (under *Series in*) to enter numbers in a row; select Columns to enter numbers in a column.

- Under Type, select the desired type of numbering scheme: linear (1, 2, 3, 4, etc.), date (Jan-91, Feb-91, etc.), or growth (1, 2, 4, 8, 16, etc.).

- Enter the increment value you would like to use in the Step Value box.

- Enter a value in the Stop Value box only if you would like to stop numbering before the end of the selected range.

- Click on OK.

Now let's use the Data, Series command to assign numbers to a series of records. First, we'll return CHAP8.XLS to its original form (as it was when you first opened it at the beginning of this chapter):

1. Open **CHAP8.XLS**. The following alert box prompt will appear:

   ```
   Revert to saved 'CHAP8.XLS'?
   ```

   This prompt is telling you that a previously saved version of your on-screen worksheet (CHAP8.XLS) exists in the current disk directory (EX4WORK). You are being asked whether you want to *revert* to this previous version, which would replace (erase) the on-screen worksheet with the previously saved version. In this case, we want to return to the original form of CHAP8.XLS. (Take care when you see a revert prompt—reverting to a previously saved file will cause the current, on-screen version to be erased.)

2. Click on **OK** to open the original version of CHAP8.XLS. Now we'll create a new field to hold the record numbers.

3. In cell **A5**, enter **1** to assign the number 1 to James Halal's record.

4. Select the range **A5:A18**. This is where we'll put the record numbers for all employees in the list.

5. Choose **Data, Series**... to open the Data, Series dialog box.

6. Observe the current settings. Series in Columns and Type Linear are selected, and the Step Value is 1.

7. Click on **OK** to accept these settings and close the dialog box. Observe the record numbers.

8. In cell **A4**, enter **NUM** to name the new field (see Figure 8.4).

Figure 8.4   **CHAP8.XLS, after using Data, Series to number records**

	A	B	C	D	E	F	G	H	I
1			***The ABC COMPANY PAYROLL for the Period Ending-->					28-Jul-92	
2									
3					DATE of	YEARS		HRLY	GROSS
4	NUM	FIRST	LAST	EMP#	HIRE	EMPLOYED	HRS	RATE	PAY
5	1	James	Halal	MPS45	5-Jun-82	10.15	35	$24.00	$840.00
6	2	Sara	Abel	CCE29	24-Dec-81	10.60	35.5	$12.50	$443.75
7	3	Sam	Binga	MPS09	5-Jul-80	12.07	35.5	$13.30	$472.15
8	4	Harry	Harper	CES25	30-Dec-85	6.58	40	$21.50	$860.00
9	5	Colleen	Culbert	CCE58	26-Jul-85	7.01	42	$16.75	$703.50
10	6	Teri	Califano	EEE55	7-Jun-83	9.15	40	$8.75	$350.00
11	7	Frank	Bally	MMS07	12-Jul-78	14.06	40	$12.60	$504.00
12	8	Theresa	Binga	MSS19	26-Feb-84	8.43	35.5	$13.30	$472.15
13	9	Barry	Keen	CES04	15-Apr-78	14.30	40	$21.50	$860.00
14	10	Sam	Freshita	MSS26	1-Feb-85	7.49	35.5	$13.30	$472.15
15	11	Shing	Chen	MPS05	8-Aug-79	12.98	35.5	$13.30	$472.15
16	12	Alice	Binga	MMS76	5-Apr-85	7.32	32	$5.50	$176.00
17	13	Bob	Abel	CCE14	25-Jan-80	12.52	35.5	$12.50	$443.75
18	14	Chris	Hall	MMS59	12-May-83	9.22	40	$7.22	$288.80
19			AVG. YRS/HRS/RATE			10.13	37.29	$14.00	
20			TOTAL GROSS PAYROLL						$7,358.40

Now let's sort the ABC Company's records:

1. Select the sort range **A5:I18**. The record numbers you just created in column A will be sorted along with the rest of the data.

2. Choose **Data, Sort**... to open the Sort dialog box.

3. Modify the settings to sort by ascending employee number. (With the **1st Key** box entry selected, click on any cell in column **D**, then select **Ascending**.)

4. Click on **OK** to perform the sort and return to the worksheet. The records are arranged alphabetically by employee identification code.

5. Note that the record numbers you created with the Data, Series command are out of order. As mentioned above, sorting a numbered list may cause the numbers to be moved out of sequence.

6. Choose **Data, Sort....**

7. Modify the settings so you can sort by years employed in descending order. (For help, see step 3.)

8. Click on **OK** to perform the sort and return to the worksheet. Observe the results.

PRACTICE YOUR SKILLS

Sort the selected records (A5:I18) in ascending order by the numbers in column A (NUM). This will return the records to their original order (1 through 14).

PERFORMING A MULTIPLE-KEY SORT

A one-key sort may not always provide enough order for your database record list. For example, if you sorted a group of employee records by last names, and four people had the last name "Smith," you would have a four-way *sort tie*. When such ties occur, Excel maintains the original order of records. This may create an undesired ordering (for instance, "John Smith" might appear before "Beverly Smith").

Excel allows you to perform multiple-key sorts to resolve sort ties. The following table displays a list of four names, the results when it is sorted by last name (one-key sort), and the results when it is sorted by last and subsorted by first name (two-key sort).

Original order	After sorting by last name	After sorting by last name and subsorting by first name
Sam Binga	Sara Abel	Bob Abel
Alice Binga	Bob Abel	Sara Abel
Sara Abel	Sam Binga	Alice Binga
Bob Abel	Alice Binga	Sam Binga

Note that the ties unresolved after sorting by last name are subsequently resolved after subsorting by first name.

To sort by two or three keys,

- Select the range of cells (records) to be sorted.

- Choose Data, Sort....

- Select Rows or Columns.

- Under 1st Key, select a cell in the column or row you would like to sort, then select Ascending or Descending order.

- Do the same for the *2nd* and, if necessary, *3rd Keys.*

- Click on OK.

Let's perform a two-key sort to arrange the selected records in alphabetical order by last and first names:

1. Select the range **A5:I18** if it is not already selected.

2. Choose **Data, Sort**....

3. Under 1st Key, select column **C** ("LAST") and **Ascending** to sort alphabetically by last name.

4. Click within the **2nd key** box to activate it. Select column **B** ("FIRST") and **Ascending** to subsort alphabetically by first names.

5. Click on **OK** to perform the sort and return to the worksheet. Observe the results (see Figure 8.5). Note that the 1st Key (last names) took sorting precedence over the 2nd Key (first names). The 2nd Key affected the sort order only when the 1st Key produced a tie (Abel and Binga).

Figure 8.5   **CHAP8.XLS, after a two-key sort**

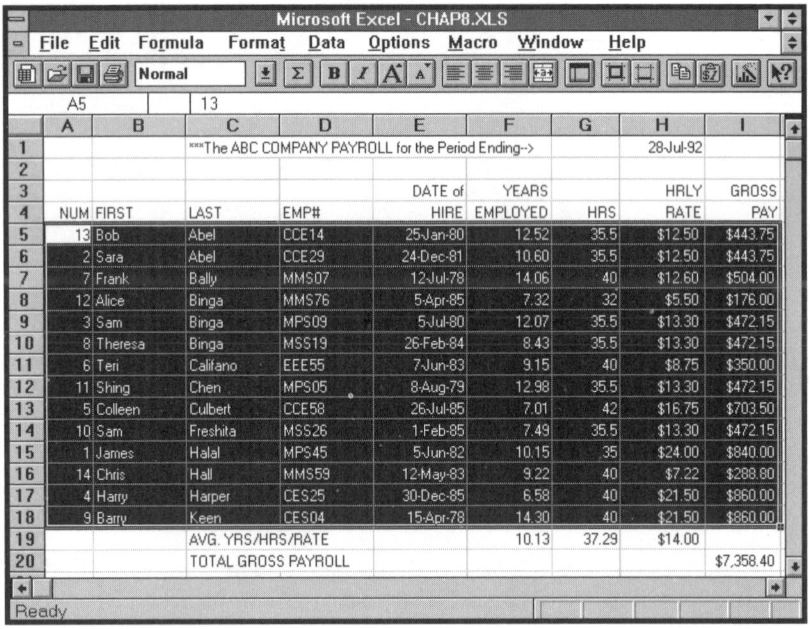

Now let's perform a second sort. We will sort by hours and subsort by hourly rate. Any ties this may produce will maintain the order of the previous sort (last name, first name):

1. Select the range **A5:I18** if it is not already selected.

2. Choose **Data, Sort**....

3. As 1st Key, choose column **G** ("HRS"), **Descending** order. As 2nd Key, choose column **H** ("HRLY RATE"), **Descending** order.

4. Click on **OK** to perform the sort and return to the worksheet (see Figure 8.6). Observe records 4 (Harry Harper) and 9 (Barry Keen). These records have the same data for both hours and hourly rate. The previous sort order (last name, first name) was retained here.

5. Observe the data in the lower half of the database (rows 11 through 16). The previous sort order was retained here also.

Finally, let's perform a three-key sort:

1. Select the range **A5:I18** if it is not already selected.

2. Choose **Data, Sort**....

Figure 8.6   **CHAP8.XLS, after a second two-key sort**

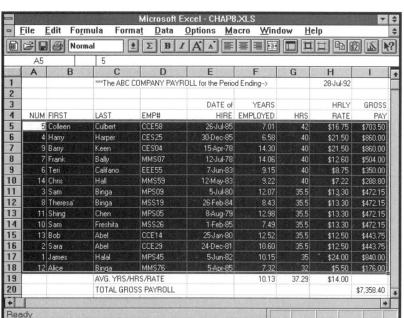

	A	B	C	D	E	F	G	H	I
1			***The ABC COMPANY PAYROLL for the Period Ending-->					28-Jul-92	
2									
3					DATE of	YEARS		HRLY	GROSS
4	NUM	FIRST	LAST	EMP#	HIRE	EMPLOYED	HRS	RATE	PAY
5	5	Colleen	Culbert	CCE58	26-Jul-85	7.01	42	$16.75	$703.50
6	4	Harry	Harper	CES25	30-Dec-85	6.58	40	$21.50	$860.00
7	9	Barry	Keen	CES04	15-Apr-78	14.30	40	$21.50	$860.00
8	7	Frank	Bally	MMS07	12-Jul-78	14.06	40	$12.60	$504.00
9	6	Teri	Califano	EEE55	7-Jun-83	9.15	40	$8.75	$350.00
10	14	Chris	Hall	MMS59	12-May-83	9.22	40	$7.22	$288.80
11	3	Sam	Binga	MPS09	5-Jul-80	12.07	35.5	$13.30	$472.15
12	8	Theresa'	Binga	MSS19	26-Feb-84	8.43	35.5	$13.30	$472.15
13	11	Shing	Chen	MPS05	8-Aug-79	12.98	35.5	$13.30	$472.15
14	10	Sam	Freshita	MSS26	1-Feb-85	7.49	35.5	$13.30	$472.15
15	13	Bob	Abel	CCE14	25-Jan-80	12.52	35.5	$12.50	$443.75
16	2	Sara	Abel	CCE29	24-Dec-81	10.60	35.5	$12.50	$443.75
17	1	James	Halal	MPS45	5-Jun-82	10.15	35	$24.00	$840.00
18	12	Alice	Binga	MMS76	5-Apr-85	7.32	32	$5.50	$176.00
19			AVG. YRS/HRS/RATE			10.13	37.29	$14.00	
20			TOTAL GROSS PAYROLL						$7,358.40

3. As 1st Key, choose column **G** ("HRS"), **Descending** order. As 2nd Key, choose column **H** ("HRLY RATE"), **Descending** order. (These are the same sort settings used in the previous task.)

4. As 3rd Key, choose column **D** ("EMP#"), **Ascending** order to create a second subsort by employee numbers.

5. Click on **OK** to perform the sort and return to the worksheet (see Figure 8.7).

6. Observe the records with ties in the hours and hourly rate fields. The records are arranged so that the employee identification codes are alphabetized where a second subsort was needed.

SORTING BY MORE THAN THREE KEYS

As seen above, when Excel performs a sort, it retains as much of the previous order as possible. You can use this fact to sort by more than three keys.

Figure 8.7   CHAP8.XLS, after a three-key sort

Microsoft Excel - CHAP8.XLS

	A	B	C	D	E	F	G	H	I
1			***The ABC COMPANY PAYROLL for the Period Ending-->					2-Sep-92	
2									
3					DATE of	YEARS		HRLY	GROSS
4	NUM	FIRST	LAST	EMP#	HIRE	EMPLOYED	HRS	RATE	PAY
5	5	Colleen	Culbert	CCE58	26-Jul-85	7.11	42	$16.75	$703.50
6	9	Barry	Keen	CES04	15-Apr-78	14.40	40	$21.50	$860.00
7	4	Harry	Harper	CES25	30-Dec-85	6.68	40	$21.50	$860.00
8	7	Frank	Bally	MMS07	12-Jul-78	14.15	40	$12.60	$504.00
9	6	Teri	Califano	EEE55	7-Jun-83	9.25	40	$8.75	$350.00
10	14	Chris	Hall	MMS59	12-May-83	9.32	40	$7.22	$288.80
11	11	Shing	Chen	MPS05	8-Aug-79	13.08	35.5	$13.30	$472.15
12	3	Sam	Binga	MPS09	5-Jul-80	12.17	35.5	$13.30	$472.15
13	8	Theresa	Binga	MSS19	26-Feb-84	8.52	35.5	$13.30	$472.15
14	10	Sam	Freshita	MSS26	1-Feb-85	7.59	35.5	$13.30	$472.15
15	13	Bob	Abel	CCE14	25-Jan-80	12.61	35.5	$12.50	$443.75
16	2	Sara	Abel	CCE29	24-Dec-81	10.70	35.5	$12.50	$443.75
17	1	James	Halal	MPS45	5-Jun-82	10.25	35	$24.00	$840.00
18	12	Alice	Binga	MMS76	5-Apr-85	7.42	32	$5.50	$176.00
19			AVG. YRS/HRS/RATE				10.23	37.29	$14.00
20			TOTAL GROSS PAYROLL						$7,358.40

To sort by more than three keys, divide the sort into two rounds. Use the least important keys for the first round of sorting. For example, to perform a five-key sort, start with a two-key sort with the fourth and fifth keys specified as 1st Key and 2nd Key, respectively. Then use the three most important keys for the second round of sorting.

PRACTICE YOUR SKILLS

1. Perform the following five-key sort on the records in range **A5:I18** of CHAP8.XLS. You will have to do two rounds of sorting. Specify the 4th and 5th Keys below as the 1st and 2nd Keys in the first round.

1st Key Column   **I** ("GROSS PAY"), **Descending** order

2nd Key Column   **F** ("YEARS EMPLOYED"), **Ascending** order

3rd Key Column   **H** ("HRLY RATE"), **Descending** order

4th Key Column   **C** ("LAST"), **Ascending** order

5th Key Column   **B** ("FIRST"), **Ascending** order

2. Compare your worksheet with the one in Figure 8.8.

Figure 8.8   **CHAP8.XLS, after a five-key sort**

	A	B	C	D	E	F	G	H	I
1			***The ABC COMPANY PAYROLL for the Period Ending-->					28-Jul-92	
2									
3					DATE of	YEARS		HRLY	GROSS
4	NUM	FIRST	LAST	EMP#	HIRE	EMPLOYED	HRS	RATE	PAY
5	4	Harry	Harper	CES25	30-Dec-85	6.58	40	$21.50	$860.00
6	9	Barry	Keen	CES04	15-Apr-78	14.30	40	$21.50	$860.00
7	1	James	Halal	MPS45	5-Jun-82	10.15	35	$24.00	$840.00
8	5	Colleen	Culbert	CCE58	26-Jul-85	7.01	42	$16.75	$703.50
9	7	Frank	Bally	MMS07	12-Jul-78	14.06	40	$12.60	$504.00
10	10	Sam	Freshita	MSS26	1-Feb-85	7.49	35.5	$13.30	$472.15
11	8	Theresa	Binga	MSS19	26-Feb-84	8.43	35.5	$13.30	$472.15
12	3	Sam	Binga	MPS09	5-Jul-80	12.07	35.5	$13.30	$472.15
13	11	Shing	Chen	MPS05	8-Aug-79	12.98	35.5	$13.30	$472.15
14	2	Sara	Abel	CCE29	24-Dec-81	10.60	35.5	$12.50	$443.75
15	13	Bob	Abel	CCE14	25-Jan-80	12.52	35.5	$12.50	$443.75
16	6	Teri	Califano	EEE55	7-Jun-83	9.15	40	$8.75	$350.00
17	14	Chris	Hall	MMS59	12-May-83	9.22	40	$7.22	$288.80
18	12	Alice	Binga	MMS76	5-Apr-85	7.32	32	$5.50	$176.00
19			AVG. YRS/HRS/RATE			10.13	37.29	$14.00	
20			TOTAL GROSS PAYROLL						$7,358.40

3. Save the file as **MYCHAP8.XLS**.

4. Close the file. (Choose **File, Close** or double-click on the **Control Menu button** of the document window—*not* of the application window.)

DATABASE DESIGN CONSIDERATIONS

Follow these design considerations when creating a database:

- Create a field for each category of data you wish to track. For example, in CHAP8.XLS, the following data are tracked: first name, last name, employee number, hire date, years employed, hours, hourly rate, and gross pay.

- Remember to leave one or more rows free at the top of the database to hold the field names ("FIRST," "LAST," "EMP#," "DATE of HIRE," and so on).

- Create the records from the items you need to track. For example, in CHAP8.XLS, each employee gets a separate record.

- If you wish, leave one column free to the left of the database for record numbers.

- Be consistent with the type of data entered into fields and records. For example, if a field contains last names, make sure to enter *only* last names in that field; if a record consists of data relating to a single employee, be sure to enter all the data in the correct order for that employee.

- If you want to include cell borders or blank rows in your database, add them *after* sorting. If cell borders or blank rows are present when a range of records is sorted, these rows will be sorted out to the bottom of the list.

Let's sort a list containing borders and blank cells:

1. Choose **File** to open the File menu. Observe the file names at the bottom of the menu. Excel "remembers" the last four files you have opened and lists them here for easy retrieval.

2. Click on **CHAP8.XLS**.

3. Maximize the document window, if necessary.

4. Press the **PgDn** key to see another version of the database you have been working with. It contains three blank cells in the "HRS" field and four blank rows (two of which, rows 28 and 35, have decorative top borders).

5. Select the sort range **B24:I41**. These are the records you want to sort.

6. Sort the list by the "HRS" field (column **G**), in **Descending** order.

7. Observe the results (you may have to scroll). The records with the blank "HRS" fields were moved to the bottom of the list, in the order in which they were found. The top-bordered records (now rows 37 and 40) were moved together with their borders.

8. Close **CHAP8.XLS** without saving the changes. (Use the **File, Close** or **Control Menu button** method).

PRACTICE YOUR SKILLS

The following activity is designed to sharpen your Excel sorting skills. Complete these steps to select a sort range and perform a three-key sort:

1. Open the file **PRU8.XLS** (Chapter 3).

2. Maximize the document window, if necessary (Chapter 3).

3. Select the range **B6:F21**. Sort the client list by the following keys:

1st Key	"BALANCE OWED"	**Ascending** order
2nd Key	"CASE TYPE"	**Ascending** order
3rd Key	"LAST NAME"	**Ascending** order

4. Press **Ctrl-Home** to deselect the sort range. Scroll down to compare your worksheet to Figure 8.9.

5. Save the sorted file as **MYPRU8.XLS** (Chapter 2).

6. Close the file (Chapter 2).

The following activity is designed to further sharpen your Excel sorting skills. Perform these steps to number a list of records and perform several sorts:

1. Open the file **OPT8.XLS** (Chapter 3).

2. Maximize the document window, if necessary (Chapter 3).

3. Using cells **A6:A38**, assign each book a sequential record number.

4. Perform the following two-key sort: sort by author in alphabetical order, and subsort by catalog number ("CAT #") in ascending order. (Hints: Before performing the sort, orient the screen so that you can see the first record. Do not select any records from the database in columns I through M.)

5. Observe the sort order where there are duplicate authors.

Figure 8.9   **PRU8.XLS, after sorting**

A	B	C	D	E	F	
4					BALANCE	
5	CASE #	LAST NAME	FIRST NAME	CASE TYPE	OWED	
6	E3254	Demmings	Brian	real estate	$50	
7	E5687	Treaves	Arthur	real estate	$50	
8	D3240	Mead	David	collections	$518	
9	C8693	Coin	Katherine	collections	$750	
10	E8958	Bartles	James	collections	$841	
11	D3221	Seidel	Ariel	corporate	$1,000	
12	D3427	Stiers	Andrew	corporate	$1,000	
13	C4539	Hooey	Kimberly	real estate	$1,090	
14	E6970	Dwyer	Gregory	corporate	$2,000	
15	D2354	Coin	Susan	collections	$5,500	
16	A3456	Bunker	Hillary	corporate	$12,000	
17	D4537	Difasi	Angie	corporate	$12,000	
18	A3421	Lojacono	Gerald	corporate	$12,000	
19	E2342	Hindemith	George	disability	$12,500	
20	A3427	Horn	Carol	real estate	$12,500	
21	A3423	Eschelwhite	Monica	corporate	$13,000	
22						
23						

6. Sort the same list by the following keys, in ascending order:

    1st Key   "FLOOR NUMBER"

    2nd Key   "LOCATION IN LIBRARY"

    3rd Key   "AUTHOR"

7. Press **Ctrl-Home** to deselect your sort range. Compare your worksheet to Figure 8.10.

8. Scroll to the right until your screen displays columns I through M. There is a duplicate list of books.

9. Sort the list in columns **I** through **M** (I6:M38) in ascending order, first by **location**, then by **floor number**, and last by **author**.

10. Select cell **I1** and compare your worksheet to Figure 8.11.

11. Save the file as **MYOPT8.XLS** (Chapter 2).

Figure 8.10   OPT8.XLS, after two rounds of sorting

	A	B	C	D	E	F
1		MILTON COUNTY PUBLIC LIBRARY		07/28/92		
2		Books that need to be put away...				
3					LOCATION	FLOOR
4		TITLE	AUTHOR	CAT #	IN LIBRARY	NUMBER
5						
6	32	Boy in the Egg, The	Boosler	F559-8	Annex	1
7	22	Early Wind, An	Coor	G533-1	Annex	1
8	14	Jack of Hearts	Coin	A557-8	Center	1
9	6	Canyon, The	Coin	I871-4	Center	1
10	18	Starling, The	Longtemps	I573-1	Center	1
11	28	Innkeeper, The	Thomas	E227-2	Center	1
12	13	Field of Stars	Artbark	H988-7	North Wing	1
13	27	Screen Shock	Hoffburg	J196-4	North Wing	1
14	2	Sante Fe Kid, The	Soule	C317-3	North Wing	1
15	15	Death of a Plowman	Browne	C344-8	South Wing	1
16	23	Golden Hand, The	Rubeling	I180-2	South Wing	1
17	33	Archangel	Sullivan	C782-8	South Wing	1
18	7	Museum, The	Wolf	D268-1	South Wing	1
19	5	My Soldier, My Son	Hardcastle	D968-7	West Wing	1
20	9	Golden Hand, The	Ansick	B955-1	Annex	2

Figure 8.11   OPT8.XLS, after sorting the duplicate list

	I	J	K	L	M
1	MILTON COUNTY PUBLIC LIBRARY		07/28/92		
2	Books that need to be put away...				
3				LOCATION	FLOOR
4	TITLE	AUTHOR	CAT #	IN LIBRARY	NUMBER
5					
6	Boy in the Egg, The	Boosler	F559-8	Annex	1
7	Early Wind, An	Coor	G533-1	Annex	1
8	Early Wind, An	Ansick	D672-9	Annex	2
9	Golden Hand, The	Ansick	B955-1	Annex	2
10	Adventure on Bourbon Street	Ansick	G994-7	Annex	2
11	Wormclaw	Applegate	A457-8	Annex	2
12	Shagwood, A Mystery	Graham	A277-7	Annex	2
13	Headsteam	Pasqua	F935-1	Annex	2
14	Canyon, The	Coin	I871-4	Center	1
15	Jack of Hearts	Coin	A557-8	Center	1
16	Starling, The	Longtemps	I573-1	Center	1
17	Innkeeper, The	Thomas	E227-2	Center	1
18	Sisters and Saints	Arlee	D788-7	Center	2
19	Structures	Raymond	D221-4	Center	2
20	King of Possum County, The	Seidel	C474-2	Center	2

12. Close the file (Chapter 2).

CHAPTER SUMMARY

This chapter introduced you to the second major topic of this book: Excel's database-management system. You learned the basics of database-management terminology and were shown how to create, modify, and sort an Excel database.

Here is a quick reference guide to the Excel features introduced in this chapter:

Desired Result	How to Do It
Perform a one- to three-key sort	Select records, choose **Data, Sort...**, select **Rows** or **Columns**, fill in **1st, 2nd, 3rd Key**, select **Ascending** or **Descending**, click on **OK**
Perform a four- to six-key sort	Sort in two rounds: keys 4 through 6 in round one, keys 1 through 3 in round two
Undo a sort	Choose **Edit, Undo Sort**
Redo a sort	Choose **Edit, Redo [u] Sort**
Number records	Enter starting cell number, select records, choose **Data, Series...**, select **Rows** or **Columns**, select **Linear, Date,** or **Growth**, set **Step Value**, if necessary set **Stop Value**, click on **OK**

In the next chapter, you will continue to build your database-management skills by learning to instruct Excel to locate specific records in a database, such as employees whose hourly wage exceeds $16 or invoices for amounts greater than $500.

IF YOU'RE STOPPING HERE

If you need to break off here, please exit from Excel. If you want to proceed directly to the next chapter, please do so now.

CHAPTER 9: FINDING DATABASE RECORDS

The Basics of Using Data, Find

Setting the Database and Criteria Ranges

Using the Data, Find Command

Text Comparison Criteria

Numeric Comparison Criteria

In working with a database, you will sometimes need to locate a specific record or group of records. For example, you might need to examine the record of an employee with ID number G2358 or obtain a listing of all clients with an advertising budget of $25,000 or more. In this chapter, you will learn how to perform such a *matching record search* by using Excel's Data, Find command.

When you're done working through this chapter, you will know

- How to set a database and criteria range
- How to find and edit database records
- How to use text comparison criteria
- How to use numeric comparison criteria

THE BASICS OF USING DATA, FIND

To find a specific record or group of records in a database, you must first define

- The *database range*, which is the collection of records to be searched
- The *search criteria*, which specify the conditions these records must meet to be found
- The *criteria range*, which is the range of cells that contain the search criteria

After you define these items (see below, "Setting the Database and Criteria Ranges"), you can issue a *Data, Find* command to find all the records that match the specified search criteria.

If you are not running Excel, please start it now. If there is a worksheet on your screen, please close it. Your screen should be empty except for a maximized Excel application window.

Let's use Data, Find to locate a record containing a specific employee number:

1. Open **C9PREVW.XLS** from your EX4WORK directory and maximize the document window, if necessary. Note that the worksheet is divided into two sections: a company payroll database in columns A through H and a search criteria range in column J. The database range (A6:H19) and criteria range (J1:J2) are already defined for this file.

2. Observe cells J1 and J2. These two cells contain search criteria instructing Excel to find all the record(s) in the payroll database with the employee last name of Binga.

3. Choose **Data, Find**. Excel finds Record 3 (see Figure 9.1).

Figure 9.1   **C9PREVW.XLS, after using Data, Find**

Microsoft Excel
File   Edit   Formula   Format   Data   Options   Macro   Window   Help

	A	B	C	D	E	F	G	H	I	J	K	L
6	NUM	LAST	EMP#	HIRE	BEN	HRS	RATE	PAY				
7	1	Halal	CS45	5-Jun-82	hdr	35	$24.00	$840.00				
8	2	Abel	CE29	24-Dec-81	hd	35.5	$12.50	$443.75				
9	3	Binga	ES09	5-Jul-80	hr	35.5	$13.30	$472.15				
10	4	Harper	CS25	30-Dec-85	r	40	$21.50	$860.00				
11	5	Culbert	CE58	26-Jul-85		42	$16.75	$703.50				
12	6	Califano	EE55	7-Jun-83	dr	40	$8.75	$350.00				
13	7	Bally	ES07	12-Jul-78	hdr	40	$12.60	$504.00				
14	8	Binga	CS19	26-Feb-84	hdr	35.5	$13.30	$472.15				
15	9	Keen	SN04	15-Apr-78	hdr	40	$21.50	$860.00				
16	10	Freshita	ES26	1-Feb-85		35.5	$13.30	$472.15				
17	11	Chen	SL05	8-Aug-79	hd	35.5	$13.30	$472.15				
18	12	Binga	CS76	5-Apr-85	r	32	$5.50	$176.00				
19	13	Abel	CE14	25-Jan-80	r	35.5	$12.50	$443.75				
20												
21												
22												
23												

Use arrow keys to view records

4. Observe the screen. Note that the document window scroll bars are filled with diagonal lines and that the status bar displays the message

```
Use arrow keys to view records
```

These changes indicate that you have moved from Ready mode (the normal Excel worksheet operating mode) to *Find* mode (the operating mode you enter when you issue a Data, Find command). You will remain in Find mode until you issue a Data, Exit Find command (or press Esc).

5. Press the **Down Arrow** key to find the next Binga record (8). In Find mode, the Up and Down Arrow keys move to previous and subsequent records that match your search criteria.

6. Press the **Down Arrow** key again to find the next Binga record (12). Press the **Down Arrow** key once again. Nothing happens, because Record 12 is the last Binga record in the database.

7. Press the **Up Arrow** key twice to move to the two previously found records (8 and 3). Press the **Up Arrow** key again; nothing happens. Record 3 is the first Binga record in the database.

8. Choose **Data, Exit Find** to exit from Find mode to Ready mode. Note that the diagonal lines disappear from the scroll bars and that the status bar reads "Ready."

9. Close the document window without saving the changes.

SETTING THE DATABASE AND CRITERIA RANGES

As mentioned above, before you can use Data, Find to locate records in an Excel database, you must first set a database range, then create and set a criteria range.

SETTING A DATABASE RANGE

To set a database range,

- Select the entire range of records that make up the database, being careful to include the database field names ("NUM," "LAST," "EMP#," "HIRE"). This range should *not* include the criteria range.

- If the field names take up two or more rows (for instance, "DATE of HIRE" or "HRLY RATE"), include in your selection only the names in the *bottom* row, the one closest to the database proper. If you include two or more field-name rows in a database range, your Data, Find operations will fail.

- Choose *Data, Set Database*.

Let's set a database range in a new worksheet:

1. Open **CHAP9.XLS** and maximize the document window, if necessary.

2. Select the range **A6:H19**. This range will become your database, the group of records to be searched using Data, Find. Note that only the single, lowest row of field names (row 6) is included in the database range.

3. Choose **Data, Set Database**. Your database range is now set to A6:H19. You won't see any changes on the screen when you

set a database range; Excel performs this operation behind the scenes.

CREATING AND SETTING A CRITERIA RANGE

When you *create* a criteria range, you specify the field that will contain the data you wish to find (for instance, EMP#), and the data itself (MMS76). When you *set* the criteria range, you tell Excel the location of the cells that contain the above information.

To create a Data, Find criteria range,

- In a cell, enter the name of the data field you wish to search. For example, to search through the field EMP# for a specific employee number, you would enter EMP#. Emp# or emp# are also correct; spelling must be exact, but capitalization is insignificant.

- In the cell directly beneath the field name you just entered, insert the criteria (the specific data) of your search. For example, to search through the EMP# field for a record containing the employee number CCE58, you would enter CCE58 (or cce58, Cce58, etc.).

To set your criteria range,

- Select the cells containing both your field name and search criteria.

- Choose *Data, Set Criteria*.

Now let's create and set a criteria range:

1. In cell **J1**, enter the field name **emp#**. Remember, when entering search criteria data, spelling is significant, but capitalization is not.

2. In cell **J2**, enter the search criteria **eee55**. You can use any empty, adjacent pair of cells in the same column to create your criteria range, but it is best to keep the criteria off to the side for visual clarity.

3. Select the range **J1:J2**.

4. Choose **Data, Set Criteria**. The criteria range is now defined as cells J1 and J2 (see Figure 9.2).

Note: The figure's current date (cell H3) will differ from that on your worksheet.

Figure 9.2 **CHAP9.XLS, after setting the database and criteria ranges**

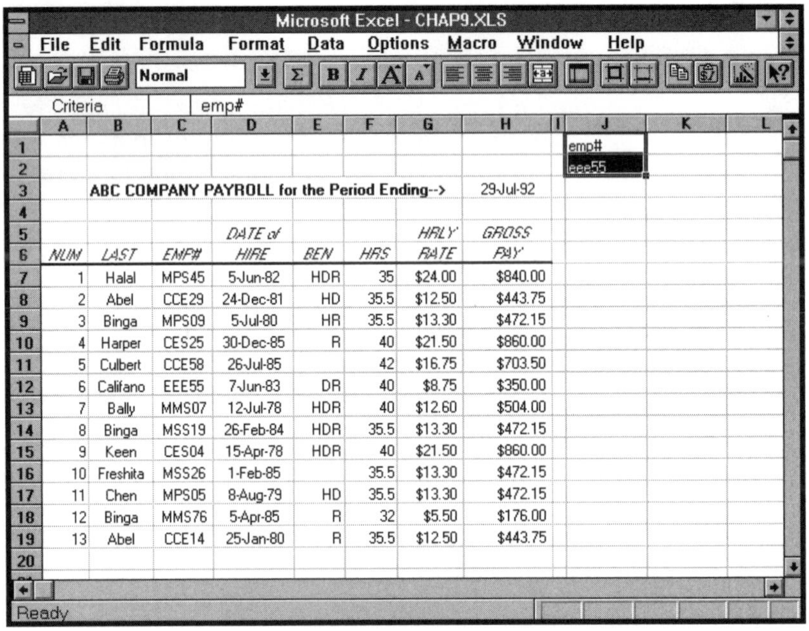

NUM	LAST	EMP#	DATE of HIRE	BEN	HRS	HRLY RATE	GROSS PAY
1	Halal	MPS45	5-Jun-82	HDR	35	$24.00	$840.00
2	Abel	CCE29	24-Dec-81	HD	35.5	$12.50	$443.75
3	Binga	MPS09	5-Jul-80	HR	35.5	$13.30	$472.15
4	Harper	CES25	30-Dec-85	R	40	$21.50	$860.00
5	Culbert	CCE58	26-Jul-85		42	$16.75	$703.50
6	Califano	EEE55	7-Jun-83	DR	40	$8.75	$350.00
7	Bally	MMS07	12-Jul-78	HDR	40	$12.60	$504.00
8	Binga	MSS19	26-Feb-84	HDR	35.5	$13.30	$472.15
9	Keen	CES04	15-Apr-78	HDR	40	$21.50	$860.00
10	Freshita	MSS26	1-Feb-85		35.5	$13.30	$472.15
11	Chen	MPS05	8-Aug-79	HD	35.5	$13.30	$472.15
12	Binga	MMS76	5-Apr-85	R	32	$5.50	$176.00
13	Abel	CCE14	25-Jan-80	R	35.5	$12.50	$443.75

USING THE DATA, FIND COMMAND

Once you have set the database range, and created and set the criteria range, you are ready to tell Excel to find the database records that match your search criteria.

To perform a Data, Find operation,

- Set the database and criteria ranges as described above.
- Choose Data, Find. If Excel finds a record that matches your criteria, it will select it and change to Find mode. In Find mode, you can use the Down Arrow and Up Arrow keys to select individual found records. When a record is selected, you can move from cell to cell using Tab or Enter.
- You can also edit a selected record in Find mode. If you click on the enter box to save your editing changes, you will remain in Find mode; if you press Enter to enter the changes, you will be returned to Ready mode.

- To return to Ready mode (if you have not pressed Enter while editing a record), choose *Data, Exit Find* or press Esc.

Let's have Excel find the record(s) that match the criteria range you just created:

1. Choose **Data, Find** to find all employees with ID number EEE55. Record 6 (Califano) is highlighted.

2. Observe the status bar message

   ```
   Use arrow keys to view records
   ```

   This, and the scroll-bar diagonals, indicate that you are in Find mode.

3. Press the **Down Arrow** key and then the **Up Arrow** key. Nothing happens, because no other records match your search criteria.

4. Press **Esc** to return to Ready mode. (You can use **Data, Exit Find** to do the same thing.)

USING DEFINED NAMES

When you define the database and criteria ranges, Excel creates two defined names: "Database" and "Criteria." Remember, a defined name is a descriptive label that refers to a cell or cell range. You can use defined names to easily move between specified areas of your worksheet.

To obtain a listing of all current defined names and determine which cell(s) each of these names refers to,

- Choose Formula, Define Name....

- Click on the desired name (in the Names In Sheet list box).

- Observe the cell or range reference (in the Refers To list box).

- Click on OK.

Let's use Formula, Define Name to examine some defined names:

1. Choose **Formula, Define Name...** to open the Define Name dialog box. There are two defined names in this worksheet: "Database" and "Criteria." They were created by Excel when you used the Set Database and Set Criteria commands.

2. Click on **Criteria**. (Do not double-click—this would close the dialog box.) Observe the Refers To box. "Criteria" refers to $J$1:$J$2.

3. Click on **Database**. "Database" refers to $A$6:$H$19.

4. Click on **Close** to close the Define Name dialog box.

To select the cell(s) referred to by a defined name, choose Formula, Goto, or press F5. Click on the desired name, and then click on OK. Or, double-click on the desired name.

Now let's use Formula, Goto to select the ranges that Database and Criteria refer to:

1. Choose **Formula, Goto...** to open the Goto dialog box.

2. Click on **Database**, then click on **OK** to select the range you defined earlier with the Set Database command (A6:H19).

3. Press **F5** and double-click on **Criteria** to select your defined criteria range (J1:J2).

EDITING A FOUND RECORD

As mentioned above, you can edit found records from within Find mode. This allows you to edit a series of found records without having to repeatedly reissue the Data, Find command. Let's change the search criteria, then find and edit a record.

1. Change the contents of cell **J2** to **cce58**. This is your new employee number search criterion.

2. Choose **Data, Find** to find the employee with ID number CCE58 (Culbert). Since you did not change the location of your search criteria (J1:J2), you did not have to re-set the criteria range.

3. Press the **Up Arrow** and **Down Arrow** keys. Nothing happens. Culbert is the only employee whose record matches your new search criteria.

4. Press **Tab** six times to select cell G11, Culbert's current hourly rate ($16.75).

5. Type **18** and press **Enter** to give Culbert a raise. Note that Culbert's gross pay jumped from $703.50 to $756.00 (compare Figures 9.2 and 9.3). Note also that pressing Enter caused you

to exit from Find mode to Ready mode. If you had clicked on the Enter box, you would have remained in Find mode.

Figure 9.3 **CHAP9.XLS, after giving Culbert a raise**

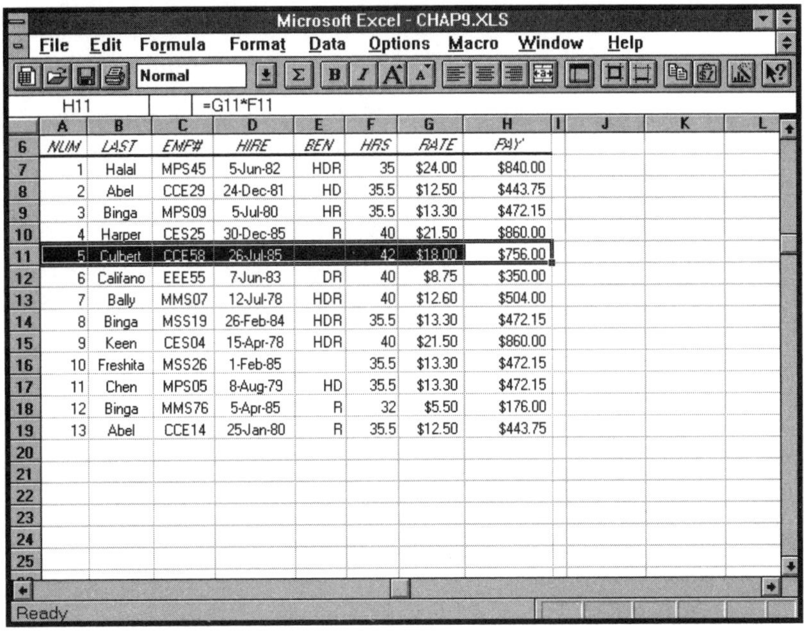

	A	B	C	D	E	F	G	H
6	NUM	LAST	EMP#	HIRE	BEN	HRS	RATE	PAY
7	1	Halal	MPS45	5-Jun-82	HDR	35	$24.00	$840.00
8	2	Abel	CCE29	24-Dec-81	HD	35.5	$12.50	$443.75
9	3	Binga	MPS09	5-Jul-80	HR	35.5	$13.30	$472.15
10	4	Harper	CES25	30-Dec-85	R	40	$21.50	$860.00
11	5	Culbert	CCE58	26-Jul-85		42	$18.00	$756.00
12	6	Califano	EEE55	7-Jun-83	DR	40	$8.75	$350.00
13	7	Bally	MMS07	12-Jul-78	HDR	40	$12.60	$504.00
14	8	Binga	MSS19	26-Feb-84	HDR	35.5	$13.30	$472.15
15	9	Keen	CES04	15-Apr-78	HDR	40	$21.50	$860.00
16	10	Freshita	MSS26	1-Feb-85		35.5	$13.30	$472.15
17	11	Chen	MPS05	8-Aug-79	HD	35.5	$13.30	$472.15
18	12	Binga	MMS76	5-Apr-85	R	32	$5.50	$176.00
19	13	Abel	CCE14	25-Jan-80	R	35.5	$12.50	$443.75

TEXT COMPARISON CRITERIA

Up to now, you have set your criteria to search for specific data (the ID numbers MMS76, EEE55, and CCE58). You can, however, search for nonspecific data—for example, *all* the ID numbers that begin with the letter *M* or end with the number 5. To do so, you must create *comparison criteria*, criteria that describe limits within which a found record may fall.

Excel uses two types of comparison criteria: text and numeric. *Text comparison criteria* are used to search for text data, such as last names or ID codes; *numeric comparison criteria* are used to search for numeric data, such as hourly rates or gross salaries. When creating text comparison criteria, you can use the *lead-edge* and/or *wildcard* searching techniques.

PERFORMING A LEAD-EDGE SEARCH

If you asked Excel to search for all records whose FIRST NAME field contained "Rob," it would find Rob, Robert, Roberta, Robbie, and so on—any FIRST NAME entry beginning with the letters *R-O-B*. This technique is known as a *lead-edge search*, because only the lead edge of the search criteria needs to be specified. For example, if you wanted to find all the entries in the LAST NAME field that began with the letter *M*, you would simply enter M as your criteria.

Let's perform a lead-edge search to find all records whose employee numbers begin with the letter *C*:

1. Choose **Formula, Goto... (or press F5)** and double-click on **Criteria** to select the criteria range, cells J1 and J2.

2. In cell **J2**, enter **C** to find all employee numbers that begin with the letter *C*. (Capitalization is insignificant.)

3. Choose **Data, Find** to locate the first match, Record 2. Note the employee number: CCE29.

4. Press the **Down Arrow** key four times to find the rest of the employee numbers beginning with *C*.

5. Press **Esc** to return to Ready mode.

PRACTICE YOUR SKILLS

1. Select the criteria range.

2. Enter the appropriate criteria to find all employee numbers that begin with *M*.

3. Find all records that match these criteria (seven in all).

4. Return to Ready mode.

PERFORMING A WILDCARD SEARCH

A wildcard is a symbol that stands for one or more arbitrary characters (letters, numbers, or punctuation marks). There are two wildcards you can use in Excel: the asterisk (*) and the question mark (?).

The asterisk (*) stands for one or more arbitrary characters. Searching for *son in a LAST NAME field finds the records of all employees whose last names (no matter how many characters long) end with "son" (for example, Mason, Peterson). Because of Excel's lead-edge feature, *son also finds records whose names extend beyond the letters *S-O-N*, such as Reasoner or Sonnenberg.

The question mark (?) stands for one arbitrary character. Searching for ?s in an ID_CODE field would find all records whose employee ID codes had an *S* as their second character, such as ES10, LS204, or 1SS20614.

USING THE * WILDCARD

To set your criteria for the following activity, you will need to be familiar with ABC Company's division and department codes, as they are used in the EMP# field:

Division	Department	Code
Chemicals	Chemical Engineering	CCE
Chemicals	Engineering Support	CES
Electronics	Electrical Engineering	EEE
Marketing	Marketing Support	MMS
Marketing	Product Support	MPS
Marketing	Sales Support	MSS

Let's perform a * wildcard search:

1. Press **F5** (Goto) and double-click on **Criteria**.

2. In cell **J2**, enter ***e** to find all employee ID numbers that contain the letter *E* (this will be true for everyone in an engineering department). See Figure 9.4.

3. Find all records matching your criteria (choose **Data, Find**). There are six.

4. Return to Ready mode. (Press **Esc** or choose **Data, Exit Find**.)

Figure 9.4   **Performing a * wildcard search**

Microsoft Excel - CHAP9.XLS											
<u>F</u>ile	<u>E</u>dit	For<u>m</u>ula	Forma<u>t</u>	<u>D</u>ata	<u>O</u>ptions	<u>M</u>acro	<u>W</u>indow	<u>H</u>elp			

Criteria | emp#

	A	B	C	D	E	F	G	H	I	J	K	L
1										emp#		
2										*e		
3		ABC COMPANY PAYROLL for the Period Ending-->						29-Jul-92				
4												
5				DATE of			HRLY	GROSS				
6	NUM	LAST	EMP#	HIRE	BEN	HRS	RATE	PAY				
7	1	Halal	MPS45	5-Jun-82	HDR	35	$24.00	$840.00				
8	2	Abel	CCE29	24-Dec-81	HD	35.5	$12.50	$443.75				
9	3	Binga	MPS09	5-Jul-80	HR	35.5	$13.30	$472.15				
10	4	Harper	CES25	30-Dec-85	R	40	$21.50	$860.00				
11	5	Culbert	CCE58	26-Jul-85		42	$18.00	$756.00				
12	6	Califano	EEE55	7-Jun-83	DR	40	$8.75	$350.00				
13	7	Bally	MMS07	12-Jul-78	HDR	40	$12.60	$504.00				
14	8	Binga	MSS19	26-Feb-84	HDR	35.5	$13.30	$472.15				
15	9	Keen	CES04	15-Apr-78	HDR	40	$21.50	$860.00				
16	10	Freshita	MSS26	1-Feb-85		35.5	$13.30	$472.15				
17	11	Chen	MPS05	8-Aug-79	HD	35.5	$13.30	$472.15				
18	12	Binga	MMS76	5-Apr-85	R	32	$5.50	$176.00				
19	13	Abel	CCE14	25-Jan-80	R	35.5	$12.50	$443.75				
20												

Ready

PRACTICE YOUR SKILLS

1. Modify the search criteria to find all employee ID numbers that contain the letter *S*.

2. Find the matching records (nine in all), and return to Ready mode.

USING THE ? WILDCARD

Now let's perform a ? wildcard search:

1. In cell **J2**, enter the search criterion **?s** to find all employee numbers in which an *S* appears as the second character.

2. Find the matching records (choose **Data, Find**). The two employee numbers in the sales support department are found.

3. In cell **J2**, enter the search criterion **???1** to find all records with employee numbers that contain the number 1 as the fourth character.

4. Find the matching records. There are two.

5. Press **Esc** to return to Ready mode.

PRACTICE YOUR SKILLS

The BEN (benefits) field of CHAP9.XLS contains codes for the various benefit plans that ABC offers its employees. "H" stands for health plan, "D" for dental plan, and "R" for retirement plan.

1. Enter the search criteria to find all employees who participate in the retirement plan. (Hint: You'll have to change the contents of both **J1** and **J2**.)

2. Find the matching records. There are nine.

3. Enter the search criterion (cell **J2** only) to find all employees who participate in both the health and dental plan. (Hint: Codes are always listed in this order: HDR.)

4. Find the matching records. There are six.

5. Find the records of all employees who participate in all three benefits plans. There are four.

NUMERIC COMPARISON CRITERIA

Until now, you have set your criteria to search for text data. (Employee ID codes, even though they contain numbers, are considered to be text: they cannot be added, subtracted, used in a formula, and so on.) Excel also allows you to search for numeric data. For example, you could set your search criteria to find all employees whose hourly rate of pay is $14.50.

As in text searches, you can specify exact criteria (for instance, 14.50) or comparison criteria which describe the numeric limits within which a record should fall (in this case, <14.50 would find all employees whose hourly rate was less than $14.50).

The following are Excel's numeric comparison operators and their functions:

Numeric Comparison Operator	Function
=	Equal to

Numeric Comparison Operator	Function
>	Greater than
<	Less than
>=	Greater than or equal to
<=	Less than or equal to
<>	Not equal to

Let's perform a search using a criteria range that contains a numeric value:

1. Enter the field name **hrs** in cell **J1**. Because the database field is named "HRS" (instead of "HOURS"), you must use this abbreviated spelling. You can, however, ignore the capitalization.

2. In cell **J2**, enter the numeric search criterion **40**.

3. Find the matching records and return to Ready mode. Four employees work exactly 40 hours per week.

Now let's perform a search using numeric comparison criteria:

1. In cell **J2**, enter the comparison criterion **<40** to find the records of employees who work less than 40 hours per week.

2. Find the matching records. There are eight.

3. In cell **J2**, enter **>=40** to find the records of employees who work 40 hours or more per week.

4. Find the matching records. There are five matches. The >=40 criterion found the four employees who work exactly 40 hours per week and the one employee who works 42 hours per week.

5. In cell **J2**, enter **<>35.5** to find the records of all employees who do not work exactly 35.5 hours per week (see Figure 9.5).

6. Find the matching records. There are seven.

7. Save the worksheet as **MYCHAP9.XLS**.

8. Close the document window.

Note: You can also use numeric comparison operators with date or time criteria. For example, you could find all the employees who have been employed since January 4, 1988, by specifying the search criterion >=1/4/88.

Figure 9.5 **Using numeric comparison criteria**

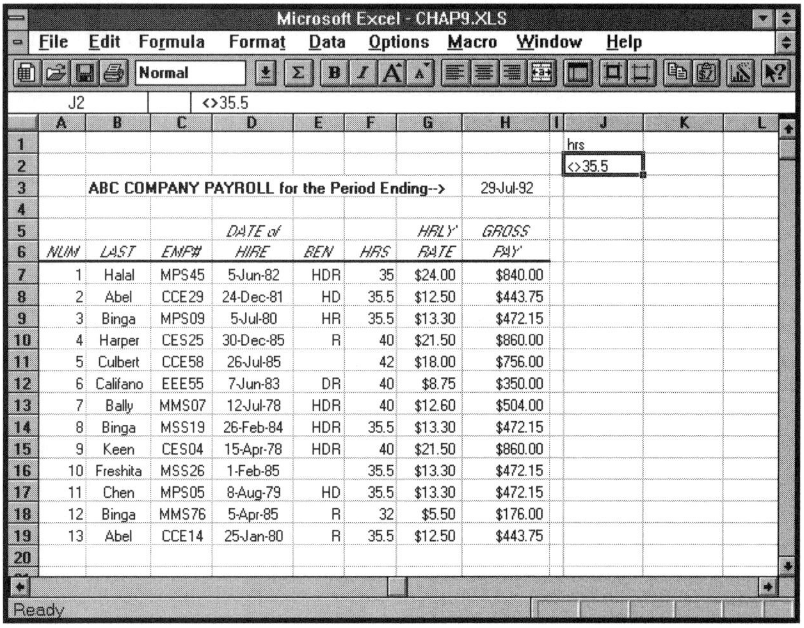

NUM	LAST	EMP#	DATE of HIRE	BEN	HRS	HRLY RATE	GROSS PAY
1	Halal	MPS45	5-Jun-82	HDR	35	$24.00	$840.00
2	Abel	CCE29	24-Dec-81	HD	35.5	$12.50	$443.75
3	Binga	MPS09	5-Jul-80	HR	35.5	$13.30	$472.15
4	Harper	CES25	30-Dec-85	R	40	$21.50	$860.00
5	Culbert	CCE58	26-Jul-85		42	$18.00	$756.00
6	Califano	EEE55	7-Jun-83	DR	40	$8.75	$350.00
7	Bally	MMS07	12-Jul-78	HDR	40	$12.60	$504.00
8	Binga	MSS19	26-Feb-84	HDR	35.5	$13.30	$472.15
9	Keen	CES04	15-Apr-78	HDR	40	$21.50	$860.00
10	Freshita	MSS26	1-Feb-85		35.5	$13.30	$472.15
11	Chen	MPS05	8-Aug-79	HD	35.5	$13.30	$472.15
12	Binga	MMS76	5-Apr-85	R	32	$5.50	$176.00
13	Abel	CCE14	25-Jan-80	R	35.5	$12.50	$443.75

CHAPTER SUMMARY

In this chapter, you added the Data, Find command to your Excel database-management skills. You learned how to set a database and criteria range, find and edit database records, and use text and numeric comparison criteria for your Data, Find searches.

Here is a quick reference guide to the Excel features introduced in this chapter:

Desired Result	**How to Do It**
Set a database range	Select database records (including bottom row of field names), choose **Data, Set Database**

Desired Result	How to Do It
Set a criteria range	Create criteria, select criteria range, choose **Data, Set Criteria**
Find database record(s)	Set database range, create and set criteria range, choose **Data, Find**
Exit Find mode	Choose **Data, Exit Find**; or press **Esc**
Select next/previous matching record in Find mode	Press the **Down/Up Arrow** keys
Select next cell in Find mode	Press **Tab**
Select previous cell in Find mode	Press **Shift-Tab**
View a defined name's range	Choose **Formula, Define Name...**, click on name
Select a defined name's range	Choose **Formula, Goto...** (or press **F5**), click twice on name (or click once on name, click on **OK**)
Perform a lead-edge search	Enter search criterion consisting of first letter(s) of item to search
Perform a wildcard search	Use ***** to search for one or more characters, **?** to search for one character
Perform a numeric comparison search	Use **=, >, <, >=, <=,** or **<>**

In the next chapter, you will continue to expand your database-management skills by learning how to extract (retrieve) the records found with Data, Find and copy them to another area of your worksheet.

IF YOU'RE STOPPING HERE

If you need to break off here, please exit from Excel. If you want to proceed directly to the next chapter, please do so now.

CHAPTER 10: EXTRACTING DATABASE RECORDS

Extracting Records From a Database

Sorting and Printing an Extract Range

In the last chapter, you learned how to find a specific record or group of records in a database. In this chapter, you will learn how to *extract* (retrieve) these found records and copy them to another area of your worksheet. Extraction is a powerful tool for summarizing the relevant information in a database. It may be used, for example, to prepare a list of all clients with outstanding debits of $1,000 or more, or of all employees whose hourly rate exceeds $12.

When you're done working through this chapter, you will know

- How to set an extract range
- How to extract records from a database
- How to sort and print an extract range

EXTRACTING RECORDS FROM A DATABASE

As you learned in the last chapter, you can use the Data, Find command to locate database records that match specific search criteria. You can use the *Data, Extract* command to retrieve these found records and copy them to another area of the worksheet, called the *extract range*. Before performing an extract, you must set the database, criteria, and extract ranges. (For help with setting the database and criteria ranges, see Chapter 9.)

 SETTING AN EXTRACT RANGE

To set an extract range,

- Select a range of empty, horizontally adjacent cells (ones that lie next to each other within the same row).

- In this range, enter the field names containing the data you wish to extract. For example, if you wanted to extract an employee's last name, ID number, hourly rate, and gross pay, you would enter in four adjacent cells: "LAST," "EMP#," "RATE," and "PAY."

- Field names must be spelled exactly as they appear in the database. Capitalization is insignificant, so a field named "HRS" could be represented as hrs, HRS, or Hrs (but not as hrs. or hours).

- Select the range containing the row of field names you just entered. Or, select the range containing the row of field names and as many rows beneath these names as you want to reserve for your data extraction(s). For instructions on when to use one or the other of these selection techniques, see below, "Specifying the Size of Your Extract Range."

- Choose Data, Set Extract.

PERFORMING A DATABASE EXTRACT

To perform an extract,

- Set the database, criteria, and extract ranges.
- Choose Data, Extract.
- Click on OK.

Note: If your database contains duplicate records and you would like to extract only one copy of each found record, check *Unique Records Only* before clicking on OK.

If you are not running Excel, please start it now. If there is a worksheet on your screen, please close it. Your screen should be empty except for a maximized Excel application window.

Now let's open a worksheet and use Formula, Define Name to examine the database and criteria ranges:

1. Open **CHAP10.XLS** from your EX4WORK directory and maximize the document window, if necessary. Note that this worksheet already contains search criteria (as you see on your screen in cells I1:I2).

2. Choose **Formula, Define Name...** to open the Define Name dialog box. Observe that CHAP10.XLS has two defined names: "Criteria" and "Database." As you learned in the last chapter, this means that the criteria and database ranges have been set using the Set Criteria and Set Database commands.

3. Click on **Criteria**; it refers to the range $I$1:$I$2. The current search criteria instruct Excel to search for the records of all employees whose hourly rate equals or exceeds $13.30.

4. Click on **Database**; it refers to the range $A$6:$G$19.

5. Click on **Close** to close the Define Name dialog box.

6. Choose **Data, Find** to find all employees who earn $13.30 or more per hour. There are eight.

7. Press **Esc** to exit from Find mode to Ready mode.

Now let's extract the records that match the search criteria:

1. Press **Ctrl-Home** to reorient the screen.

2. Select the range **I6:K6**. These cells will be used to create an extract range.

3. In cell **I6**, enter the field name **rate**.

4. In cell **J6**, enter the field name **last**.

5. In cell **K6**, enter the field name **emp#**. You can extract information from all fields of your database or only the specific fields you are interested in.

6. With I6:K6 still selected, choose **Data, Set Extract** to set the extract range to these three cells. You won't see any changes on the screen when you set the extract range; Excel performs this operation behind the scenes. Your database, criteria, and extract ranges are now all set; you are ready to perform the extract.

7. Choose **Data, Extract**.... Observe the Unique Records Only option in the dialog box. As mentioned above, you use this option when a database contains duplicate records and you want to extract only one copy of each found record. In the current data base, all employee codes are unique (not duplicated) so it is not necessary to select the Unique Records Only option.

8. Click on **OK** to perform the extract and return to the worksheet (see Figure 10.1). Note that the records are extracted in the order they were found in the database. To rearrange this order (for example, alphabetically), you would use the Data, Sort command (see below, "Sorting and Printing an Extract Range").

SPECIFYING THE SIZE OF YOUR EXTRACT RANGE

If you define a single row of field names as your extract range (as you did above with I6:K6), Excel will clear (erase) the contents of all the cells that lie beneath this range when it performs the extract. If any of these cells happens to contain data, you will lose it *permanently*—a Data, Extract command cannot be reversed with Undo.

For this reason, you should get in the habit of defining an extract range large enough to hold all the records that will be extracted from your database. Simply make the extract range equal in size (number of rows) to the database range; that way, no possible extract could exceed the extract range.

Let's see what can happen when you define a single row of field names as your extract range:

1. In cell **I20**, enter your initials.

2. Choose **Data, Extract...** and click on **OK** to re-execute the last extract. Observe cell I20. Your initials no longer appear there. Remember that when you define a single row of field names as your extract range, Excel will clear (erase) all cells that lie beneath it.

3. Click on **Edit** to drop the Edit menu. Note that "Can't Undo" appears at the top of the menu. As mentioned above, the Data, Extract command cannot be undone.

Figure 10.1   **CHAP10.XLS, after extracting records**

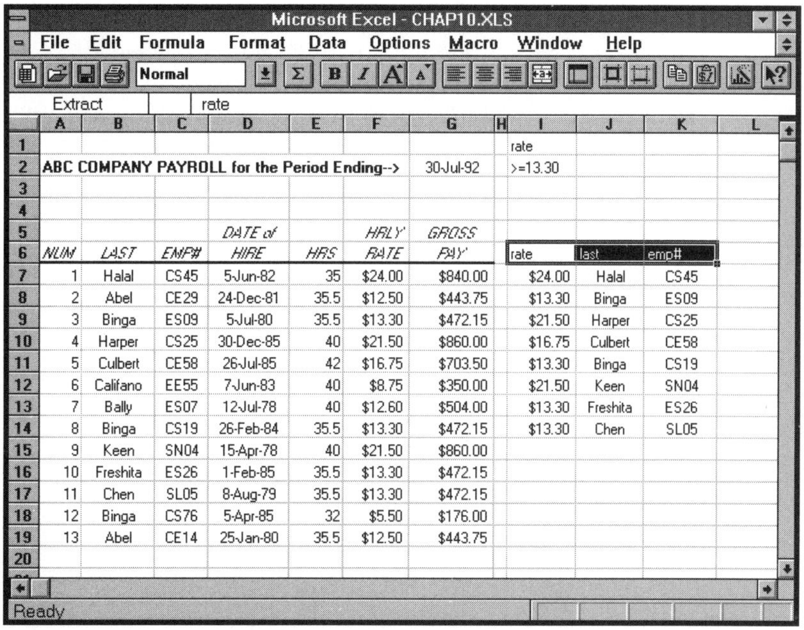

Now let's select an extract range as large as the database:

1. Erase the range **I7:K14**. (Select the range, press **Delete** or choose **Edit, Clear**; then click on **OK**.) You don't have to erase your extracted records before performing another extract, but it simplifies the task of changing the extract range.

2. In cell **I1**, enter **pay**.

3. In cell **I2**, enter **>500**. Your search criteria are now set to find all employees whose gross pay is greater than $500 per week.

4. In cell **I6**, enter **pay**. Your extract range is now set to extract the GROSS PAY, LAST, and EMP# fields of all employee records meeting the above search criteria. Note that the extract columns do not have to be in the same order as the database columns.

5. Select the range **I6:K19** and choose **Data, Set Extract** to define an extract range as large as your database. Locating the database and extract side by side in your worksheet greatly simplifies this task. (Note: Just as with the Set Database and Set Criteria commands, you won't see any changes on the screen when you issue a Set Extract command; Excel performs this operation behind the scenes.)

6. Reenter your initials in cell **I20**.

7. Choose **Data, Extract...** and click on **OK** to perform the extract. Note that your initials are still intact (see Figure 10.2). Since the defined extract range was larger than one row and ended *above* your initials, Excel did not clear the initials.

Figure 10.2   **Setting an extract range as large as your database**

	A	B	C	D	E	F	G	H	I	J	K	L
1									pay			
2	ABC COMPANY PAYROLL for the Period Ending-->					30-Jul-92			>500			
3												
4												
5				DATE of		HRLY	GROSS					
6	NUM	LAST	EMP#	HIRE	HRS	RATE	PAY		pay	last	emp#	
7	1	Halal	CS45	5-Jun-82	35	$24.00	$840.00		$840.00	Halal	CS45	
8	2	Abel	CE29	24-Dec-81	35.5	$12.50	$443.75		$860.00	Harper	CS25	
9	3	Binga	ES09	5-Jul-80	35.5	$13.30	$472.15		$703.50	Culbert	CE58	
10	4	Harper	CS25	30-Dec-85	40	$21.50	$860.00		$504.00	Bally	ES07	
11	5	Culbert	CE58	26-Jul-85	42	$16.75	$703.50		$860.00	Keen	SN04	
12	6	Califano	EE55	7-Jun-83	40	$8.75	$350.00					
13	7	Bally	ES07	12-Jul-78	40	$12.60	$504.00					
14	8	Binga	CS19	26-Feb-84	35.5	$13.30	$472.15					
15	9	Keen	SN04	15-Apr-78	40	$21.50	$860.00					
16	10	Freshita	ES26	1-Feb-85	35.5	$13.30	$472.15					
17	11	Chen	SL05	8-Aug-79	35.5	$13.30	$472.15					
18	12	Binga	CS76	5-Apr-85	32	$5.50	$176.00					
19	13	Abel	CE14	25-Jan-80	35.5	$12.50	$443.75					
20									rpps			

Let's take a moment to observe a unique characteristic of the Data, Extract command:

1. Select cell **G7** and examine the formula bar. It contains the formula =F7*E7.

2. Now examine cell **I7**. It contains the constant value 840. Both of these cells contain Halal's gross pay, yet one contains a formula and one a constant. Data, Extract only extracts constant values and text from a database, not formulas or functions.

Now let's select an extract range too small to hold the extract:

1. Erase the extracted records in cells **I7:K11**. (Use **Delete** or **Edit, Clear**.)

2. Select the range **I6:K9** and choose **Data, Set Extract** to define an area that is too small to hold the records you will be extracting.

3. Choose **Data, Extract...** and click on **OK**. An alert box appears, informing you that the extract range is full. Whenever an extract range is not large enough to hold the extracted records, Excel will issue you this warning.

4. Click on **OK** to continue.

Note that Excel extracts three records, the maximum number that fit in the extract range you just defined (I6:K9). Allowing a partial extract like this to occur could cause problems; you might, at some later date, forget the alert message and assume that the full extract consisted of only three records. The solution, once again, is to take the precaution of defining your extract range to include exactly as many rows as your database.

PRACTICE YOUR SKILLS

1. Define cells **I6:K19** as the extract range.

2. Perform the extract. (Five records will be extracted.)

SORTING AND PRINTING AN EXTRACT RANGE

You can sort and print an extract range just as you would any other range of your worksheet.

To sort an extract range,

- Select the records to be sorted.

- Choose Data, Sort....
- Select Rows or Columns, fill in 1st (2nd, 3rd) Key, select Ascending or Descending.
- Click on OK.

To preview or print an extract range,

- Select the records to be previewed or printed.
- Choose Options, Set Print Area.
- To preview the printout, choose File, Print Preview.
- To print, choose File, Print..., set the desired print options and click on OK.

For further help, please refer to the procedures outlined in Chapter 6 (for printing) and Chapter 8 (for sorting).

Let's sort the records you extracted in the above Practice Your Skills activity:

1. Select the range **I7:K11**.

2. Choose **Data, Sort...**.

3. Select any cell in column **J** as the **1st Key** and click on **OK** to sort by last names in alphabetical order. Note that an extract-range sort functions exactly like a database sort.

Now let's preview and save the extracted records:

1. Select the range **I6:K11**.

2. Choose **Options, Set Print Area** to define the extract range as the print area.

3. Choose **File, Print Preview**.

4. Place the mouse pointer over the upper-left corner of the pre-viewed page; it will change to a magnifying glass. Click once to obtain an actual-size page view (see Figure 10.3).

5. If you wish to print this out now, use **Setup...** and/or **Margins** to set your print options, then click on **Print** and **OK**. If not, click on **Close** to return to your worksheet.

6. Save the file as **MYCHAP10.XLS**.

7. Close the document window.

Figure 10.3   Magnified print preview of CHAP10.XLS sorted extract

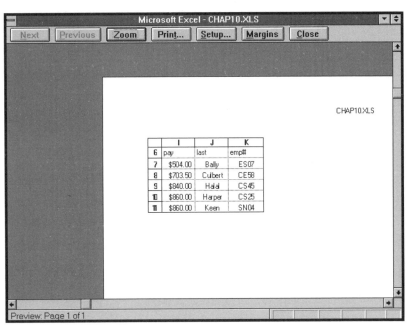

PRACTICE YOUR SKILLS

The following activity is designed to sharpen your Excel finding and extracting skills. Perform these steps to modify the file PRU9&10.XLS to match Figure 10.4:

1. Open **PRU9&10.XLS** (Chapter 3).

2. Maximize the document window, if necessary (Chapter 3).

3. In cell **M4**, enter the name of the field where employees's weekly hours are recorded (Chapter 9).

4. In cell **M5**, enter the comparison criterion required to find all employees who work 40 hours or more each week (Chapter 9).

5. Select the range **M4** through **M5** and define this as the criteria range. (Chapter 9)

6. Select the range **A4** through **K31** and define this as the database range (Chapter 9).

7. Find the records that match the criterion (Chapter 9). There should be 15.

Figure 10.4   **Extracted records of PRU9&10.XLS**

	H	I	J	K	L	M	N	O	P	Q
	Extract		first							
4	EMPLOYED	HRS	RATE	PAY		hrs				
5	10.61	35.5	$12.50	$443.75		>=40				
6	12.08	35.5	$13.30	$472.15						
7	7.02	42	$16.75	$703.50						
8	9.15	40	$8.75	$350.00		first	last	emp#	hrs	
9	14.06	40	$12.60	$504.00		Colleen	Culbert	CCE58	42	
10	10.16	35	$24.00	$840.00		Teri	Califano	EEE55	40	
11	8.43	35	$12.10	$423.50		Frank	Bally	MMS07	40	
12	14.30	40	$21.50	$860.00		Barry	Keen	CES04	40	
13	7.50	35.5	$13.30	$472.15		Harry	Harper	CES25	40	
14	6.59	40	$21.50	$860.00		Chris	Hall	MMS59	40	
15	12.99	35.5	$13.30	$472.15		Robert	Dollar	MMS47	40	
16	7.32	32	$5.50	$176.00		Len	Lacey	MMS18	40	
17	12.52	35.5	$12.50	$443.75		Dominick	Osowski	MMS57	40	
18	9.23	40	$7.22	$288.80		Deanne	Verta	EEE49	40	
19	10.15	40	$12.60	$504.00		Jane	Martin	EEE03	40	
20	10.81	35.5	$13.30	$472.15		Bill	Young	CCE04	40	
21	12.24	40	$22.00	$880.00		Jane	Tree	EEE07	40	
22	9.62	40	$22.00	$880.00		Kon	Song	CCE49	40	
23	10.11	40	$15.00	$600.00		Brad	Daley	CCE15	40	

8. Type the following field names into the corresponding cells:

	M	N	O	P
8	**first**	**last**	**emp#**	**hrs**

9. Select the range **M8** through **P8** and define this as the extract range. (Since there is no data contained in the cells beneath this range, we did *not* have to select a multi-row extract range.)

10. Extract the matching records.

11. Compare the extracted records to those in Figure 10.4.

12. Save the file as **MYPR9&10.XLS** (Chapter 2).

13. Close the file (Chapter 2).

The following activity is designed to further sharpen your Excel finding and extracting skills. Perform these steps to modify the file OPT9&10.XLS to match Figure 10.5:

1. Open **OPT9&10.XLS** (Chapter 3).

Figure 10.5   **Extracted and sorted records of OPT9&10.XLS**

	J	K	L	M	N	O	P	Q	R	S
4	RATE	PAY		last	first	hire	employed			
5	$12.50	$443.75		Young	Bill	8-Mar-76	16.41			
6	$13.30	$472.15		Keen	Barry	15-Apr-78	14.30			
7	$16.75	$703.50		Bally	Frank	12-Jul-78	14.06			
8	$8.75	$350.00		Martin	Jane	2-Feb-79	13.50			
9	$12.60	$504.00		Quick	Julia	17-Feb-79	13.46			
10	$24.00	$840.00		Tree	Jane	8-Apr-79	13.32			
11	$12.10	$423.50		Chen	Shing	8-Aug-79	12.99			
12	$21.50	$860.00		Abel	Bob	25-Jan-80	12.52			
13	$13.30	$472.15		Lacey	Len	7-May-80	12.24			
14	$21.50	$860.00		Binga	Sam	5-Jul-80	12.08			
15	$13.30	$472.15		Daley	Brad	8-Nov-80	11.73			
16	$5.50	$176.00		Ackle	Carol	21-Jul-81	11.03			
17	$12.50	$443.75		Binga	Alice	11-Oct-81	10.81			
18	$7.22	$288.80		Abel	Sara	24-Dec-81	10.61			
19	$12.60	$504.00		Halal	James	5-Jun-82	10.16			
20	$13.30	$472.15		Dollar	Robert	10-Jun-82	10.15			
21	$22.00	$880.00		Verta	Deanne	23-Jun-82	10.11			
22	$22.00	$880.00		Osowski	Dominick	19-Dec-82	9.62			
23	$15.00	$600.00		Hall	Chris	12-May-83	9.23			

2. Maximize the document window, if necessary (Chapter 3).

3. Your boss needs a list of all personnel who have been employed for more than nine years. Extract a list containing the following information (Chapters 8 and 9; see Hints, below):

   • Their last names (LAST)

   • Their first names (FIRST)

   • The dates they were hired (HIRE)

   • The number of years they have been employed (EMPLOYED)

   Hints: Remember to include the bottom field-name row when setting the database range (Chapter 9). Also remember to include both the bottom field name and the search criterion when setting the criteria range (Chapter 9).

4. Arrange the extracted employee list in order of decreasing period of employment (Chapter 8). Hint: Do *not* include the field-name row when sorting the extracted records (Chapter 8).

5. Compare the extracted and sorted records to those in Figure 10.5.

6. Save the file as **MYOP9&10.XLS** (Chapter 3).

7. Close the file (Chapter 2).

CHAPTER SUMMARY

In this chapter, you learned the basics of data extraction, a powerful technique used to retrieve specific information from a database. You now know how to set an extract range, extract records from a database, and sort and print these extracted records.

Here is a quick reference guide to the Excel features introduced in this chapter:

Desired Result	How to Do It
Set an extract range	Create row of database field names to extract, select this row and as many rows as desired beneath it (preferably the same number of rows as are in database range), choose **Data, Set Extract**
Extract database records	Set database, criteria, and extract ranges, choose **Data, Extract**, click on **OK**
Sort an extract range	Select extract records to be sorted, choose **Data, Sort...**, select **Rows** or **Columns**, fill in **1st (2nd, 3rd) Key**, select **Ascending** or **Descending**, click on **OK**
Print an extract range	Select extracted records to be printed, choose **Options, Set Print Area**, choose **File, Print...**, set the desired print options, click on **OK**
Preview an extract range	Select extracted records to be previewed, choose **Options, Set Print Area**, choose **File, Print Preview**

In the next chapter, you will learn how to create expanded search criteria and how to add records to an existing database range. You will also learn how to use the Data, Delete command to erase, rather than find or extract, the records that match your search criteria.

IF YOU'RE STOPPING HERE

If you need to break off here, please exit from Excel. If you want to proceed directly to the next chapter, please do so now.

CHAPTER 11: ADVANCED DATABASE-MANAGEMENT TECHNIQUES

Performing
Multiple-Criteria
and and/or
Searches

Using the Data,
Form Command

Using Database
Functions

Deleting Found
Records

In Chapters 8 through 10, you learned the basics of database management: how to design a database; how to sort, find, and extract records from a database; and how to print part or all of a database. In this chapter, we'll introduce you to several advanced database-management techniques. You'll learn how to perform *multiple-criteria* (AND and OR) *searches*; how to use a special class of functions called *database functions*; and new ways to edit, add, find, and delete records from a database. These techniques will supplement your basic database skills and prepare you for the kinds of situations you're likely to encounter in your real-world database-management work.

This chapter completes your foundation in Excel database-management skills. In the remaining chapters, you will explore Excel's extensive charting capabilities.

When you're done working through this chapter, you will know

- How to perform multiple-criteria AND and OR searches

- How to use the Data, Form command to edit, add, and find records in a database

- How to use database functions to perform calculations on records that match your specified search criteria

- How to delete found records from a database

PERFORMING MULTIPLE-CRITERIA AND AND/OR SEARCHES

In your find and extract operations up to now, you have always specified a single search criterion (for example, a last name beginning with *S* or an hourly rate of $13). At times, however, you may need to search for multiple criteria. Excel allows you to do this by performing an *AND search* and an *OR search*.

An AND search instructs Excel to find records that match *all* of a set of multiple criteria (such as all employees whose hire date precedes January 1, 1985, *and* whose gross pay exceeds $35,000). An OR search instructs Excel to find records that match at least *one* of a set of multiple criteria (all employees whose hire date precedes January 1, 1985, *or* whose gross pay exceeds $35,000).

PERFORMING AN AND SEARCH

To perform an AND search—to find records that match *all* of a set of multiple search criteria—you must first create a criteria range that contains these multiple criteria.

The following single criteria range instructs Excel to find the records of all employees who work exactly 40 hours per week:

```
HOURS
40
```

The following multiple criteria range instructs Excel to find the records of all employees who work 40 hours per week *and* earn more than $500 per week:

```
HOURS   PAY
40      >500
```

Note that the second set of search criteria (PAY, >500) was added to the right of the first set (HOURS, 40). AND criteria are added in columns to the right of the existing criteria.

If you are not running Excel, please start it. If there is a worksheet on your screen, please close it. Your screen should be empty except for a maximized Excel application window. Now let's open a file and perform a simple AND search:

1. Open **CHAP11.XLS** from your EX4WORK directory and maximize the document window, if necessary. Observe the criteria range, cells I1 and I2. This file has been set up to extract data from the records of employees who earn more than $500 gross per week.

2. Change the criteria to find employees who earn more than $450 gross per week. (Enter **>450** in cell I2.)

3. Choose **Formula, Define Name** to verify that the database, criteria, and extract ranges have all been set. (We set them up when creating this worksheet file.) Click on **Close** to return to the worksheet.

4. Choose **Data, Extract...** and click on **OK** to extract data from employee records matching your modified search criteria. There are nine matches.

5. Now we'll enter a second set of criteria to prepare for an AND search. In cell **J1**, enter **emp#**; in cell **J2**, enter **c**. By adding a column to your criteria range, you have created an AND condition. This new column instructs Excel to find all employees who work in a chemicals division (whose ID code begins with the letter *C*).

6. Select the range **I1:J2** and choose **Data, Set Criteria**. When you change the size of the criteria range, you must use Data, Set Criteria to reset this range. The criteria range does *not* automatically update when you add or remove criteria.

7. Choose **Data, Extract...** and click on **OK** to extract data from records of employees who earn more than $450 gross *and* who work in a chemicals division.

8. Observe the extract range. Only three records—Harper, Culbert, and Keen—satisfy *both* of your AND criteria.

PRACTICE YOUR SKILLS

1. Modify your search criteria to find all marketing employees who earn more than $450 gross per week. (A marketing employee's ID code begins with an *M*.)

2. Extract the matching records. There will be six (see Figure 11.1).

Figure 11.1 **CHAP11.XLS, after performing an AND search**

	Microsoft Excel - CHAP11.XLS									

File Edit Formula Format Data Options Macro Window Help

| Normal | | | | Σ | B | I | A A | ≡≡≡ | | | | | | | | |

J2 | m

	A	B	C	D	E	F	G	H	I	J	K
1									pay	emp#	
2									>450	m	
3											
4		***The ABC COMPANY PAYROLL for the Period Ending-->					3-Aug-92				
5											
6				DATE of		HRLY	GROSS				
7	NUM	LAST	EMP#	HIRE	HRS	RATE	PAY		pay	last	emp#
8	1	Halal	MPS45	5-Jun-82	35	$24.00	$840.00		$840.00	Halal	MPS45
9	2	Abel	CCE29	24-Dec-81	35.5	$12.50	$443.75		$472.15	Binga	MPS09
10	3	Binga	MPS09	5-Jul-80	35.5	$13.30	$472.15		$504.00	Bally	MMS07
11	4	Harper	CES25	30-Dec-85	40	$21.50	$860.00		$472.15	Binga	MSS19
12	5	Culbert	CCE58	26-Jul-85	42	$16.75	$703.50		$472.15	Freshita	MSS26
13	6	Califano	EEE55	7-Jun-83	40	$8.75	$350.00		$472.15	Chen	MPS05
14	7	Bally	MMS07	12-Jul-78	40	$12.60	$504.00				
15	8	Binga	MSS19	26-Feb-84	35.5	$13.30	$472.15				
16	9	Keen	CES04	15-Apr-78	40	$21.50	$860.00				
17	10	Freshita	MSS26	1-Feb-85	35.5	$13.30	$472.15				
18	11	Chen	MPS05	8-Aug-79	35.5	$13.30	$472.15				
19	12	Binga	MMS76	5-Apr-85	32	$5.50	$176.00				
20	13	Abel	CCE14	25-Jan-80	35.5	$12.50	$443.75				

Ready

PERFORMING AN OR SEARCH

To perform an OR search—to find records that match at least *one* of a set of search criteria—you must first create a criteria range that contains these multiple criteria.

The following multiple criteria range instructs Excel to find the records of all employees who work 40 *or* 42 hours per week:

```
HOURS
40
42
```

Note that the second search criterion (42) was added *beneath* the first criterion (40). OR criteria are added in rows beneath the existing criteria.

Let's perform a simple OR search:

1. In cell **J3**, enter **??e**. By adding a new row to the criteria range, you have created an OR condition. This new row instructs Excel to find all employees who work in an engineering department (whose ID codes have the letter *E* as the third letter).

2. Note that cell I3 is blank; no AND condition was set for the ??e criterion in cell J3. *Any* employee in an engineering department, regardless of gross pay, will be found with this criteria setup.

3. Choose **Data, Extract...** and click on **OK**. No new records were extracted, because we left out a crucial step in the criteria modification process: resetting the criteria range.

4. Select the range **I1:J3** and choose **Data, Set Criteria** to define this as the new criteria range. Remember that when you expand your criteria range, you must reset it; it does not automatically update.

5. Choose **Data, Extract...** and click on **OK** to extract data from records of employees who

   • Work in an engineering department (criteria contained in cells I3:J3), *or*

   • Earn more than $450 gross *and* work in marketing (criteria contained in I2:J2).

   There are ten matching records. Note in particular Califano, whose gross pay is $350; as mentioned above, this criteria setup finds any engineering employee, regardless of gross pay.

Now see what happens if we add an AND for the ??e criterion condition in cell J3:

1. In cell **I3**, enter **>550**. You don't need to reset the criteria range, because the range that you set in the last activity (I1:J3) includes cell I3.

2. Choose **Data, Extract...** and click on **OK** to extract data from records of employees who

   • Earn more than $550 gross *and* work in an engineering department (cells I3:J3), *or*

- Earn more than $450 gross *and* work in marketing (cells I2:J2)

3. Note that the number of found records was reduced from ten in step 5 of the last activity to seven here. Note also that Califano ($350 gross earnings) is gone (see Figure 11.2).

Figure 11.2   **CHAP11.XLS, after performing an AND/OR search**

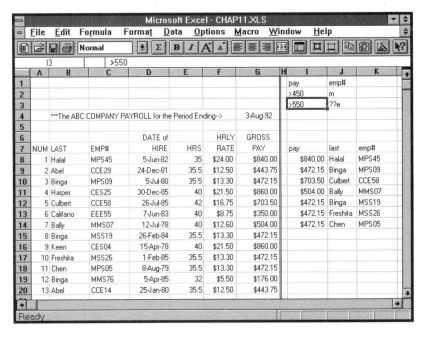

 REDUCING THE SIZE OF THE CRITERIA RANGE

In the last activity, you saw the problems that can arise when you expand your search criteria without resetting the criteria range. Now let's try reducing the criteria without resetting the range:

1. Clear the contents of **I1:J3**. (Use **Delete** or **Edit, Clear**.)

2. In cell **I1**, enter **rate** and in cell **I2**, enter **8.75** to find the records of all employees who earn exactly $8.75 per hour.

3. Change cell **I7** to **rate** to include data from the HRLY RATE field in the extract.

4. Choose **Data, Extract...** and click on **OK**. Note that data from every record in the database was extracted. Let's see why this happened.

5. Press **F5** (Goto) and double-click on **Criteria**. According to Excel, cells I1 through J3 contain the search criteria. Excel interpreted cell I3 as a blank OR condition. That is, it processed the criteria by finding the records of all employees who earn $8.75 per hour *or* who earn any amount per hour (blank cell I3). This interpretation led Excel to extract data from every record.

6. Select the range **I1:I2** and choose **Data, Set Criteria** to reset the criteria range.

7. Choose **Data, Extract...** and click on **OK**. The extract now proceeds as intended. Only one person in the list earns exactly $8.75 per hour (Califano).

SPECIFYING MULTIPLE CRITERIA FOR A SINGLE DATA FIELD

Excel allows you to specify more than one search criterion for a single data field. Let's investigate how this works:

1. In cell **I2**, enter **>10**. This criterion will find the records of all employees who earn more than $10 per hour.

2. In cell **J1**, enter **rate** and in cell **J2**, enter **<20**. This criterion will find the records of all employees who earn less than $20 per hour.

3. Select the range **I1:J2** and choose **Data, Set Criteria** to include the new data in the criteria range. You have now set multiple criteria (>10 and <20) for a single data field (HRLY RATE).

4. Choose **Data, Extract...** and click on **OK** to extract data from the records of employees who earn more than $10 *and* less than $20 per hour. Eight people match the criteria (see Figure 11.3).

5. Save the file as **MYCHAP11.XLS**.

USING THE DATA, FORM COMMAND

When working with an Excel database, you will need to edit, add, and delete records. The techniques you've learned so far for performing these tasks—editing a cell with the mouse or Edit key (F2); adding records with Edit, Insert; and deleting records with Edit,

Delete—can be tedious and time-consuming, especially if you are working with a large database (50 records or more). Fortunately, Excel provides a feature that greatly simplifies these tasks: the *Data, Form* command.

Figure 11.3 **Extracting data, after specifying multiple HRLY RATE criteria**

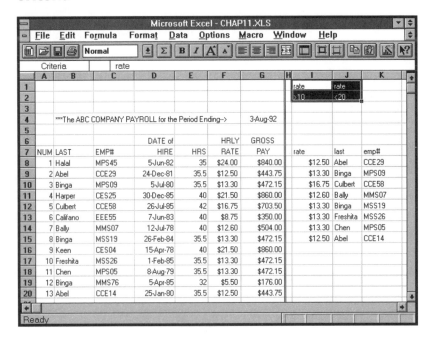

 ADDING A RECORD TO THE DATABASE

To add a record to your database using the Data, Form command,

- Set the database range using the Data, Set Database command, if you have not already done so.

- Choose Data, Form to display the *data form* of the database.

- Click on New.

- Type in the field data for the new database record (to move from field to field, use the mouse pointer or Tab key).

- Click on Close to leave the data form and return to the worksheet. Your new record will be entered as the last record of the database.

Note: It is not necessary to reset the database range after adding or deleting a record with Data, Form; Excel updates the range automatically.

Let's use Data, Form to add a record to MYCHAP11.XLS:

1. Choose **Data, Form...** to display the data form of the database (see Figure 11.4). Note that Record 1 is displayed with all its data fields listed (NUM, LAST, EMP#, HIRE, and so on). Note also that a text box appears next to every field except for the last one (PAY). These boxes contain constant data; PAY does not have a box because it contains a formula, not data.

Figure 11.4   **The Data, Form dialog box**

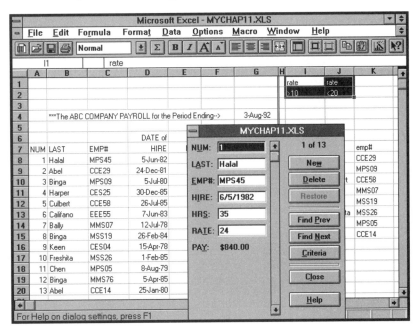

2. Click on the **down scroll arrow** inside the dialog box several times to display Records 2, 3, 4, and so on.

3. Press the **Up Arrow** key several times to return to Record 1. You can use the mouse or keyboard to scroll through records in a data form.

4. Click on **New** to display a blank record. Note the insertion point in the NUM field; the text you type will be entered here.

5. Type **14** to assign the number 14 to the new record.

6. Press **Tab** (not Enter) to move down to the next data field. Pressing Tab moves to the next *field*; pressing Enter moves to the next *record*. (You can also use the mouse to move among fields.)

7. Type **Hall** and press **Tab** to enter a last name and move down to the next field.

PRACTICE YOUR SKILLS

Complete this record using the following data:

EMP#	**MMS59** (use uppercase letters as shown)
HIRE	***today's date*** (use dd/mm/yy format; for example, 11/17/94)
HRS	**40**
RATE	**12.50**

Press **Enter** to add the record to the database. Your screen will blink a few times as Excel processes the new data. Note that the Data, Form dialog box remains on the screen and a new blank record appears.

EDITING A RECORD

To edit a database record using the Data, Form command,

• Choose Data, Form.

• Use the scroll arrows or Arrow keys to select the record you wish to edit.

• Use the mouse or Tab key to select the data you want to edit.

• Type in the new data.

• Click on Close to leave the data form and return to the worksheet. Your new data will be entered in the database.

Let's use Data, Form to edit a record (the data form box should still be displayed on the screen):

1. Scroll to Record 8, one of the Bingas. (Use the mouse or keyboard.)

2. Select the data in the RATE field text box (**13.3**).

3. Type **15**.

4. Click on **Close** to enter the new information and return to your worksheet.

5. Observe Record 8. Binga's hourly rate is now $15.00 and his salary has been updated to $532.50 (see Figure 11.5).

Figure 11.5   **MYCHAP11.XLS, after using the Data, Form command**

	A	B	C	D	E	F	G	H	I	J	K
									rate	rate	
1									>10	<20	
2											
3											
4		***The ABC COMPANY PAYROLL for the Period Ending-->					3-Aug-92				
5											
6				DATE of		HRLY	GROSS				
7	NUM	LAST	EMP#	HIRE	HRS	RATE	PAY		rate	last	emp#
8	1	Halal	MPS45	5-Jun-82	35	$24.00	$840.00		$12.50	Abel	CCE29
9	2	Abel	CCE29	24-Dec-81	35.5	$12.50	$443.75		$13.30	Binga	MPS09
10	3	Binga	MPS09	5-Jul-80	35.5	$13.30	$472.15		$16.75	Culbert	CCE58
11	4	Harper	CES25	30-Dec-85	40	$21.50	$860.00		$12.60	Bally	MMS07
12	5	Culbert	CCE58	26-Jul-85	42	$16.75	$703.50		$13.30	Binga	MSS19
13	6	Califano	EEE55	7-Jun-83	40	$8.75	$350.00		$13.30	Freshita	MSS26
14	7	Bally	MMS07	12-Jul-78	40	$12.60	$504.00		$13.30	Chen	MPS05
15	8	Binga	MSS19	26-Feb-84	35.5	$15.00	$532.50		$12.50	Abel	CCE14
16	9	Keen	CES04	15-Apr-78	40	$21.50	$860.00				
17	10	Freshita	MSS26	1-Feb-85	35.5	$13.30	$472.15				
18	11	Chen	MPS05	8-Aug-79	35.5	$13.30	$472.15				
19	12	Binga	MMS76	5-Apr-85	32	$5.50	$176.00				
20	13	Abel	CCE14	25-Jan-80	35.5	$12.50	$443.75				

Now let's examine the database range:

1. Choose **Formula, Define Name...**, and click on **Database**.
   Observe the database range: $A$7:$G$21. This range contains the record you just added (Hall). As mentioned above, when

you use Data, Form to add a record to your database, Excel automatically updates your database range.

2. Click on **Close** to return to the worksheet.

3. Choose **Data, Extract...** and click on **OK** to update the extract. Hall's record meets the current search criteria and is added to the extract.

 FINDING A RECORD

In addition to adding and editing a record, Excel allows you to search for a specific record within a data form. To do this:

- Choose Data, Form... .

- Click on Criteria.

- Type the desired search criteria in the appropriate data-field box(es). The criteria you enter here are completely independent of any search criteria you may have already entered in the worksheet.

- Click on Find Next to find the first matching record in the data form. Continue clicking on Find Next or Find Prev to view other matching records.

- Click on Close to exit the data form and return to the worksheet.

Let's use this procedure to find the records of all employees who earn less than $10 an hour:

1. Choose **Data, Form...** .

2. Click on **Criteria**. A blank employee record appears.

3. In the RATE text box, type **<10**. Note that this criterion is different from either of the criteria currently entered in the worksheet (cells I1:J2). As mentioned, when you perform a search within a data form, Excel ignores the worksheet criteria.

4. Click on **Find Next**. Califano's record is found ($8.75 an hour).

5. Click on **Find Next** again. Binga's record is found ($5.50 an hour).

6. Click on **Find Next** again. Nothing happens. Only two records match your data-form search criterion (<10).

7. Click on **Find Prev**. Califano's record is found again.

8. Click on **Close** to exit the data form and return to the work-sheet. Note that Califano's record is *not* selected. Finding a record within a data form does not cause it to be selected when you exit the data form.

USING DATABASE FUNCTIONS

Excel provides a category of functions, called *database functions*, that you can use to perform calculations upon data from a specified field in those records that match your current search criteria. For example, later on in this section, we'll use the *DSUM* database function to add up the values in the GROSS PAY field for employees whose records match the following search criteria:

```
RATE  RATE
>10   <20
```

To use a database function, you must specify three arguments: the database range, the field on which the function is to act, and the search criteria that determine which records are to be used. The syntax of a database function is

D*FUNCTION*(*database,field,criteria*)

- D*FUNCTION* is the name of the database function (DSUM, DAV-ERAGE, and so on).

- The *database* argument defines the database range upon which the function will act. If you have used the Set Database command to set a database range, you can use the defined name Database as this argument.

- The *field* argument defines the field on which the function will act by specifying the field header. This argument can be expressed as text enclosed by quotes (such as "HRS" or "pay") or as a cell reference (such as e7 or g7).

- The *criteria* argument defines the range containing the search criteria used to determine the records upon which the function will act. If you have used the Set Criteria command to set a search criteria range, you can use the defined name Criteria as this argument.

For example, if you have used the Set Database and Set Criteria commands to define your database and criteria ranges, and the current search criteria are

```
HRS
40
```

you can use the database function

```
DSUM(Database,"pay",Criteria)
```

to find the total gross pay (as specified by the "pay" argument) for employees who work exactly 40 hours per week.

MYCHAP11.XLS uses a database function called DAVERAGE to calculate the average number of weekly work hours for employees whose records match the currently specified search criteria (in cells I1:J2). Let's take a look at this function:

1. Select cell **E23**. Observe the DAVERAGE function in the formula bar. Note that it contains the standard database-function arguments enclosed in parentheses: the database argument, Database; the field argument, E7; and the criteria argument, Criteria.

2. Observe the database argument, Database. This defines the database range. Because this range has already been set, the argument uses the defined name Database.

3. Observe the field argument, E7. This defines the field which DAVERAGE will act upon. The cell E7 identifies the field as HRS. ("HRS" or "hrs" could have been used instead of E7 as the argument.)

4. Examine the criteria argument, Criteria. This defines the search criteria range. Only records matching the criteria in this range will be acted upon by DAVERAGE. The current search criteria (in cells I1:J2) are set to find records of employees who earn between $10 and $20 an hour. The average weekly work hours of these employees is displayed in cell E23.

Now let's enter a database function in cell G24 to calculate the total gross pay of all employees whose records match the current criteria:

1. Select cell **G24**. Choose **Formula, Paste Function...** to open the Paste Function dialog box.

2. In the Function Category list box, select **Database**.

3. In the Paste Function list box, select **DSUM**. (You'll need to scroll.) Verify that **Paste Arguments** is checked. When pasting a database function, it is often useful to paste arguments also, because the *database* and *criteria* arguments are usually left unchanged (as you'll see in step 5).

4. Click on **OK** to paste the DSUM function and its arguments into cell G24.

5. In the formula bar, observe the pasted arguments, *database*, *field*, and *criteria*. Because Database and Criteria are already defined in the worksheet, you do not need to change these arguments.

6. Double-click on the **field** argument to select it. This argument must contain a reference to the name of the field on which the DSUM function will operate.

7. Type **"pay"** (include the quotes) to specify GROSS PAY as the field to be summed. (You could have entered g7 or "PAY" instead of "pay" to specify this field.)

8. Enter the function and observe the results (see Figure 11.6). The calculated value represents the total gross pay for all employees whose hourly rate is between $10 and $20 (as defined by the search criteria in cells I1:J2).

DELETING FOUND RECORDS

You have learned how to find records and how to extract found records. Excel also allows you to *delete* found records from your database. Record deletion is particularly useful for database updating. For example, at the beginning of fiscal year 1992, you could use Data, Delete to delete all records with a transaction date of 1991 or earlier.

To use the Data, Delete command to delete found records,

• Save your worksheet file.

• Set the database range using the Data, Set Database command, if you have not already done so.

• Enter your search criteria for the records to be deleted, and set the criteria range using the Data, Set Criteria command.

• Choose Data, Delete to delete the records that match your search criteria.

Figure 11.6 **Using the DSUM database function**

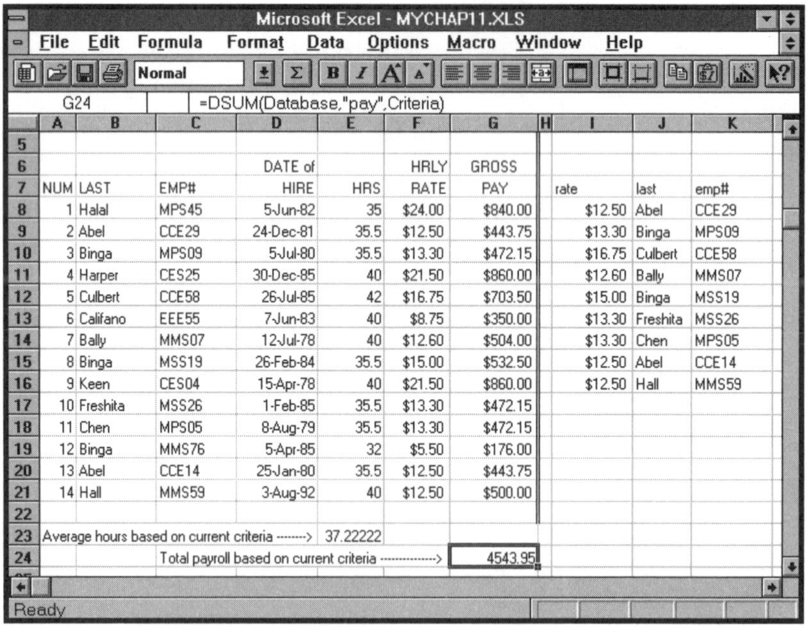

	A	B	C	D	E	F	G	H	I	J	K
5											
6				DATE of		HRLY	GROSS				
7	NUM	LAST	EMP#	HIRE	HRS	RATE	PAY		rate	last	emp#
8	1	Halal	MPS45	5-Jun-82	35	$24.00	$840.00		$12.50	Abel	CCE29
9	2	Abel	CCE29	24-Dec-81	35.5	$12.50	$443.75		$13.30	Binga	MPS09
10	3	Binga	MPS09	5-Jul-80	35.5	$13.30	$472.15		$16.75	Culbert	CCE58
11	4	Harper	CES25	30-Dec-85	40	$21.50	$860.00		$12.60	Bally	MMS07
12	5	Culbert	CCE58	26-Jul-85	42	$16.75	$703.50		$15.00	Binga	MSS19
13	6	Califano	EEE55	7-Jun-83	40	$8.75	$350.00		$13.30	Freshita	MSS26
14	7	Bally	MMS07	12-Jul-78	40	$12.60	$504.00		$13.30	Chen	MPS05
15	8	Binga	MSS19	26-Feb-84	35.5	$15.00	$532.50		$12.50	Abel	CCE14
16	9	Keen	CES04	15-Apr-78	40	$21.50	$860.00		$12.50	Hall	MMS59
17	10	Freshita	MSS26	1-Feb-85	35.5	$13.30	$472.15				
18	11	Chen	MPS05	8-Aug-79	35.5	$13.30	$472.15				
19	12	Binga	MMS76	5-Apr-85	32	$5.50	$176.00				
20	13	Abel	CCE14	25-Jan-80	35.5	$12.50	$443.75				
21	14	Hall	MMS59	3-Aug-92	40	$12.50	$500.00				
22											
23	Average hours based on current criteria ------->				37.22222						
24			Total payroll based on current criteria -------------->				4543.95				

Be forewarned that a Data, Delete command cannot be undone. For this reason, you should save your file immediately before using Data, Delete. You might also want to extract the records and examine them before you delete them.

Now let's perform a found-record deletion using Data, Delete:

1. Choose **File, Save** to update **MYCHAP11.XLS**. Remember to save your file before using Data, Delete.
2. Observe the criteria range. The search criteria are set to find all employees earning between $10 and $20 per hour.
3. Choose **Data, Extract**... and click on **OK**. Observe the extracted records. It's a good habit to examine the records you will be deleting before you actually delete them.
4. Choose **Data, Delete.** An alert box appears, informing you that if you continue, all records that match the criteria will be permanently deleted. Remember that you cannot undo a Data, Delete command.

5. Click on **OK** to delete the records of all employees earning between $10 and $20 per hour.
6. Observe the modified database. The only records left are those of employees who earn less than $10 or more than $20 per hour (see Figure 11.7).

Figure 11.7 **MYCHAP11.XLS, after using Data, Delete to erase records**

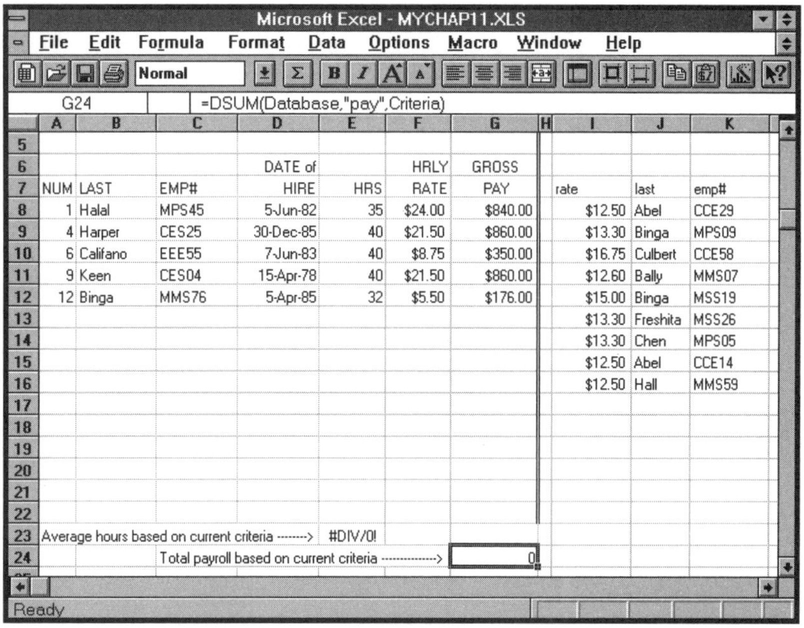

	A	B	C	D	E	F	G	H	I	J	K
5											
6				DATE of		HRLY	GROSS				
7	NUM	LAST	EMP#	HIRE	HRS	RATE	PAY		rate	last	emp#
8	1	Halal	MPS45	5-Jun-82	35	$24.00	$840.00		$12.50	Abel	CCE29
9	4	Harper	CES25	30-Dec-85	40	$21.50	$860.00		$13.30	Binga	MPS09
10	6	Califano	EEE55	7-Jun-83	40	$8.75	$350.00		$16.75	Culbert	CCE58
11	9	Keen	CES04	15-Apr-78	40	$21.50	$860.00		$12.60	Bally	MMS07
12	12	Binga	MMS76	5-Apr-85	32	$5.50	$176.00		$15.00	Binga	MSS19
13									$13.30	Freshita	MSS26
14									$13.30	Chen	MPS05
15									$12.50	Abel	CCE14
16									$12.50	Hall	MMS59
17											
18											
19											
20											
21											
22											
23	Average hours based on current criteria ------->				#DIV/0!						
24			Total payroll based on current criteria ---------------->				0				

7. Click on **Edit** in the menu bar. Note the Can't Undo entry. If you needed to reverse the Data, Delete operation, you could use File, Open to open MYCHAP11.XLS and revert to the version of the worksheet you saved before issuing the Data, Delete command. (Do not do this now.)
8. Observe cell **E23,** which displays

   `#DIV/0!`

   This is an error code indicating that the DAVERAGE function in this cell tried to divide by zero (0), a mathematical taboo. Let's take a moment to reconstruct the logic that resulted in this error code. You used Data, Delete to delete the record of all employees matching the search criteria. The DAVERAGE function in cell E23, however, is set up to act only upon these same, now-deleted records. When DAVERAGE divided the total hours by the total number of records to calculate its average, it attempted to divide by zero—the total number of now-matching records.

9. Observe cell **G24**. It displays "0," which represents the total gross pay of all employees whose records match the search criteria. Again, because you just deleted all these matching employee records, the sum is zero. (No #DIV/0! error code appears because the DSUM function does not divide.)

PRACTICE YOUR SKILLS

1. Change the criteria to find all employees who earn less than $10 an hour. (Hint: Remember to reset the criteria range.) Note the modified values in cells E23 and G24.

2. Close the file without saving the changes.

PRACTICE YOUR SKILLS

The following activity is designed to review the major topics covered in the database-management section of this book, Chapters 8 through 11. Perform these steps upon the file EXERDB.XLS to extract records to match those in Figure 11.8:

1. Open **EXERDB.XLS** (Chapter 3).

2. Maximize the document window, if necessary (Chapter 3).

3. Enter the following information in the specified cells:

M1 Field name for employee number

N1 Field name for employees' hours per week

O1 Field name for employees' hourly rate

Figure 11.8 **Printout of EXERDB.XLS, after an extract and three-key sort**

EXERDB.XLS

FIRST	LAST	EMP#	HRS	RATE
Robert	Abot	MMS08	40	$12.60
Todd	Allen	MMS69	40	$12.60
Frank	Bally	MMS07	40	$12.60
Dominick	Bono	MMS09	40	$21.50
Brad	Brower	MMS12	40	$22.00
Robert	Dollar	MMS47	40	$12.60
Theresa	Footer	MMS79	40	$12.60
Harry	Harper	CES25	40	$21.50
Kyle	Jansen	MMS16	40	$22.00
Barry	Keen	CES04	40	$21.50
Len	Lacey	MMS18	40	$22.00
Harry	Noan	CES20	40	$21.50
Dominick	Osowski	MMS57	40	$22.00
Molly	Perkins	MMS65	40	$22.00
Paul	Ulman	CES02	40	$21.50
Bill	James	MMS05	38	$15.50
Greg	James	MMS49	38	$15.50
Carol	Lynn	MMS14	38	$15.50
Fred	Thomas	MMS06	38	$15.50
Doug	Whitney	MMS40	38	$15.50
Alice	Binga	MSS11	35.5	$13.30
Bill	Binga	MSS03	35.5	$13.30
Sam	Binga	MPS09	35.5	$13.30
Shing	Chen	MPS05	35.5	$13.30
Sam	Freshita	MSS26	35.5	$13.30
Theresa	Binga	MSS19	35	$12.10
Laura	Brainard	MMS25	35	$24.00
Jane	Gregg	MSS23	35	$12.10
James	Halal	MPS45	35	$24.00
Laura	Hoffman	MMS77	35	$24.00
Brooks	Kaufman	MMS21	35	$24.00
Jane	Killim	MSS29	35	$12.10
Jane	Liner	MSS17	35	$12.10
Jane	Noah	MSS45	35	$12.10
Mako	Zee	MMS28	35	$24.00

4. In cell **M2**, enter a criterion to find all support department employees (Chapter 9). Hint: Support department employees have an *S* as the third character of their employee numbers.

5. In cell **N2**, enter a criterion to find all employees who work 35 hours or more per week (Chapter 9).

6. In cell **O2**, enter a criterion to find all employees who earn more than $12 per hour (Chapter 9).

7. Type or copy these field names into the specified cells:

	M	N	O	P	Q
4	**FIRST**	**LAST**	**EMP#**	**HRS**	**RATE**

8. Select the range **A4** through **K99** and define this as the database range (Chapter 9).

9. Select the range **M1** through **O2** and define this as the criteria range (Chapter 9).

10. Select the range **M4** through **Q99** and define this as the extract range (Chapter 10).

11. Extract the matching records (Chapter 10).

12. Sort the extracted records, based on the following keys (Chapter 8):

Key	Field	Order
1st Key	**HRS** (column P)	**Descending**
2nd Key	**LAST** (column N)	**Ascending**
3rd Key	**FIRST** (column M)	**Ascending**

13. Use the toolbar to right-align the contents of cells **P4** ("HRS") and **Q4** ("RATE") (Chapter 6).

14. Select the range **M4** through **Q39**, and define this as the print area (Chapter 10).

15. Print the extracted records, using all the current print settings (Chapter 10).

16. Compare your printout to Figure 11.8.

17. Save the file as **MYEXERDB.XLS** (Chapter 2).

18. Close the file (Chapter 2).

The following activity is designed to further review your Excel database-management skills. Perform these steps upon the file OPTEXDB.XLS to extract records to match those in Figure 11.9:

1. Open **OPTEXDB.XLS** (Chapter 3).

2. Maximize the document window, if necessary (Chapter 3).

3. Assign record numbers to all the records in the database (Chapter 8). Hint: Type the start number (**1**) in cell **A5** before using the Data menu.

4. Enter the field name **NUM** in cell **A4**.

5. Rearrange the records in the database in alphabetical order (ascending) by last name (Chapter 8). Hint: Do not include the field names when sorting the database.

6. Your boss needs a combined list of all employees who meet the following criteria:

   GROUP 1

   • Works in an engineering department (Chapter 9), *and*

   • Was hired after January 1, 1980 (use a comparison operator) (Chapter 9), *and*

   • Was hired before December 31, 1985 (use a comparison operator) (Chapter 9)

   GROUP 2

   • Works for a chemicals division (Chapter 9), *and*

   • Earns more than $12.50 per hour (Chapter 9)

   Hints: Use the EMP# field when specifying division and department criteria. Include the field names and all the records when setting the database range. Also include both the field names and the criteria when setting the criteria range.

7. Extract the following information about the above group of employees (Chapter 10):

   • Division

Figure 11.9   **Printout of OPTEXDB.XLS, after an extract and two-key sort**

OPTEXDB.XLS

DIVISION	DEPT	FIRST	LAST	HIRE	RATE
Chemicals	Chemical Engineering	Sara	Abel	24-Dec-81	$12.50
Chemicals	Chemical Engineering	Bob	Abel	25-Jan-80	$12.50
Chemicals	Chemical Engineering	Mary	Abrams	25-Nov-82	$12.50
Chemicals	Chemical Engineering	George	Abromo	3-Dec-82	$12.50
Chemicals	Chemical Engineering	Carol	Ackle	21-Jul-81	$12.50
Chemicals	Chemical Engineering	Sam	Chin	27-Oct-84	$15.50
Chemicals	Chemical Engineering	Bill	Conner	5-Nov-83	$19.50
Chemicals	Chemical Engineering	Colleen	Culbert	26-Jul-85	$16.75
Chemicals	Chemical Engineering	Colleen	Culbert	2-Sep-81	$16.75
Chemicals	Chemical Engineering	Brad	Daley	8-Nov-80	$19.50
Chemicals	Chemical Engineering	Sue	Laly	30-Nov-79	$15.50
Chemicals	Chemical Engineering	Bill	Reagan	4-Oct-81	$19.50
Chemicals	Chemical Engineering	Kim	Sen	27-Nov-84	$16.75
Chemicals	Chemical Engineering	Kon	Song	15-Nov-84	$15.50
Chemicals	Chemical Engineering	Colleen	Taube	12-Jan-82	$16.75
Chemicals	Chemical Engineering	Colleen	Traber	3-May-85	$16.75
Chemicals	Chemical Engineering	Bill	Travel	12-Jan-77	$19.50
Chemicals	Chemical Engineering	Bill	Young	8-Mar-76	$19.50
Chemicals	Chemical Engineering	Sam	Zalwa	28-Nov-78	$15.50
Chemicals	Chemical Engineering	Jerry	Zambito	7-Jul-77	$15.50
Chemicals	Engineering Support	Holly	Brown	17-Aug-79	$6.50
Chemicals	Engineering Support	Harry	Flack	23-Jan-84	$6.50
Chemicals	Engineering Support	Paula	Garan	7-Dec-82	$6.50
Chemicals	Engineering Support	Mata	Hari	9-Sep-82	$6.50
Chemicals	Engineering Support	Harry	Harper	30-Dec-85	$21.50
Chemicals	Engineering Support	Barry	Keen	15-Apr-78	$21.50
Chemicals	Engineering Support	Harry	Noan	28-Oct-82	$21.50
Chemicals	Engineering Support	Paul	Ulman	19-Apr-74	$21.50
Electronics	Electrical Engineering	Steve	Allen	5-Oct-81	$21.50
Electronics	Electrical Engineering	Ester	Easter	13-Dec-81	$15.00
Electronics	Electrical Engineering	Joshua	Randall	23-Jan-86	$21.50
Electronics	Electrical Engineering	Deanne	Verta	23-Jun-82	$15.00
Electronics	Electrical Engineering	Ester	Winter	24-Dec-82	$15.00
Electronics	Electrical Engineering	Elba	Zapts	8-Apr-86	$15.00

- Department
- First name
- Last name
- Date of employment
- Hourly pay

Hint: Use the spelling of the field names as they appear in the worksheet ("DEPT," "HIRE," and so on).

8. Arrange the extracted records by division in ascending order, and by department in ascending order (Chapter 8). Hint: Do not include the field names when sorting the extracted records.

9. Right-align the extract-range field names "HIRE" and "RATE" (Chapter 6).

10. Print—without row and column headings or gridlines—the extracted records and field names (Chapters 7 and 10).

11. Compare your printout to Figure 11.9.

12. In cell **H101**, enter a database function to calculate the average number of years employed for all employees whose records match the current search criteria (Chapter 11).

13. In cell **K102**, enter a database function to calculate the total gross pay for all employees whose records match the current search criteria (Chapter 11).

14. Compare your screen to Figure 11.10. (Note: Your average years employed value in cell H101 will differ, because it is dependent upon the current date.)

15. Save the file as **MYOPTDB.XLS** (Chapter 2).

16. Close the file (Chapter 2).

CHAPTER SUMMARY

In this chapter, you learned several advanced database-management techniques. You now know how to expand your search criteria to perform AND and OR searches; how to use the Data, Form command to edit, add, and find database records; how to use database functions; and how to use the Data, Delete command to delete records that match your search criteria.

Figure 11.10   **Using database functions to average and sum**

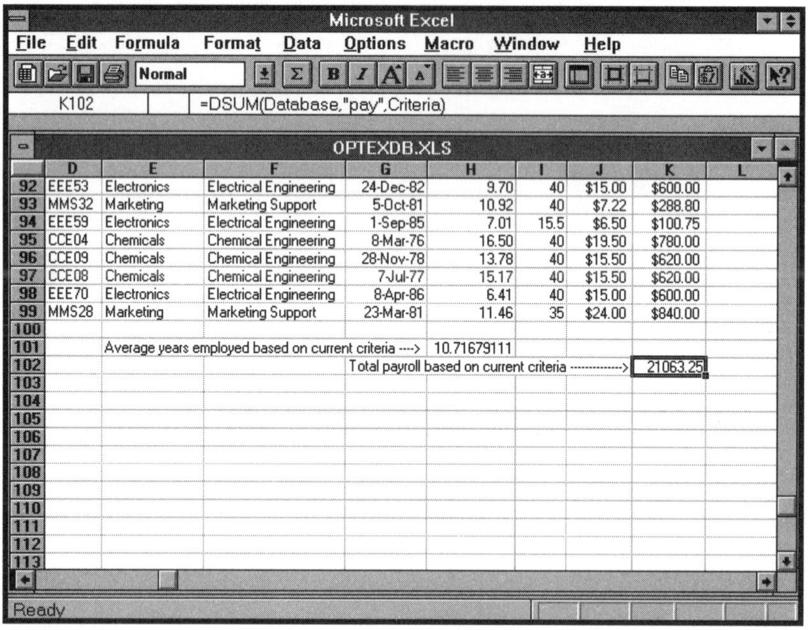

With this chapter, your foundation in Excel database-management techniques is complete. Congratulations! You now possess the skills to perform sophisticated database-management tasks.

Here is a quick reference guide to the Excel features introduced in this chapter:

Desired Result	How to Do It
Perform an AND or OR search	Expand/modify criteria range to include desired AND or OR condition(s), reset criteria range, if necessary set database and extract ranges, choose **Data, Find...** or **Data, Extract...**
Add a record to the database	Choose **Data, Form...**, click on **New**, type field data, click on **Close**
Edit a database record	Choose **Data, Form...**, edit desired field data, click on **Close**

Desired Result	How to Do It
Find records within a data form	Choose **Data, Form...**, click on **Criteria**, type desired search criteria in appropriate data-field box(es), click on **Find Next** or **Find Prev** to find next or previous matching record, click on **Close** to exit data form and return to worksheet
Use a database function	Use **Formula, Paste** to paste desired function with its arguments, specify arguments, change search criteria if necessary
Delete found records	Save worksheet, create search criteria for records to be deleted, set criteria range, if necessary set database range, choose **Data, Delete...**

The remaining chapters of this book are devoted to Excel's charting system. In Chapter 12, you will learn how to create a simple chart (graph) from your worksheet data; how to enhance and customize this chart; and, finally, how to save and print it.

IF YOU'RE STOPPING HERE

If you need to break off here, please exit from Excel. If you want to proceed directly to the next chapter, please do so now.

CHAPTER 12:
CREATING AND
PRINTING A CHART

It is often much easier to understand overall trends and patterns in numeric data by viewing these data in graphic form, rather than as columns of numbers in a worksheet. For this reason, visually accessible data prove particularly effective in business presentations and reports. This chapter introduces the third and final major topic of the book: *charting*, the display of worksheet data in graphic (chart) form.

When you're done working through this chapter, you will know

- How to create a standard column chart
- How to add a legend and text labels to a chart
- How to change the chart type
- How to save and print a chart
- How to create multiple charts from a single worksheet
- How Excel links a chart to a worksheet

CHART TERMINOLOGY

Before you begin creating and modifying Excel charts, you should be familiar with the following terms (see Figure 12.1):

Chart	A graphic representation of worksheet data. Each chart you create appears in its own document window.
Chart menu bar	The bar that displays the menu options available for use with charts.
Data marker	A symbol that marks a data value in a chart. This symbol varies with the chart type. Column and bar charts (see Figure 12.1) use rectangular-bar data markers; pie charts use wedge shapes; line charts use dots.
Gridlines	Optional lines that extend across the plot area to make it easier to view data values.
Chart text	Text that describes data or objects in a chart. *Attached text* is a label attached to a particular chart object, such as a data marker; an attached text label can be moved only when the object to which it is attached is moved. *Unattached text* is text you add to a chart by typing at any point within the chart and then pressing Enter; unattached text can be moved anywhere on the chart.
Legend	A caption box that identifies the data markers of a chart data series.

Figure 12.1 **Chart terminology**

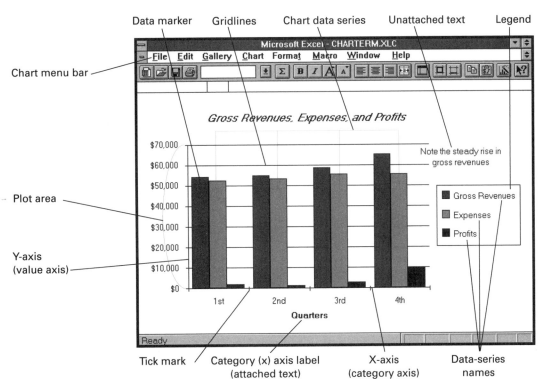

Data marker Gridlines Chart data series Unattached text Legend

Chart menu bar

Plot area

Y-axis
(value axis)

Tick mark Category (x) axis label
(attached text) X-axis
(category axis) Data-series
names

Axis	A reference line along which chart data is plotted. Categories (row headings) are plotted along a *category axis*, or *x-axis* ("1st," "2nd," "3rd," "4th" in Figure 12.1). Data values (numeric values) are plotted along a *value axis*, or *y-axis*.
Tick mark	A small line that intersects an axis and is used to delineate categories and data values.
Plot area	The area in which data are plotted, including all axes and data markers.
Chart data series	A series of related data values (in Figure 12.1, the expense data for all four quarters). A chart data series typically includes all the values in a single worksheet column.

CREATING A STANDARD COLUMN CHART

To create a standard column chart,

- Create a worksheet.

- Select the range to chart, including both the numeric data and the row/column headings that should appear as labels in the chart (see below, "Selecting the Range to Chart").

- Choose File, New.

- Select *Chart*, then click on OK.

If you are not running Excel, please start it now. If there is a worksheet on your screen, close it. Your screen should be empty except for a maximized Excel application window. Now let's open a worksheet and create a standard column chart:

1. Open **CHAP12.XLS** from your EX4WORK directory. Do not maximize the document window. (If it already is maximized, leave it as is.)

2. Select the range **C4:E8**. You will be charting four quarters of gross revenues and expenses.

3. Choose **File, New...** .

4. Click on **Chart**, then click on **OK**. Excel opens a new window in which it creates a chart depicting the selected worksheet data. Note that the Chart toolbar automatically appears at the bottom of the screen. (If this toolbar does not appear on your screen, don't worry; this simply means that your Excel 4.0 program is configured slightly differently from ours. We'll take care of this discrepancy in a later activity.)

5. Maximize the chart window. (Use the same method as for a worksheet window: click on the **Maximize button** or press **Ctrl-F10**.) Observe the chart (see Figure 12.2). Excel displays your selected worksheet data in standard, column-chart form. Note the chart file name, Chart1. Note also that the Excel menu bar has changed; two new charting options, Gallery and Chart, are displayed.

Figure 12.2   **Chart1, newly created**

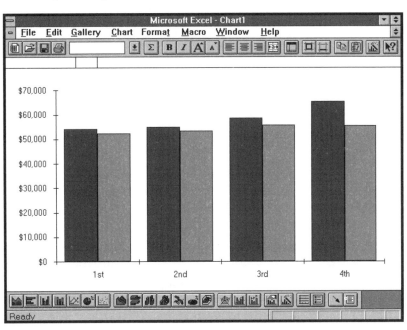

SELECTING THE RANGE TO CHART

The shape and content of the range of cells you select in your worksheet determine the layout of the resultant chart. For this reason, you should be aware that

- The far-left column of your worksheet selection should contain text labels, not data—these will be the category (x-axis) labels on the chart ("1st," "2nd," "3rd," and "4th" in the above activity).

- The top row of your worksheet selection should also contain text labels—these will be the data-series labels in your chart legend (you will create this legend in the next activity; the data-series labels will read "Gross Revenues" and "Expenses").

- The remainder of your worksheet selection should contain the numeric data you would like Excel to plot.

Excel's charting assumptions will be discussed further in Chapter 14.

LABELING A CHART

Excel provides you with extensive text-labeling options to enhance a chart's clarity and appearance. You can add a legend, attached text (such as a title), and unattached text to your chart.

ADDING A LEGEND

To add a legend to a chart,

* Select the chart to be modified.

* Choose *Chart, Add Legend*—the legend will appear to the right of the chart.

Let's add a legend to Chart1. Since the chart is already selected (active), we can skip the first of the two steps above.

1. Choose **Chart, Add Legend**. The legend appears to the right of the chart and serves to identify the screen patterns (colors) that are assigned to the data markers, Gross Revenues and Expenses. Note that the plot area has been redrawn to make room for the legend. The black selection squares surrounding the legend indicate that it can be moved.

2. Move the legend to the middle of the screen. (Position the mouse pointer over the legend and drag.) Note that the plot area has again been redrawn, this time filling the entire screen. Anytime you move a legend away from the edge of a chart, Excel redraws the plot area at full size.

3. Choose **Edit, Undo Move** to move the legend back to its original location. Note that the plot area has once again adjusted to accommodate the legend.

ATTACHING TEXT

As mentioned above, there are two kinds of text you can add to a chart: attached and unattached. Attached text is bound to a chart object (axis, data marker) and can be moved only if that object is moved. Unattached text is not bound to any object and can be moved anywhere within the chart. (The procedure used to create unattached text will be covered in the next chapter.)

To attach text to a chart,

- Select the chart to be modified.
- Choose *Chart, Attach Text...* .
- Select the chart object (data marker or axis, for example) to which you want to attach the text.
- Click on OK.
- Type the text and press Enter.

Let's attach text to Chart1:

1. Choose **Chart, Attach Text...** .

2. Select **Chart Title**, then click on **OK**. "Title" appears at the top of the chart and is surrounded by white selection squares. As mentioned above, black selection squares indicate that an object can be moved; white squares indicate that an object *cannot* be moved.

3. Type the new chart title **ABC Company Revenues and Expenses**, then press **Enter**.

4. Observe the Bold button on the toolbar. The button is selected because Excel automatically bolded your title.

5. Click on the **Bold button** to remove the bold formatting. Click again on the **Bold button** to make the title bold again. You can use the Standard toolbar to modify chart text just as you would use it to modify worksheet text.

PRACTICE YOUR SKILLS

Attach the text label **Quarters** to the category (x) axis label of Chart1. (Use the **Chart, Attach Text** command.) Press **Esc** to deselect the axis label. Compare your chart with Figure 12.3.

CHART TYPES

So far, we have looked at just one type of chart, a standard column chart. Excel offers fourteen chart types; the one you choose will vary according to your data. Here is a list of Excel's chart types and brief descriptions of their primary uses:

Use This Type of Chart	To Demonstrate
Area	The relative importance of data values over a period of time
Bar	Individual data values for comparison
Column	Individual data values for comparison over a period of time
Line	Trends in data over a period of time
Pie	The relationship of parts to a whole within a single chart data series
Radar	Relative comparison between numeric data
XY (Scatter)	Relationships among numeric values in different groups of data
Combination	Relationships among data shown by superimposing two types of charts
3-D Area	A three-dimensional view of an area chart
3-D Bar	A three-dimensional view of a bar chart
3-D Column	A three-dimensional view of a column chart
3-D Line	A three-dimensional view of a line chart
3-D Pie	A three-dimensional view of a pie chart
3-D Surface	A variation on a 3-D column chart

For each chart type, Excel offers you several formats (visual arrangements) to choose from. The format you choose will vary according to personal preference and the nature of your data.

Figure 12.3   Chart1, after adding a legend, title, and axis label

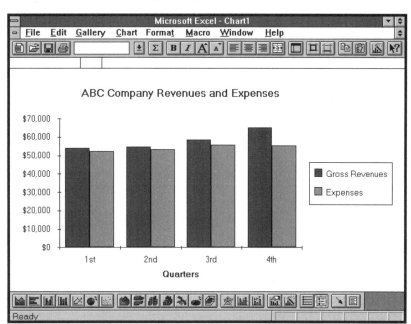

CHANGING THE CHART TYPE

To change the type of your chart by using the Gallery menu,

- Select the chart to be modified.
- Choose Gallery.
- Select the desired chart type.
- Select the desired chart format.
- Click on OK.

To change the type of your chart by using the Chart Toolbar,

- Select the chart to be modified.
- Display the Chart toolbar, if it is hidden.
- Click on the desired chart-type button on the toolbar.

Figure 12.4 identifies the Chart toolbar buttons.

Let's use the Gallery menu and the Chart toolbar to experiment with different chart types and formats. In order to do this, the

Chart toolbar must be displayed on your screen. If it is not displayed, please perform steps 1 through 4 below. If it is displayed, please skip directly to step 5.

Figure 12.4   **The Chart toolbar buttons**

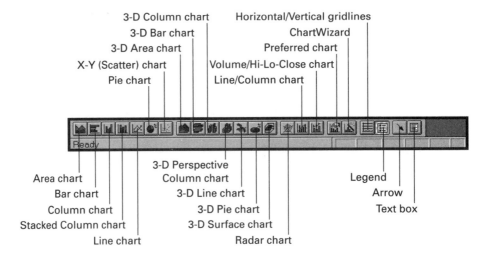

1. Choose **Window, 1 CHAP12.XLS** to activate the CHAP12.XLS worksheet. Toolbars are shown/hidden from the worksheet menu, not a chart menu.

2. Choose **Options, Toolbars...** to open the Toolbars dialog box.

3. In the Show Toolbars list box, select (click once on) **Chart**. Click on **Show** to display the Chart toolbar.

4. Choose **Window, 2 Chart1** to activate the chart.

5. If the Chart toolbar is not shown as a long, narrow rectangle at the bottom of the screen (as in Figure 12.3), use the mouse to drag it to this position.

6. Choose **Gallery, Bar...** to change your chart type from column to bar. A dialog box appears, offering you a variety of bar-chart formats.

7. Click on format option **6**, then click on **OK** to create your bar chart. As mentioned above, bar charts are used to compare individual data values. A bar chart is essentially a column chart

flipped on its side: categories (in this case, quarters) are displayed on the vertical axis rather than on the horizontal axis.

8. Choose **Gallery, Line...** to change your chart type from bar to line. Observe the line-format dialog box. Note that format option 1 displays lines and markers.

9. Double-click on format option **1** (this is equivalent to clicking on option 1 and then clicking on OK) to create your line chart. Line charts are used to show trends in data over a period of time.

10. Choose **Gallery, Area...** to change your chart type from line to area.

11. Double-click on format option **5** to create your area chart. Area charts are used to show the relative importance of data values over a period of time.

12. Choose **Edit, Undo Area** to undo the area formatting. The line chart reppears.

13. Now click on the **Area Chart button** in the Chart toolbar (the leftmost button, as shown in Figure 12.4). A standard area chart appears.

14. Click on the **3-D Area Chart button** in the Chart toolbar (the eighth button from the left) to change your chart type from area to 3-D area (see Figure 12.5).

15. Choose **Gallery, 3-D Area...** . Note the seven available 3-D area chart variations. Use the Chart toolbar to create a standard chart type; use the Gallery menu to create a specific variation.

16. Double-click on format option **1** to create your modified 3-D area chart.

PRACTICE YOUR SKILLS

1. Use **Edit, Undo** and **Edit, Redo** to switch back and forth between your two 3-D area charts—the one you created with the Chart toolbar and the one you created with the Gallery menu. Observe the similarities in structure.

2. Use the Gallery menu to return the chart type to column, format option 1.

Figure 12.5   **Chart1 in 3-D area view**

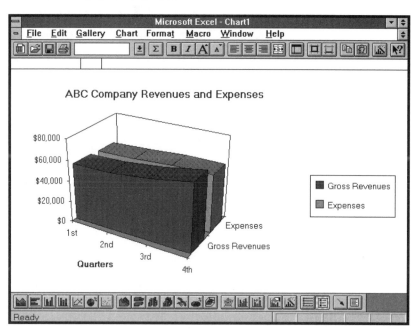

SAVING AND PRINTING A CHART

A chart created with the File, New, Chart command is treated by Excel as an independent document; it is saved and printed separately from the worksheet on which it is based.

SAVING A CHART

To save a chart,

- Select the chart to be saved.

- Choose File, Save As... (the first time a chart is saved) or File, Save... (to update an existing chart with the same name).

- Type a file name up to eight characters long (the naming rules for worksheets apply here, too).

- Click on OK. Excel automatically adds the extension .XLC (instead of .XLS) to the end of your chart file name; this stands for "Excel Chart."

Let's save your chart:

1. Choose **File, Save As...** . Note that the standard chart name is CHART1.XLC.

2. Type **mychart**, then click on **OK** to save the chart as MYCHART.XLC. Remember, Excel automatically adds the .XLC; you don't need to include it in your file name.

PRINTING A CHART

To print a chart,

- Select the chart to be printed.

- Choose File, Print Preview to see how the printed chart will look.

- Click on Setup... to change any desired print options.

- Click on Print, then click on OK to print the chart.

Note: If you don't want to preview the printout, you can use File, Page Setup to set the desired print options and File, Print to print.

Now let's preview your chart, then print it:

1. Choose **File, Print Preview**. If you wish to change any print options, use **Setup...** to do this now.

2. Click on **Print**, then click on **OK** to print MYCHART.XLC using the current settings. When the printing is finished, you will be exited from print preview to your chart.

CREATING MULTIPLE CHARTS FROM A SINGLE WORKSHEET

At times, you may wish to create two or more charts from a single worksheet to depict different aspects of the worksheet data. For example, you might want to present both a bar chart and a 3-D area chart for the same set of data; or you might want to create several different charts, each based on a unique selection of data from the same worksheet. Excel allows you to create an unlimited number of charts from a single worksheet.

To create a new chart from a worksheet,

- Select the worksheet range you want to chart.

- Choose File, New, Chart and click on OK. Or, press F11.

Let's create a second chart from CHAP12.XLS:

1. Choose **Window**. Note that there are two windows available, CHAP12.XLS and MYCHART.XLC.

2. Choose **CHAP12.XLS**.

3. Observe the formula in cell F5. It calculates profit by subtracting expenses (E5) from revenues (D5).

4. Select the range **C4:C8**. This range contains the "Quarters" column heading and the quarter names.

5. While holding down **Ctrl**, select the range **F4:F8** to include the Profits column in your data selection.

6. Press **F11** if you have this key on your keyboard; if not, choose **File, New...** and double-click on **Chart**. Either of these methods will create a standard column chart from the selected worksheet data.

7. Note that your new chart has been automatically entitled "Profits." When you select only one data-series column in your worksheet—in this case, column F, Profits (column C contains category labels, not data)—Excel uses the heading of this column for the chart title. Select the title and bold it.

8. Choose **Gallery, Pie...** .

9. Double-click on format option **1** to display the profits data as a pie. Pie charts are used to show the relationship of parts to a whole within a single chart data series (Profits).

10. Click on the Chart toolbar **Pie Chart button** (the sixth button from the left). Each piece of the pie represents a percentage of the whole; the Pie Chart button displays these percentages.

11. Click on the Chart toolbar **Legend button** (the third button from the right) to create a legend for the pie pieces. Each piece represents the sales for one quarter. (Clicking on the Legend button is equivalent to choosing Chart, Add Legend.)

12. Press **Esc** to deselect the legend. See Figure 12.6.

Figure 12.6   **Chart2, after adding a legend**

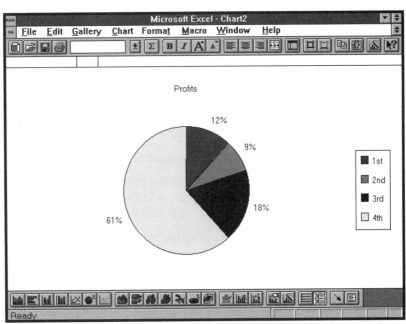

THE WORKSHEET/CHART LINK

A worksheet is automatically linked to all the charts you create from it. When you change labels or numeric data in the worksheet, Excel redraws the associated charts to reflect these changes.

As you learned in Chapter 7, when you have multiple documents open (for example, a worksheet and its associated charts), you can use the Window, Arrange All command to display these documents side by side. This is helpful when you are doing "what if" analysis on charted data; when you change numbers in the worksheet window, you can immediately see the effect on trends and percentages displayed in your chart(s).

You currently have three documents open: Chart 2, CHAP12.XLS, and MYCHART.XLC. Chart 2 should be active; if not, please select it. Now let's examine the link between a worksheet and its associated chart:

1. Press **Ctrl-F10** to *restore* (reduce) the size of Chart 2, enabling you to see both the chart and the worksheet on the screen at once.

2. Now choose **Window, Arrange...**, select **Tiled**, and click on **OK** to see all three documents at once: Chart 2, CHAP12.XLS, and MYCHART.XLC.

3. Click on the MYCHART.XLC window to activate it. Note the appearance of a Control Menu button and Maximize button to identify the active window. (Chart windows do not have scroll bars.) Close **MYCHART.XLC** without saving the changes.

4. Choose **Window, Arrange...** and click on **OK** again to see Chart 2 and CHAP12.XLS side by side.

5. Click on the **CHAP12.XLS** window to activate it.

6. Click on the scroll arrows until you can see columns D, E, and F in the window. These columns contain the Gross Revenues, Expenses, and Profits data.

7. Observe the percentages for each piece of the pie chart. In the next step, you will increase a fourth-quarter expense; this will cause a corresponding decrease in fourth-quarter profits.

8. In cell **E8**, enter **65000**. Observe the change in profit in both column F and the pie chart. The fourth-quarter segment was 61% of the pie before the change; it is now 5% of the pie. The other percentages have adjusted accordingly (see Figure 12.7).

9. Choose **Edit, Undo Entry** to undo the last data entry.

10. Select the chart window. Choose **File, Save As...** , type **mychart2**, and press **Enter** to save a copy of the chart as MYCHART2.XLC.

11. Close both windows. (Hold down **Shift** and choose **File, Close All**.) Don't save the changes in the worksheet CHAP12.XLS.

PRACTICE YOUR SKILLS

The following activity is designed to hone the Excel charting skills that you've acquired in this chapter. Perform these steps to transform the data in PRU12.XLS to a chart that matches Figure 12.7:

1. Open **PRU12.XLS** (Chapter 3).

2. Maximize the document window, if necessary (Chapter 3).

3. Select the range **E5** through **E16**.

4. Create a chart.

Figure 12.7   **Chart2, after modifying the worksheet data**

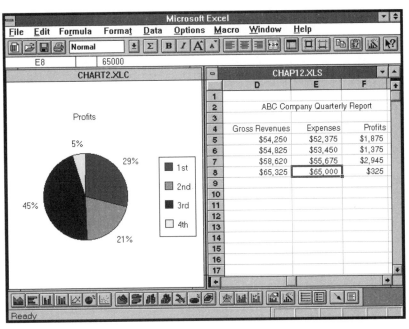

5. Change the chart type to line by using the Chart toolbar.

6. Add the following title: **ABC Company Profits**. Press **Esc** to deselect the title.

7. Compare your chart to Figure 12.8.

8. Save the chart as **MYPRU12.XLC**.

9. Preview the chart as an alternative to printing. Change any print settings you wish.

10. Use **File, Close All** to close all windows without saving the changes (Chapter 7).

The following activity is designed to further sharpen your Excel charting skills. Perform these steps to transform the data in OPT12.XLS to a chart that matches Figure 12.9:

1. Open **OPT12.XLS** (Chapter 3).

2. Maximize the document window, if necessary (Chapter 3).

Figure 12.8   **The completed chart of PRU12.XLS**

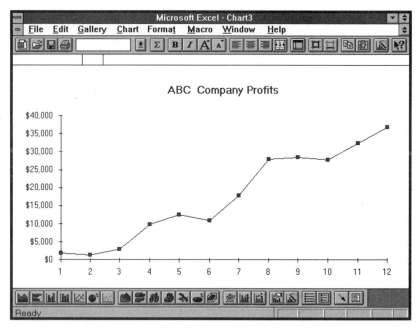

Figure 12.9   **The completed chart of OPT12.XLS**

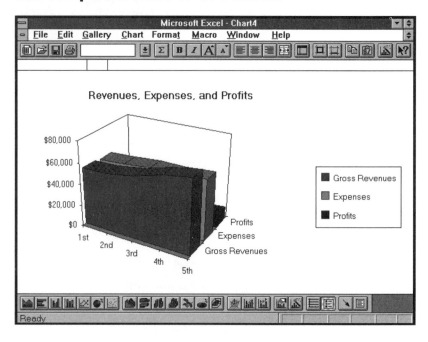

3. Your boss wants you to create the chart shown in Figure 12.9. The worksheet file must be changed before you can create the chart. Change the number in cell **C5** ($159,000) to **$54,250**. Hint: Do *not* type the dollar sign ($) or comma (,) when entering numbers into the worksheet.

4. Create the chart shown in Figure 12.9. Hints: Select the range containing the quarters headings (1st, 2nd, 3rd, 4th, and 5th) and all three data series (Gross Reserves, Expenses, and Profits); then open the new chart file. Add the title by using the **Chart, Attach Text** command. Add a legend, using the Chart toolbar. Change the chart type to 3-D area by using Gallery option **5**.

5. Save the chart as **MYOPT12.XLC**.

6. Preview the chart as an alternative to printing. Change any print settings you wish.

7. Save the worksheet (*not* the chart) as **MYOPT12.XLS**.

8. Use **File, Close All** to close all windows without saving the changes (Chapter 7).

CHAPTER SUMMARY

This chapter introduced charting, the third and final major topic of this book. After learning the basics of chart terminology, you discovered how to create a chart, add a legend and text to the chart, change the chart type, print or preview the chart, and save it.

Here is a quick reference guide to the Excel features introduced in this chapter:

Desired Result	How to Do It
Create a standard column chart	Create worksheet, select range to plot, choose **File, New** and double-click on **Chart** (or press **F11**)
Add a legend to a chart	Select chart, choose **Chart, Add Legend** or click on Chart toolbar legend button
Attach text to a chart	Select chart, choose **Chart, Attach Text...** , select chart object to attach to, click on **OK**, type text, press **Enter**

Desired Result	How to Do It
Change chart type	Select chart, choose **Gallery**, select desired chart type, select desired chart format, click on **OK**; or select chart, click on desired Chart tool-bar button
Save a chart	Select chart, choose **File, Save As...** (for a new file) or File, Save... (to update existing file), type file name, click on **OK**
Print a chart	Select chart, choose **File, Print Preview**, change desired print options with **Setup...** , click on **Print**, click on **OK**

In the next chapter, you will learn several new Excel charting techniques, such as positioning the legend, adding arrows, editing text, and changing marker patterns. You will also learn how to create a chart that is embedded in a worksheet.

IF YOU'RE STOPPING HERE

If you need to break off here, please exit from Excel. If you want to proceed directly to the next chapter, please do so now.

CHAPTER 13: CUSTOMIZING AND EMBEDDING YOUR CHART

Using File, Links to View a Chart 's Supporting Documents

Customizing a Chart Legend

Adding Arrows and Unattached Text to a Chart

Editing Chart Text

Additional Formatting Techniques

Embedding a Chart in a Worksheet

Excel allows you to customize the format, content, and layout of a chart to meet your specific presentation needs. The techniques described in this chapter give you almost unlimited control over the appearance of the final chart. You will learn how to create and customize legends, arrows, unattached text, font styles and sizes, data marker patterns, and value-axis scales. In addition, you will learn how to embed a chart in a worksheet, a technique that affords you the convenience of treating a worksheet and its dependent chart as a single document.

When you're done working through this chapter, you will know

- How to customize a chart legend
- How to add arrows and unattached text to a chart
- How to edit chart text
- How to format chart text
- How to change data marker patterns
- How to change the scale of a chart's value axis
- How to create overlapping data markers
- How to create a chart embedded in a worksheet

USING FILE, LINKS TO VIEW A CHART'S SUPPORTING DOCUMENTS

As you learned in Chapter 12, a chart is linked to the worksheet from which it was created. When you change worksheet data, Excel will automatically redraw the chart to reflect these changes. In a chart/worksheet relationship, the chart is the *dependent* document (it depends upon worksheet data), and the worksheet is the *supporting* document (its data supports the chart). To view a list of the worksheet(s) that support a chart, use the *File, Links* command.

If you are not running Excel, please start it now. If there is a worksheet on your screen, please close it. Your screen should be empty except for a maximized Excel application window. Now let's begin by opening a chart stored in your work directory and then using the File, Links command to view and open its supporting worksheet:

1. Open **CHP13CHT.XLC** from your EX4WORK directory. The following message appears:

   ```
   Update references to unopened documents?
   ```

   Excel is telling you that the chart you are about to open is dependent upon data in a currently unopened (not on-screen) worksheet. You are being asked whether you want any changes that were made to this worksheet (data values, text headings) to be incorporated in the chart.

2. Click on **Yes**. Excel will now update the chart to reflect any changes made to its supporting worksheet. Maximize the chart, if necessary (see Figure 13.1).

Figure 13.1   **The CHP13CHT.XLC chart, updated and maximized**

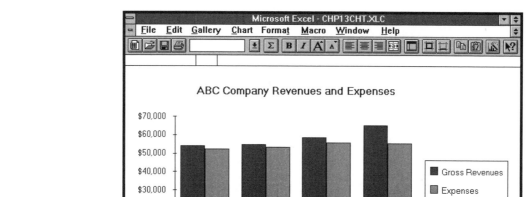

3. Choose **File, Links...** to see the name of the supporting worksheet, C:\ EX4WORK\CHAP13.XLS. (C:\ EX4WORK\ indicates that the file CHAP13.XLS is stored in the EX4WORK directory on disk drive C.)

4. Click on the **Help button** in the Links dialog box to see the Help screen for the File, Links command. Take a moment to scroll through the available information. When you are finished, close the Help window.

5. Select (click once on) the **CHAP13.XLS** entry in the Links dialog box.

6. Click on **Open** to open CHAP13.XLS. You can use the File, Links command to open, as well as view, a chart's supporting documents.

7. Choose **Window, 2 CHP13CHT.XLC** to activate the chart.

CUSTOMIZING A CHART LEGEND

When you add a legend to a chart, Excel places it in a standard location (to the right of the plot area) and formats it with a standard font style and size (10-point Helvetica). Should you find that you want to customize the appearance of your chart legend, Excel allows you to move the legend, change the legend font and data marker patterns, and add a shadow border to the legend box.

 ## MOVING A LEGEND WITH THE MOUSE OR THE FORMAT, LEGEND COMMAND

First, let's look at moving a legend within a chart. Excel provides you with two techniques to move the legend to a new chart location: using the mouse and using the *Format, Legend* command.

You learned in the last chapter to move a legend with the mouse by pointing to the legend and dragging it to the desired location. To avoid overlapping the chart plot area, you should drag the legend to an edge of the window.

To move a legend with the Format, Legend command, choose Format, Legend, select the desired legend location, and click on OK.

Let's practice moving the legend of CHP13CHT.XLC using both the mouse and Format, Legend techniques:

1. Select the legend. Observe the cell-reference area (the rectangular box to the left of the formula bar); the word "Legend" is displayed. Whenever you select a chart object, Excel displays its name in the cell-reference area.

2. Note the black selection squares around the legend, indicating that it can be moved. Drag the legend to the space between the chart title and the data markers (the columns). Excel redraws the plot area to fill the entire window; the legend now overlaps the plot area.

3. Now choose **Format, Legend...** . The available legend positions are Bottom, Corner, Top, Right, and Left.

4. Select **Left** and click on **OK**. The legend is moved to the left of the chart. Note that Excel has redrawn the plot area so it doesn't overlap the legend; when you use Format, Legend to move your legend, Excel automatically resizes the plot area to avoid overlaps.

5. Drag the legend to the middle of the second- and third-quarter data markers. Dragging allows you to move a legend to locations not available with Format, Legend.

6. Drag the legend as far to the right of the window as possible (do not release the mouse button). Note the appearance of a vertical line. Release the mouse button. The plot area and legend do not overlap. When you drag a legend to the edge of a window, a horizontal or vertical line will appear. This line indicates that the plot area and the legend will not overlap.

PRACTICE YOUR SKILLS

1. Drag the legend to the bottom edge of the chart window. (Wait until you see the horizontal line before releasing the mouse button.)

2. Now move the legend to the bottom of the chart window automatically by using the **Format, Legend** command. Note that this command centers the legend under the chart.

 ## ADDING A SHADOW BORDER TO THE LEGEND

Excel allows you to give your legend a *shadow border:* a dark border that creates a 3-D appearance.

To add a shadow border to a legend,

• Select the legend.

• Choose *Format, Patterns...* .

• Under *Border*, check *Shadow*.

• Click on OK.

Let's add a shadow border to your chart legend:

1. Select the legend if it is not already selected.

2. Choose **Format, Patterns...** .

3. Under **Border**, check **Shadow**.

4. Click on **OK** to create a shadow border around the legend.

5. Press **Esc** to deselect the legend (see Figure 13.2).

Figure 13.2   **CHP13CHT.XLC, after adding a shadow border to the legend**

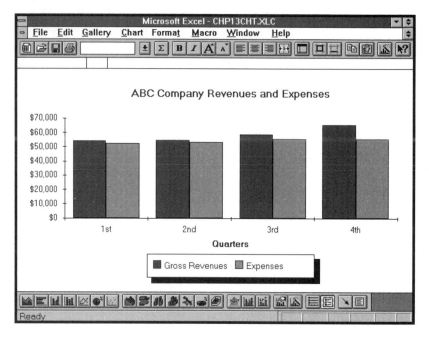

ADDING ARROWS AND UNATTACHED TEXT TO A CHART

At times, you may wish to draw attention to certain aspects of your chart—for example, to point out an important trend or explain a data anomaly. With Excel, you can accomplish this by adding arrows and unattached text to your charts.

ADDING AN ARROW TO A CHART

To add an arrow to a chart,

* Choose *Chart, Add Arrow,* or click on the *Arrow button* in the Chart toolbar (the second button from the right). An arrow will appear in your chart window.

* Drag the arrow selection squares to adjust the size and direction of the arrow.

* Drag the arrow body to move the arrow to the desired chart location, if necessary.

Let's add an arrow to CHP13CHT.XLC. (Note: In order to perform this activity, the Chart toolbar must be displayed at the bottom of your screen. If it is not displayed, activate CHAP13.XLS, use Options, Toolbars to show the Chart toolbar, activate CHP13.CHT.XLC, and move the Chart toolbar to the bottom of the screen, if necessary.) Follow these steps:

1. Click on the **Arrow button** in the Chart toolbar (the second button from the right). An arrow appears in your chart window. (Note that "Arrow1" is displayed in the cell-reference area.) The black selection squares indicate that this arrow can be moved and resized.

2. Drag the square at the head of the arrow to make it point to the upper-left corner of the fourth-quarter gross revenues marker, the highest data marker in the chart (see Figure 13.3).

Figure 13.3   **CHP13CHT.XLC, after adding an arrow and unattached text**

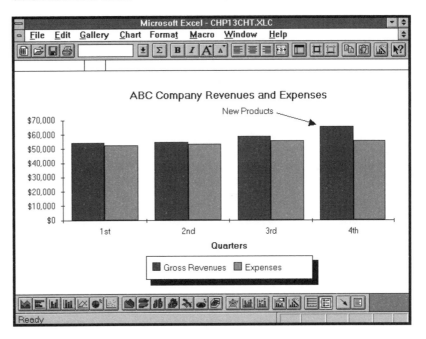

3. Shorten the arrow by dragging the square at the end. The arrow should now look like the one in Figure 13.3. (The text beside the arrow will be added in the next activity.)

ADDING UNATTACHED TEXT TO A CHART

As mentioned in the last chapter, unattached text is not bound to a chart object; you can move it anywhere within the chart window.

To add unattached text to a chart,

- Press Esc to deselect all chart objects.

- Type the desired text.

- Press Enter (your text will appear on the screen).

- Drag the text box to the desired location.

- If necessary, drag the text-box selection squares to resize the text box.

Let's add some unattached text to explain the function of the arrow you just created:

1. Press **Esc** to deselect the arrow.

2. Type **New Products** and press **Enter**. The text appears in the middle of your chart. Note that the text box is surrounded by black selection squares, indicating that it can be moved and resized.

3. Position the mouse pointer over the text and drag it to the end of the arrow. (Do not attempt to drag by the black selection squares, as this will resize the text box.)

4. Press **Esc** to deselect the text box. Your screen should match Figure 13.3. The function of the arrow is now clear: the introduction of new products in the fourth quarter resulted in a sharp increase in gross revenues.

5. Save the chart as **MYCHT13.XLC**.

PRACTICE YOUR SKILLS

1. Change the unattached arrow text ("New Products") to **Introduced plastics line**.

2. If necessary, reposition the text.

EDITING CHART TEXT

You may need to modify the text you've added to your chart; for example, you might want to revise a title or relabel an arrow. Excel allows you to edit both attached and unattached chart text.

To edit chart text,

- Select the text you would like to modify (point at it with the mouse and click).

- Click in the formula bar or press F2 to begin editing the selected text.

- Edit the text in the formula bar.

- Click on the enter box, or press Enter to enter the revised text.

Now let's revise the title of MYCHT13.XLC:

1. Click on the chart title to select it. Note that white selection squares appear around the text, indicating that it is attached and cannot be moved.

2. Observe the formula bar. The title text, "ABC Company Revenues and Expenses," is displayed.

3. Select the text **Revenues and Expenses** (double-click on **Revenues** in the formula bar and drag to **Expenses**).

4. Type **Annual Performance Summary Chart** to replace the above selection.

5. Press **Enter** to change the chart title to "ABC Company Annual Performance Summary Chart."

 CONTROLLING LINE BREAKS IN CHART TEXT

You can control the *line breaks* in your chart text—that is, how the text is broken into two or more lines—by inserting or removing these breaks manually. To do this,

- Select the desired text.

- To insert a new line break, place the formula-bar insertion point directly before the word where you want the new line to begin, and then press Alt-Enter.

- To remove an existing line break, place the formula-bar insertion point at the beginning of the line you would like to join to the previous line, and then press Backspace.

- Press Enter, or click on the enter box to enter your newly broken lines of text.

Let's use this procedure to control the line breaks of our chart title:

1. Select the title, if necessary. Note that there are no line breaks in the text; the entire title fits on a single line.

2. In the formula bar, position the insertion point directly before the word "Summary."

3. Press **Alt-Enter** to insert a line break at this point. In the formula bar, "Summary Chart" moves down to the second line.

4. Press **Enter** to enter your new two-line title, which breaks at "Summary," as expected.

5. Now let's say you changed your mind and wanted the title to break at "Annual" instead. In the formula bar, position the insertion point directly before "Annual."

6. Press **Alt-Enter** to insert a line break at this point. Note that the title is now divided into three lines:

ABC Company

Annual Performance

Summary Chart

In order to complete the task and end up with a two-line title, we have to remove the extra line break at "Summary."

7. Position the insertion point at the beginning of the line beginning with "Summary."

8. Press **Backspace** to remove the line break and join "Summary Chart" to the previous line. Note that the title now consists of two lines, broken at "Annual." This is what we want.

9. Press **Enter** to enter your modified two-line title.

10. Press **Esc** to deselect the title text box; your screen should now match Figure 13.4.

Figure 13.4   Modified two-line chart title

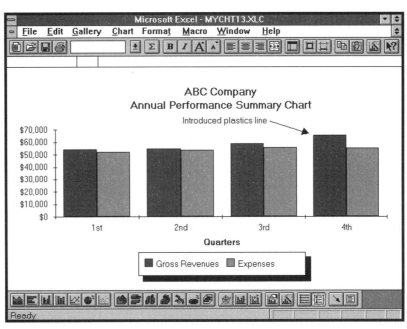

ADDITIONAL FORMATTING TECHNIQUES

In the following section, you will learn several additional techniques for formatting your charts. These techniques will allow you to

- Change the typeface of all or a portion of the chart text

- Change the patterns used to identify data markers

- Change the type of a customized chart

- Create overlapping data markers (for bar and column charts)

FORMATTING ALL THE TEXT IN A CHART

You can format all or a selected portion of your chart text.

To format all the text in a chart,

- Choose *Chart, Select Chart* to select the entire chart.

- Choose *Format, Font.*

- Select the desired font, size, and style.

- Click on OK.

Let's use the above procedure to format all the text in MYCHT13.XLC:

1. Choose **Chart, Select Chart** to select the entire chart. Note the white selection squares enclosing the chart.

2. Choose **Format, Font...** .

3. Under **Font**, choose **Tms Rmn**. Under **Size**, choose **12**.

4. Click on **OK** to change all the text in MYCHT13.XLC to 12-point Times Roman, as shown in Figure 13.5. Note that the arrow label is now misaligned; reformatting your text may change the screen position of labels.

5. Choose **Edit, Undo Font** to undo your font change and prepare for the next activity.

Figure 13.5   **MYCHT13.XLC, after changing all the text to 12-point Times Roman**

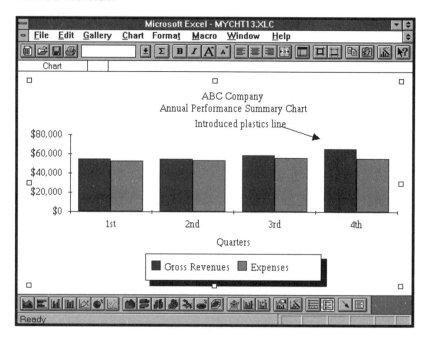

FORMATTING SELECTED TEXT IN A CHART

To format selected text in a chart,

- Select the text you would like to format.
- Choose Format, Font.
- Select the desired font, size, and style.
- Click on OK.

Now let's use the above procedure to format a selected portion, rather than all, of the text in MYCHT13.XLC:

1. Click on the chart title to select it.
2. Choose **Format, Font...** .
3. Under **Size**, choose **18** and click on **OK** to change the title size to 18 points. You can select any text object in your chart and modify its format.
4. Click on the arrow text (**Introduced plastics line**) to select it.
5. Click on the **Italic button** in the toolbar (marked "I") to italicize your text selection.
6. If necessary, reposition the text box to realign it with the arrow tail.

CHANGING THE PATTERN OF A CHART DATA MARKER

Chart data markers (bars, columns, pie slices, and so on) are given different patterns (or colors) to distinguish them from one another. Excel automatically chooses these patterns from a standard set. You may, however, change one or more of your data marker patterns for visual emphasis or clarity.

To change the pattern of a chart data marker,

- Double-click on any data marker in the desired data series; the entire series of related markers will be selected and the Patterns dialog box will open.
- Under Area, click on *Custom.*
- Click on the Pattern arrow to display the available data marker patterns.
- Click on the desired pattern.

- Click on OK.

Let's change the expenses data marker patterns in MYCHT13.XLC:

1. Double-click on any one of the Expenses data markers. (To identify the color or pattern of a data marker, observe the legend.) All the markers in the Expenses data series are selected and the Patterns dialog box is opened.

2. Under **Area**, select **Custom**. Click on the **Pattern arrow** to display the available marker patterns.

3. Click on the pattern with broad horizontal lines.

4. Click on **OK**. Note the new pattern for the Expenses data markers.

PRACTICE YOUR SKILLS

1. Change the Gross Revenues data markers to a pattern you feel effectively complements the pattern you just chose for Expenses.

2. Deselect the markers and compare your chart to Figure 13.6. (Your Gross Revenues pattern may differ.)

CHANGING THE VALUE-AXIS SCALE

You can control the scale used on the value axis of a chart. This is especially useful for emphasizing trends, as you'll see in the next activity.

To change the value-axis scale,

- Double-click on the value axis to open the Patterns dialog box.

- Click on the *Scale button* to open the Axis Scale dialog box.

- Change the Minimum, Maximum, or other options as desired. A smaller range of values will produce a more noticeable trend.

- Click on OK.

Let's change the value-axis scale of MYCHT13.XLC to emphasize its revenue trends:

1. Double-click anywhere on the value axis to open the Patterns dialog box. The value axis is the vertical line to the left of the data markers and is used, in this case, to show dollar values ($0 to $70,000). Note that "Axis 1" is displayed in the cell-reference area.

Figure 13.6   **MYCHT13.XLC, after changing the data marker patterns**

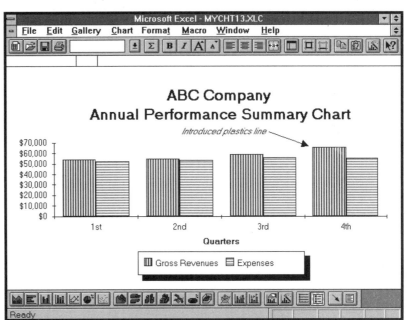

2. In the **Patterns dialog box**, click on the **Scale** button to open the Axis Scale dialog box. You can use the Patterns dialog box as an entry point into other chart-editing features by clicking on the Scale, Font, or Text buttons.

3. Change the value in the **Minimum box** to **50000**.

4. Click on **OK** to accept your change and return to the chart (see Figure 13.7). Observe the modified value-axis scale: $50,000 to $70,000 instead of $0 to $70,000. Note that this compressed scale emphasizes the upward trend in revenues.

CHANGING THE CHART TYPE OF A CUSTOMIZED CHART

You learned in Chapter 12 to change the chart type (column, bar, area) of a standard chart by using the Gallery menu and the Chart toolbar. To change the chart type of a customized chart (one whose format or layout you have modified), you should use the *Format, Main Chart* command.

Figure 13.7   **MYCHT13.XLC, after changing the value-axis scale**

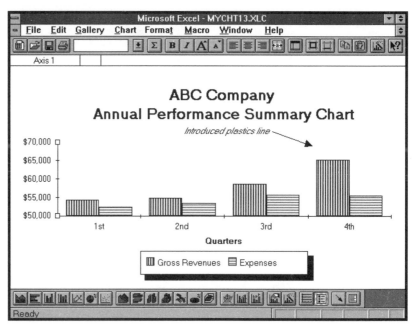

Changing the chart type using the Gallery menu or Chart toolbar will *cancel* many of the custom formats you have applied to your chart. However, changing the chart type using Format, Main Chart will *retain* all your customization. As a rule of thumb, use the Gallery menu or Chart toolbar to change the chart type when working with a new, unmodified chart; use Format, Main Chart to change your chart type when working with a customized chart.

To change the chart type of a customized chart,

- Choose Format, Main Chart.

- Select the desired chart type.

- If you are given *Data View* (data-marker display) *options*, select the appropriate one.

- Click on OK.

You will practice this technique in the next activity.

CREATING OVERLAPPING DATA MARKERS IN A COLUMN OR BAR CHART

Until now, the column and bar data markers you have worked with have all been nonoverlapping: one full column next to another full column (review Figures 13.1 through 13.7). At times, however, you may want to create overlapping data markers for visual emphasis or due to limited page space.

For example, if you created a column chart depicting the expenses for every week in your fiscal year, this chart would display 52 columns, a very large number to fit on a standard-sized page. Overlapping these columns would allow each column to be significantly wider. The resultant chart would be far more visually clear than a chart that displayed 52 nonoverlapping columns.

To create overlapping data markers in a column or bar chart,

- Choose Format, Main Chart.

- Under *Bar/Column*, enter the desired overlap percentage (the percentage that the bars or columns within a given cluster overlap each other); for example, for a 50-percent overlap, enter 50.

- Click on OK.

Let's start by misapplying the Gallery Menu to create overlapping data markers in MYCHT13.XLC:

1. Choose **Gallery, Column…** . Double-click on format option **4** to create an overlapped column chart.

2. Observe the data marker patterns and the legend. They have reverted back to their original (uncustomized) states. Remember, after you have begun to customize your chart, do *not* use the Gallery menu to change the chart type.

3. Choose **Edit, Undo Column** to undo the Gallery command you just issued. Note that the data marker patterns and legend have returned to their customized states.

Now let's use the proper method—the Format, Main Chart command—to change the type of your customized chart:

1. Choose **Format, Main Chart…** .

2. Under **Bar/Column**, change the overlap percentage from 0 to **50**.

3. Click on **OK**. Observe the data markers and their patterns. The revised marker patterns have been retained, and Excel has overlapped the markers.

Now let's preview the printout of your customized chart:

1. Choose **File, Print Preview**. Note that the chart is set to print in a landscape (widthwise), rather than portrait (lengthwise), page orientation. (Note: If your printer doesn't support landscape printing, the chart will be set to portrait orientation and the Landscape setup option in the next step will be dimmed, meaning that it is unavailable.)

2. Click on **Setup...** . Under **Orientation**, select **Portrait**. Click on **OK** to see the chart as it would appear printed lengthwise on the page.

3. Click on **Setup...** . Under **Chart Size**, select **Use Full Page**. Click on **OK**. With the Full Page option selected, Excel adjusts the height-to-width ratio of your printout to take advantage of the space available on the paper.

PRACTICE YOUR SKILLS

1. Change **Chart Size** to **Scale to Fit Page**.

2. Print the chart. Compare the printout with Figure 13.8.

3. Update the chart (use **File, Save**).

4. Close the document window.

EMBEDDING A CHART IN A WORKSHEET

As you have learned in these last two chapters, an Excel chart is formally linked to the worksheet from which it was created. For this reason, you may want to work with, save, and print your chart and worksheet together. Excel allows you to do this by using the toolbar Chart tool to *embed* a chart in its supporting worksheet.

CREATING AN EMBEDDED CHART

To create an embedded chart,

• Display the Chart toolbar, if it is not already displayed.

Figure 13.8   **Portrait printout of MYCHT13.XLC**

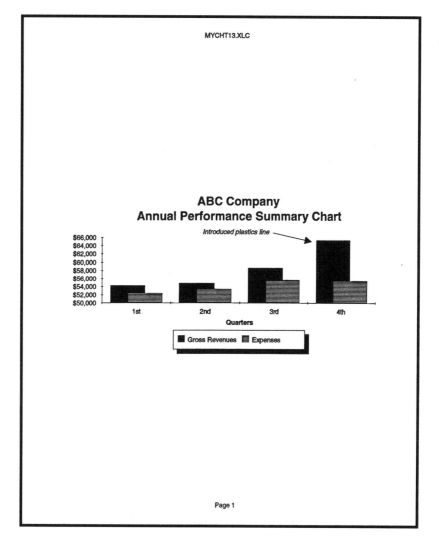

- Select the range of worksheet data you would like to chart.

- Click on the appropriate Chart toolbar button.

- Drag inside the worksheet to create an embedded chart box to create a square box, hold down the Shift key as you drag; to align the box to the worksheet's cell grid, hold down the Ctrl key as you drag.

- When you release the mouse button, the chart will be drawn.

- To resize an embedded chart, drag the selection squares surrounding the chart box.

Let's embed a chart in CHAP13.XLS:

1. CHAP13.XLS should be open and minimized on your screen. (You opened it using File, Links earlier in this chapter.) If it is not, please open and maximize it now.

2. Select the noncontiguous ranges **C4:C8** and **F4:F8**. (Use the mouse and the **Ctrl** key.)

3. Click on the Column Chart button in the Chart toolbar (the third button from the left). Observe the status bar message:

   ```
   Drag in document to create a chart
   ```

4. Move the mouse pointer to the worksheet. Note that the mouse pointer becomes a crosshair.

5. Point anywhere in cell **C11** and drag to anywhere in cell **F20**. (When dragging to a location below the bottom border of a window, simply point below the window —without releasing the mouse button—and wait for the worksheet to scroll.) You can specify any size and location you desire for your embedded chart box. Note that when you release the mouse button, the chart is automatically drawn, as in Figure 13.9.

OPENING AN EMBEDDED CHART

At times, you may want to *open* an embedded chart; that is, place the chart in its own window (as opposed to its own embedded chart box). To do this, simply double-click on the embedded chart. Once an embedded chart has been opened, the chart can be modified and saved in the same manner as a chart that was created using the File, New, Chart command.

Figure 13.9   **CHAP13.XLS, after creating an embedded chart**

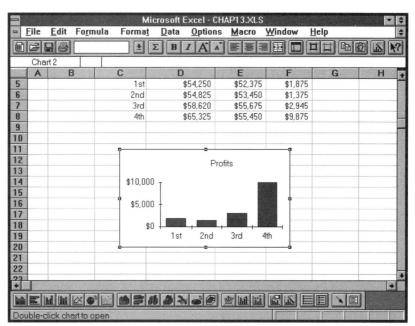

Let's open the chart you embedded in CHAP13.XLS:

1. Point to the embedded chart and double-click. Excel places the chart in a window entitled "CHAP13.XLS Chart 1." Observe the menu bar; this is the Charting menu.

2. Click on the **3-D Pie Chart button** in the Chart toolbar (the thirteenth button from the left) to create a pie chart with displayed percentages. You can change options in an opened chart just as you would in a chart created with File, New, Chart.

3. Choose **Window, Arrange...** , select **Tiled**, and click on **OK** to tile the chart and worksheet on screen. Note that the Profits chart is shown in its embedded form and in its windowed form.

4. Select cell **E8** in the worksheet. While observing the two pie charts, change the contents of cell **E8** to **60000**. The charts and worksheet are linked, so the charts change along with the worksheet data.

5. Close the CHAP13.XLS Chart 1 window.

6. Maximize CHAP13.XLS.

Let's print-preview the combination worksheet/chart, then modify some print options:

1. Set the print area to **C1:F20**. (Select **C1:F20**, then choose **Options, Set Print Area**.)

2. Choose **File, Print Preview**.

3. Click on **Setup...** .

4. Check **Center Horizontally** and **Center Vertically** to center the worksheet/chart horizontally and vertically on the paper.

5. Uncheck **Row & Column Headings** and **Cell Gridlines** to suppress the printing of row/column headings and gridlines.

6. Adjust margins and other options as desired.

7. Click on **OK** to exit Setup. Observe the changes in the print preview page layout.

8. Click on **Close** to return to the worksheet. Your worksheet/chart combination document is now ready to print.

 SAVING A WORKSHEET CONTAINING AN EMBEDDED CHART

A worksheet and its embedded chart(s) are saved together as one document. To save a worksheet containing an embedded chart, click on the worksheet to deselect the chart, then choose File, Save or File, Save As. The chart is saved in an embedded chart box within the worksheet (.XLS) file.

Let's save and then print your combination worksheet/chart:

1. Choose **File, Save As...** .

2. Type **mychap13** and click on **OK** to save the worksheet/chart file as MYCHAP13.XLS. Note that Excel added an .XLS (not .XLC) extension to the file.

3. Choose **File, Print...** and click on **OK** to print the worksheet/chart using the settings you specified in the previous activity. Compare your printout to Figure 13.10.

4. Close the document window.

Figure 13.10   **The printed worksheet/chart MYCHAP13.XLS**

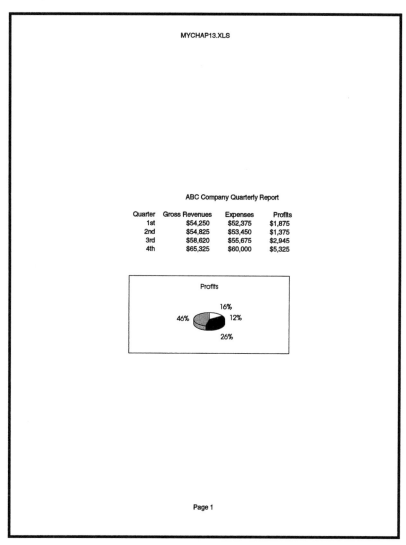

CHAPTER SUMMARY

In this chapter, you learned the basics of chart customization: moving and adding a shadow border to a legend; adding arrows and unattached text; and changing text formats, data marker patterns, and value-axis scales. You also learned to create, open, save, and print an embedded chart.

Here is a quick reference guide to the Excel features introduced in this chapter:

Desired Result	How to Do It
View/open a chart's supporting worksheets	Choose **File, Links...** ; to open a supporting worksheet, double-click on it
Move a legend	Choose **Format, Legend**, select desired legend location, click on **OK**; or select legend with mouse and drag
Add a shadow border to a legend	Select legend, choose **Format, Patterns**, check **Shadow**, click on **OK**
Add an arrow to a chart	Choose **Chart, Add Arrow**, drag selection squares to adjust arrow's size and direction, if desired drag arrow body to new location
Add unattached text to a chart	Press **Esc** to deselect all chart objects, type text, press **Enter**, select text box and drag to desired location
Edit chart text	Select text to edit, click in formula bar or press **F2** to begin editing, edit text, enter revised text
Insert a new line break in chart text	Select desired text, place formula-bar insertion point directly before word where new line is to begin, press **Alt-Enter**, press **Enter**
Remove an existing line break from chart text	Select desired text, place formula-bar insertion point at beginning of line to be joined to previous line, press **Backspace**, press **Enter**

Desired Result	How to Do It
Format all the text in a chart	Choose **Chart, Select Chart** to select entire chart, choose **Format, Font** or use Standard toolbar to make desired formatting changes
Format selected text in a chart	Select text to format, make desired formatting changes
Change a data marker pattern	Double-click on desired data marker to open Patterns dialog box, select **Custom** (under **Area**), select desired pattern, click on **OK**
Change the value-axis scale	Double-click on value axis to open Patterns dialog box, click on **Scale button** to open Axis Scale dialog box, change scaling options as desired, click on **OK**
Change the chart type of a customized chart	Choose **Format, Main Chart**, select desired chart type, select appropriate **Data View** (if given), click on **OK**
Create overlapping data markers in customized bar and column charts	Choose **Format, Main Chart**, under **Bar/Column** enter desired overlap percentage, click on **OK**
Create an embedded chart	Select range of worksheet data to chart, click on appropriate Chart toolbar button, drag inside worksheet to create embedded chart box
Open an embedded chart	Double-click on embedded chart
Save a worksheet containing an embedded chart	Click on worksheet to deselect the chart, choose **File, Save** or **File, Save As...**

In the next chapter, you will learn how to further customize your charts by using several advanced charting techniques. You'll learn how to add a new data series to a chart and how to edit an existing data series. We'll introduce you to ChartWizard, a powerful utility designed to facilitate the creation and modification of charts. You'll also learn how to create a chart that combines two chart types (column and line, for example), how to add a second value axis to such a combination chart, and how to attach a data-point label to a chart's data marker.

IF YOU'RE STOPPING HERE

If you need to break off here, please exit from Excel. If you want to proceed directly to the next chapter, please do so now.

CHAPTER 14: ADVANCED CHARTING TECHNIQUES

Using ChartWizard to Create and Modify Charts

Creating a Combination Chart

Attaching a Data-point Label to a Data Marker

In this, the last chapter in our three-part series on charts, we'll introduce you to a selection of advanced charting techniques. You'll begin by exploring *ChartWizard*, a powerful and flexible utility designed to assist you in the creation and modification of a chart. Next, you'll learn how to create a *combination chart*, a chart that combines two different chart types (for example, column and line) into a single hybrid chart. Finally, you'll learn how to use a new kind of label to identify the data markers in your charts. Mastery of these techniques will go a long way in helping you to create professional-looking charts quickly and easily.

This chapter completes your foundation in Excel charting skills. In the next and final chapter of this book, you will explore some advanced printing features.

When you're done working through this chapter, you will know

- How to use ChartWizard to create and modify charts

- How to create a combination chart

- How to attach a data-point label to a data marker

USING CHARTWIZARD TO CREATE AND MODIFY CHARTS

ChartWizard leads you, step by step, through the process of creating an embedded chart. Along the way, it offers you sample views of the chart and provides continual on-line Help at the click of a button.

To create an embedded chart by using ChartWizard,

- Select the range of worksheet cells containing the data that you want to chart.

- Click on the *ChartWizard button*. This button, which depicts a column chart with a magic wand above it, is on both the Standard and Chart toolbars; you can use either.

- Drag in the worksheet to create an embedded chart box. To create a square box, hold down the Shift key as you drag; to align the box to the worksheet's cell grid, hold down the Ctrl key as you drag.

- ChartWizard will now lead you through a five-step chart-creation process. Each step is represented by its own dialog box. Follow the instructions that appear in these dialog boxes. You can use the following dialog-box buttons:

Next>	Moves to the next ChartWizard step
<Back	Moves to the previous ChartWizard step
>>	Creates a chart using the options you have selected and then exits ChartWizard
l<<	Returns to the first step of ChartWizard
Cancel	Cancels ChartWizard and returns to the worksheet
Help	Opens the Help window

If you are not running Excel, please start it now. If there is a work-sheet on your screen, please close it. Your screen should be empty except for a maximized Excel application window. Let's begin by opening a worksheet and using ChartWizard to create an embed-ded chart in it:

1. Open **CHAP14.XLS** from your EX4WORK directory and maxi-mize it, if necessary. This worksheet keeps track of monthly sales totals by product group.

2. Select the range **B4:G6**. You will use this data to create a chart.

3. Click on the **ChartWizard button** (the second button from the right in the Standard toolbar, or the fifth button from the right in the Chart toolbar.) Observe the status-bar prompt:

   `Drag in document to create a chart`

4. Drag from the middle of cell **B8** to the middle of cell **H20** to define the box in which your embedded chart will be drawn.

5. Observe the screen. Note that the embedded chart box you just defined does not appear. Instead, ChartWizard displays the first of its five dialog boxes (see Figure 14.1). As mentioned above, these boxes walk you through a five-step process of cre-ating an embedded chart. The Step 1 dialog box prompts you to define the range containing the data to chart. Verify that the range you selected before clicking on the ChartWizard button ($B$4:$G$6) appears in the Range text box.

6. Click on **Next>** to accept this range and move to the Step 2 dia-log box. Examine the box; it prompts you to select a chart type. Note that all 14 chart types that appear in the Gallery menu are available, and that the default choice is a column chart.

7. Observe the buttons at the bottom of the dialog box. The func-tions of these buttons were described earlier in this section.

8. Click on **Next>** to accept the default chart type (column) and move to the Step 3 dialog box. Examine the box; it prompts you to pick a format for your selected chart type. Again, these are the same format options that appear when you use the Gallery menu.

9. Select option **9** and click on **Next>** to select a stacked-column chart and move to the Step 4 dialog box. Examine the box; it shows a sample chart depicting your selected worksheet data, chart type, and chart format. The Data Series In option on the

right side of this dialog box allows you to specify whether to plot the rows or columns of your selected worksheet data as the chart's data series. We'll take a closer look at this very important option in the upcoming section, "Plotting Rows or Columns as Data Series."

Figure 14.1   **The first of five ChartWizard dialog boxes**

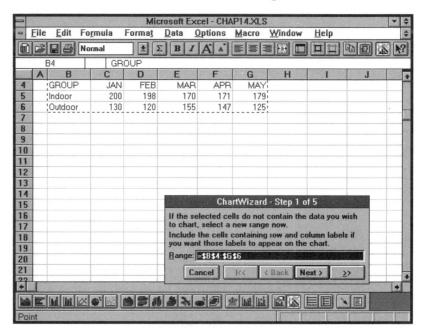

10. Observe the sample chart. Although it depicts the selected data accurately ("Indoor" product sales versus "Outdoor" product sales), this chart format does not effectively communicate how the indoor sales *compare* to the outdoor sales. A side-by-side column format is far more appropriate for this.

11. Click on **<Back** to return to the Step 3 dialog box. Select format option **4** and click on **Next>** to select a side-by-side, overlapped column format and move to the Step 4 dialog box. Examine the sample chart; it has changed to reflect your new format option. Note that this format depicts the indoor/outdoor sales comparison much more effectively.

12. Click on **Next>** to accept the sample chart and move to the Step 5 dialog box. This final dialog box allows you to add or remove a legend, chart title, and axis title(s).

13. Click in the **Chart Title text box** and type **ABC Sales Report**. When you are finished typing, pause for a moment (do not press Enter) to let the title appear in the sample chart.

14. Click on **OK** to draw the embedded chart in your specified chart box (B8:G20), using your specified charting options. Compare your screen with Figure 14.2.

Figure 14.2   **Creating an embedded chart using ChartWizard**

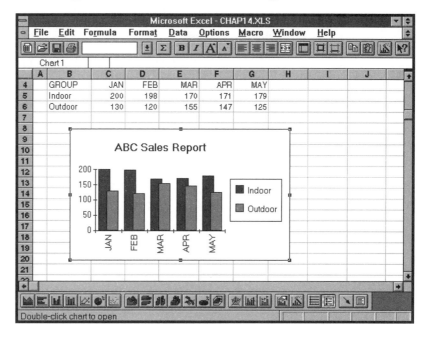

 ADDING DATA TO A CHART

After you have created a chart, you can use ChartWizard to add data to it. You can add data in two ways: by adding a new data series or by adding new data to an existing data series. As you'll recall from Chapter 12, a data series is a set of related data values that is usually—but not always—stored in a single worksheet row.

CHAP14.XLS, for example, contains the two data series, Indoor and Outdoor.

Indoor	200	198	170	171	179
Outdoor	130	120	155	147	125

To add data to a chart,

- Add the data to the supporting worksheet.
- If the chart you are modifying is in a window (rather than embedded in the worksheet), use Window, Arrange to tile the chart and worksheet, fitting them both on screen.
- Select the embedded chart, or activate the windowed chart to which you want to add your new worksheet data.
- Click on the ChartWizard tool. The Step 1 dialog box appears.
- In the supporting worksheet, select the range containing all the data to be charted, including the data you want to add.
- Click on the >> button in the ChartWizard dialog box.

Let's use this procedure to add a new data series to the embedded chart we just created:

1. In row 7 of the worksheet, enter the following data series for a new product group called "All Season":

	B	C	D	E	F	G
7	All Season	166	170	175	177	190

2. Select (click once on) the embedded chart.

3. Click on the **ChartWizard button** (in the Standard or Chart toolbar). Examine the selected range in the Step 1 dialog box.

4. In the worksheet, select the range **B4:G7** to include your new data series (All Season) in the embedded chart.

5. In the ChartWizard dialog box, click on **>>** to skip the remaining ChartWizard steps. The embedded chart is immediately redrawn using your newly selected range.

6. Examine the resultant chart (see Figure 14.3). The "All Season" product group is now included.

Figure 14.3   **Adding a data series to a chart**

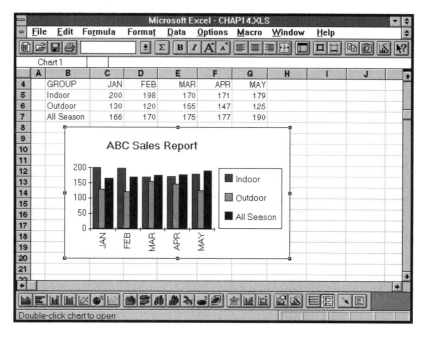

Now let's use ChartWizard to add new data to the existing data series, Indoor, Outdoor, and All Season:

1. In row **H** of the worksheet, enter the following new June sales data:

	H
4	**JUN**
5	**175**
6	**151**
7	**181**

2. Select the embedded chart.

3. Click on the **ChartWizard button**. Examine the selected range in the Step 1 dialog box.

4. In the worksheet, select the range **B4:H7** to include the new June category data in the embedded chart.

5. In the Step 1 dialog box, click on **>>** to skip the remaining ChartWizard steps. The embedded chart is immediately redrawn using the new range.

6. Observe your new data (marked "JUN") on the chart (see Figure 14.4).

7. Save the worksheet as **MYCOLUMN.XLS**. The embedded chart is saved along with the worksheet.

Figure 14.4   **Adding data to existing data series**

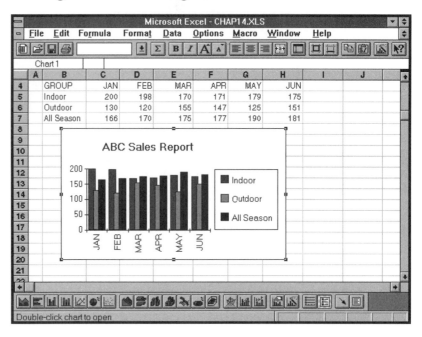

PLOTTING ROWS OR COLUMNS AS DATA SERIES

As mentioned earlier, a chart's data series are not always stored in worksheet rows; sometimes they are stored in worksheet columns. When you select a worksheet range and create a chart, Excel tries to determine where the data series are stored. Excel assumes that you want more categories (JAN, FEB, and so on) than data series (Indoor, Outdoor, and All Season) in your chart; therefore, if the range you select to chart has more columns than rows, Excel plots columns as categories and rows as data series. Conversely, if the selected range has more rows than columns, Excel plots rows as categories and columns as data series.

At times, you may need to override Excel's assumptions and tell it whether to plot the rows or the columns of your selected worksheet range as the data series. To do this,

- If you are creating a new chart, activate the supporting work-sheet and select the range to be charted. If you are modifying an existing chart, select or activate the chart.

- Click on the ChartWizard button.

- If you are creating a new chart, drag to create your embedded chart box.

- Verify that the range in the Step 1 dialog box is correct.

- If you are creating a new chart, complete steps 2 through 3 of the ChartWizard procedure, and then click on Next> to move to the Step 4 dialog box. If you are modifying an existing chart, click on Next> to move to the Step 2 dialog box.

- Under Data Series In, select Rows or Columns. Observe the sample chart to verify the results.

- If you are creating a new chart, complete step 5 of the Chart-Wizard procedure, and then click on OK to draw the chart. If you are modifying an existing chart, click on OK to draw the chart.

Let's tell Excel to plot columns, instead of rows, as the data series in our embedded chart:

1. Select the embedded chart, if it is not already selected.

2. Click on the **ChartWizard button** to open the Step 1 dialog box. Verify that the data range is correct.

3. Click on **Next>** to move to the Step 2 dialog box. Note the title, "ChartWizard—Step 2 of 2." When you are modifying an existing chart, the ChartWizard procedure consists of two steps (instead of five).

4. Under **Data Series In**, click on **Columns** to tell Excel to plot columns (instead of rows) as the chart data series. Observe the sample chart. The worksheet columns (JAN, FEB, and so on) are now plotted as data series (y-axis), and the worksheet rows (Indoor, Outdoor, and All Season) are now plotted as categories (x-axis).

5. Click on **OK** to redraw the embedded chart and return to the worksheet (see Figure 14.5).

Figure 14.5   **Plotting columns as data series**

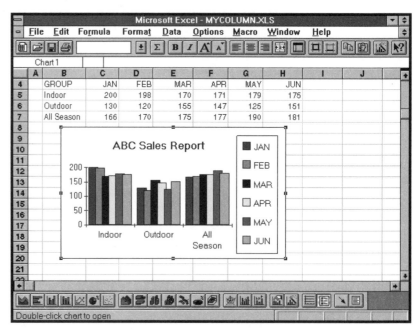

6. Save the worksheet as **MYCOL2.XLS**.

7. Close the worksheet.

CREATING A COMBINATION CHART

At times, you may wish to use a chart to compare two related sets of data (for example, a company's projected earnings versus actual earnings for a fiscal year). Excel allows you to do this by creating a *combination chart* that consists of a *main chart* and, superimposed over this, an *overlay chart*. Each of these charts plots a different set of data. The contrast (or similarity) between your data sets can easily be seen.

- To create a new combination chart, select the range of worksheet data to be charted, create a chart, choose *Gallery, Combination*, and double-click on the desired chart format.

- To create a combination chart from an existing, uncustomized chart, choose *Gallery, Combination*, and double-click on the desired chart format.

- To create a combination chart from an existing customized chart, choose *Chart, Add Overlay* and double-click on the desired overlay chart.

- To specify which data series appear on the main chart and which appear on the overlay chart, choose *Format, Overlay*. Then, under *Series Distribution*, click on *First Overlay Series* and enter the number of the first series to appear on the overlay chart.

Let's open a new worksheet and create a combination chart to depict its data trends:

1. Open **CHAP14B.XLS** and maximize the worksheet window, if necessary. Note that this worksheet is a close variant of the previous, CHAP14.XLS.

2. Select the range **B5:H8**. Then, press and hold **Ctrl** and select **B10:H10**. The noncontiguous range B5:H8 and B10:H10 should now be selected. These cells contain the data we wish to chart.

3. Press **F11** (or choose **File, New**, select **Chart**, and click on **OK**) to create a standard column chart depicting your selected data.

4. Choose **Gallery, Combination...** and double-click on format option **1** (a column chart overlaid with a line chart).

5. Choose **Chart, Add Legend** to add a legend to the chart.

Observe the results. Excel charted the first two data series as columns (Indoor, Outdoor) and the second two as lines (All Season, AVERAGES). When you create a combination chart with the Gallery,

Combination command, Excel displays the first half of your data series in the main chart, and the second half in the overlay chart.

In this case, however, we want a different data-series distribution. Because the first three data series represent product groups, they should all be charted as columns. Only the fourth series, AVERAGES, should be charted as a line. Let's remedy this situation:

1. Choose **Gallery, Combination...** .

2. Press **F1** (Help) and scroll through the Help screen. There is no mention here of how to modify the distribution of the data series between the main and overlay charts.

3. Close the Help dialog box and click on **Cancel** to return to the chart.

4. Choose **Format, Overlay...** . This is the command you must use to change the data-series distribution.

5. Under **Series Distribution**, select **First Overlay Series**; in the text box, type **4**. Click on **OK**. The fourth plotted series, and any series added in the future, will be displayed in the overlay (line) format (see Figure 14.6).

6. Save the chart as **MYCHT14.XLC**, then close it.

7. Save the worksheet as **MYCHP14B.XLS**, then close it.

 ADDING A SECOND VALUE AXIS TO A COMBINATION CHART

Combination charts sometimes depict two kinds of data that are measured in very different ways. For example, in the combination chart you'll create in the next activity, the number of books sold per month, is plotted against the monthly revenues generated from the book sales. These data are measured very differently. "Books Sold" ranges from 179 to 894 books per month; "Revenues" ranges from $903 to $4,256 per month. For clarity's sake, these two data types call for two separate value axes, where each axis reflects the range of its associated data.

To add a second value axis to a combination chart,

• Activate the combination chart.

• Choose Gallery, Combination.

• Select a format that has both left and right value axes.

Figure 14.6   **Chart1, formatted as a combination chart**

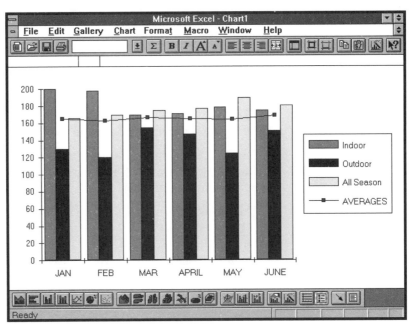

- Click on OK.
- If necessary, use the Format, Scale command to scale each axis separately.

Let's create a combination chart with two value axes:

1. Open **ABCBOOKS.XLS** and maximize it, if necessary. As mentioned earlier, this worksheet contains data on the number of books sold and on the revenues generated from these sales for a 12-month period.

2. Select the range **B4:D16**.

3. Press **F11** (or choose **File, New**, select **Chart**, and click on **OK**) to create a new chart depicting the selected data. The default chart type (column) is used.

4. Add a legend to the chart. (Use the Gallery menu or the Chart toolbar.)

5. Choose **Chart, Attach Text...** , select **Chart Title**, and then enter the title **ABC Book Sales and Revenues**.

6. Choose **Gallery, Combination…** and observe the format options. The options that have two value (y) axes—one on the right and one on the left—will allow you to have separate value axes for books sold and revenues. Only combination charts can use separate value axes.

7. Select option **2** and click on **OK** to create a column/line combination chart with two value axes. Note that Excel scales and labels each axis correctly, based on its analysis of your chart data.

Now let's attach text labels to these axes:

1. Choose **Chart, Attach Text…** , select **Value (Y) Axis**, click on **OK**, and type **Books Sold** to attach a text label to the left-hand value axis.

2. Choose **Chart, Attach Text…** , select **Overlay Value (Y) Axis**, click on **OK**, and type **Revenues** to attach a text label to the right-hand value axis. This axis is called the *overlay* value axis because it is associated with the overlay part (revenues) of the combination chart, rather than the main part (book sales).

3. Press **Esc** to deselect the Revenues text box. Your combination chart should now match the one shown in Figure 14.7.

4. Save the chart as **MYBOOKS.XLC**.

5. Close all document windows.

ATTACHING A DATA-POINT LABEL TO A DATA MARKER

You can use the Chart, Attach Text command to attach a data-point label to an individual data marker in a chart. A *data point* is a single value in a data series. For example, the Book data series in the combination chart shown in Figure 14.7 comprises twelve data points: the twelve values depicted by the book-sales columns for JAN through DEC.

To attach a data-point label to a data marker,

• Press and hold Ctrl, and then click on the desired data marker to select it.

• Choose Chart, Attach Text to open the Attach Text dialog box. Verify that the Series Number and Point Number values are correct.

• Click on OK.

Figure 14.7   **Creating a combination chart with two value axes**

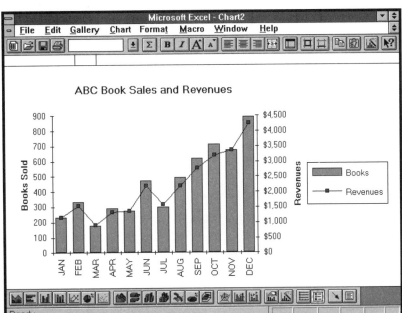

Let's open a worksheet and its associated chart, and then label a data point in this chart:

1. Open **PRODUCTS.XLS** from your EX4WORK directory.

2. Open **PIECHART.XLC**. This pie chart compares the total sales of Indoor, Outdoor, and All-Season product groups, as reported in PRODUCTS.XLS.

3. Choose **Window, Arrange...** , select **Tiled**, and click on **OK** to tile the pie chart and worksheet on your screen.

4. Activate the worksheet and scroll horizontally until the totals column (I) is visible. As mentioned earlier in this chapter, a chart's data series are usually stored in worksheet rows. Here's a good example of a data series that is stored instead in a worksheet column. The Totals data series depicted in PIECHART.XLC is stored in column I of the associated worksheet.

5. Activate the chart. Press and hold **Ctrl**, and then click on the **Indoor data marker** (pie slice) to select it. Black selection squares enclose the data marker to indicate that it is selected.

6. Choose **Chart, Attach Text...** to open the Attach Text dialog box. Verify that both Series Number and Point Number are set to **1**. The Totals (column I) data series depicted in the pie chart is the first—and only—data series in the chart; hence its designation as 1. The indoor-sales totals data (in cell I5) is the first of three data points in this series; hence its designation as 1.

7. Click on **OK** to accept these values and return to the worksheet. Press **Esc** to deselect; examine the results (see Figure 14.8). The amount $1,093 appears next to the pie chart's Indoor data marker.

Figure 14.8   **Attaching a data-point label to a data marker**

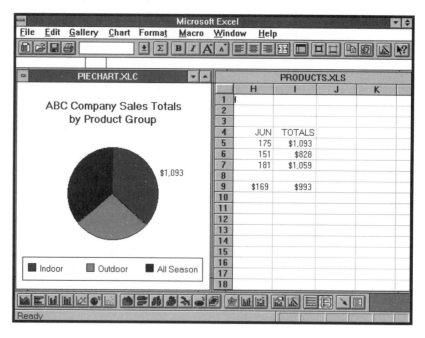

PRACTICE YOUR SKILLS

1. Attach data-point labels to the Outdoor and All Season data markers in the pie chart.

2. Save the chart as **MYPIE.XLC**.

3. Close all document windows without saving the changes.

PRACTICE YOUR SKILLS

This chapter ends with four, instead of the usual two, "Practice Your Skills" activities. The first two are designed to sharpen your ChartWizard skills. The last two review the major topics covered in the charting section of this book (Chapters 12 through 14).

Perform these steps to create an embedded chart that matches Figure 14.9, using ChartWizard:

1. Open **PRU14.XLS** and maximize it, if necessary (Chapter 3).

2. Select the appropriate range to create a chart of hardcover and paperback sales by month (Chapter 14).

3. Use ChartWizard to create an embedded type-1 line chart in the range **B8:N18**. (When setting the chart box range B8:N18, hold down the **Ctrl** key while dragging; the chart box should align with the worksheet gridlines and reach from the upper-left corner of B8 to the lower-right corner of N18, as shown in Figure 14.9.) Use ChartWizard steps to add the title **ABC Book Sales** and to add the value-axis title **Thousands of dollars** (Chapter 14).

Figure 14.9   **The completed MYPRU14.XLS worksheet/chart**

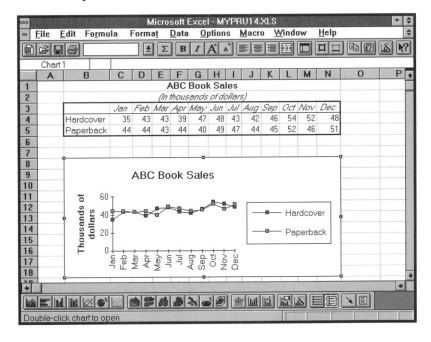

4. Save the worksheet as **MYPRU14.XLS** (Chapter 2).

5. Compare your chart to Figure 14.9.

6. Close the worksheet (Chapter 2).

Perform these steps to create a chart that matches Figure 14.10, using ChartWizard:

1. Open **OPT14.XLS** and maximize it, if necessary (Chapter 3).

2. Create a new chart (not an embedded chart) depicting the first- and second-quarter (Qtr1 and Qtr2) data for the three sales representatives (Chapter 12).

3. Add a legend to the chart (Chapter 12).

4. Use ChartWizard to tell Excel to plot rows as the chart data series (Chapter 14).

5. Add the title **ABC Company Sales Reps** (Chapter 12).

Figure 14.10   **The completed MYOPT14.XLC chart and MYOPT14.XLS worksheet**

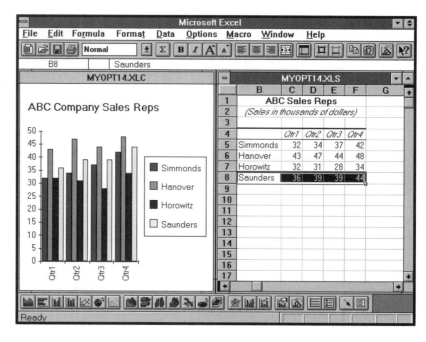

6. Tile the chart and worksheet windows on the screen (Chapter 12).

7. Activate the worksheet and add the following data for the remaining two quarters:

	Qtr3	Qtr4
Simmonds	37	42
Hanover	44	48
Horowitz	28	34

8. Activate the chart window and use ChartWizard to add the Qtr3 and Qtr4 data to the chart (Chapter 14).

9. Activate the worksheet window and add the following data for a new sales representative:

	B	C	D	E	F
8	Saunders	36	39	39	44

10. Activate the chart window and use ChartWizard to add Saunders's data to the chart (Chapter 14).

11. Save the chart as **MYOPT14.XLC** (Chapter 2).

12. Activate the worksheet and save it as **MYOPT14.XLS** (Chapter 2).

13. Compare your screen to Figure 14.10.

14. Close all windows without saving the changes (Chapter 7).

The following two activities review the major topics covered in the charting section of this book (Chapters 12 through 14).

Perform these steps to create a line chart that matches Figure 14.11:

1. Open **EXERCH.XLS** (Chapter 3) and maximize it, if necessary (Chapter 3).

2. If the Chart toolbar is not displayed, display it now (Chapter 12).

3. Select the range **B5** through **D17**.

4. Create a chart (Chapter 12).

5. Use the Chart toolbar to change the chart type to line (Chapter 12).

Figure 14.11   The printed line chart of EXERCH.XLS

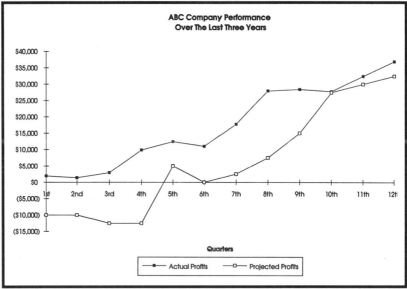

6. Use the Chart menu to add a legend to the chart (Chapter 12).

7. Move the legend from the right side of the chart to the bottom of the chart (Chapter 13).

8. Add the following chart title (Chapter 12):

    ABC Company Performance Over The Last Three Years

9. Modify the title to break to a second line at the word "Over" (Chapter 13).

10. Add the following category (x) axis label (Chapter 12):

    Quarters

11. Make the following File, Page Setup changes (Chapter 13):

    • Set **Chart Size** to **Use Full Page**

    • Set **Orientation** to **Landscape**

    • Remove (delete) the header and footer

12. Preview and then print the chart (Chapter 13).

13. Compare your printout to Figure 14.11.

14. Save the chart with the name **MYEXERCH.XLC** (Chapter 12).

15. Close all windows without saving the changes (Chapter 7).

The following activity is designed to further review your Excel charting skills. Perform these steps to create a combination chart that matches Figure 14.12.

Figure 14.12 **The printed combination chart of OPTEXCH.XLS**

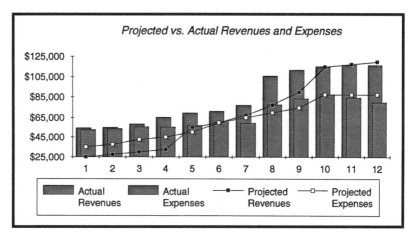

1. Open **OPTEXCH.XLS** (Chapter 3).

2. Maximize the document window, if necessary (Chapter 3).

3. Create a default column chart depicting the actual and the projected revenues and expenses data (Chapter 12). Hints: you'll have to select a noncontiguous range comprising four worksheet columns to do this. When the New Chart dialog box appears, click on **OK** to verify that the first column of your selected data (actual revenues) contains the first data series of your chart.

4. Use the Chart toolbar to change the chart type to a standard combination chart (Chapter 12).

5. Format the chart columns to overlap by **70%** (Chapter 13). Hint: Choose **Format, Main Chart**.

6. Format the chart columns to display the diagonal patterns shown in Figure 14.12 (Chapter 13).

7. Emphasize the growth trends by changing the value-axis scale to show a minimum of **$25,000** instead of $0 (Chapter 13).

8. Add the following title (Chapter 12):

    `Projected vs. Actual Revenues and Expenses`

9. Add a legend to the bottom of the chart (Chapter 12).

10. Edit the worksheet cells containing the legend text to add the words **Actual** and **Projected** to the legend (Chapter 12).

11. Format all chart text to **12-point Helvetica** (Chapter 13).

12. Format the chart title to **14-point Helvetica Italic** (Chapter 13).

13. Print the chart, using the following File, Page Setup settings (Chapter 13):

Orientation	**Portrait**
Chart Size	**Scale to Fit Page**
Header	(deleted)
Footer	(deleted)

14. Compare your printout with Figure 14.11.

15. Save the chart as **MYOPTCH.XLC** (Chapter 12).

16. Close all windows without saving the changes (Chapter 2).

CHAPTER SUMMARY

In this chapter, you experimented with several advanced chart customization techniques. You learned how to use ChartWizard to create and modify your charts, how to create a column/line combination chart, and how to attach a data-point label to a data marker.

With this chapter, your foundation in Excel charting techniques is complete. Congratulations! You now possess the skills to create sophisticated, presentation-quality charts.

Here is a quick reference guide to the Excel features introduced in this chapter:

Desired Result	How to Do It
Create an embedded chart using ChartWizard	Select range of worksheet cells containing data to chart, click on **ChartWizard button**, drag in worksheet to create embedded chart box, follow the ChartWizard dialog-box instructions
Add data to a chart	Add data to supporting worksheet, if modifying windowed chart (rather than embedded) tile chart and worksheet, select or activate chart, click on **ChartWizard tool**; in supporting worksheet, select range containing all data to be charted (including data you want to add), click on **>> button** in the ChartWizard dialog box
Plot rows or columns as data series	If creating new chart, activate supporting worksheet and select range to be charted; if modifying existing chart, select or activate chart; click on **ChartWizard button**; if new chart, drag to create embedded chart box, verify range in Step 1 dialog box, complete steps 2 through 3 and click on Next> to move to Step 4 dialog box; if existing chart, click on Next> to move to Step 2 dialog box, under Data Series In select Rows or Columns; if new chart complete step 5, click on **OK** to draw chart
Create a new combination chart	Select range of worksheet data to be charted, create chart, choose **Gallery, Combination**, double-click on desired chart format
Create a combination chart from an uncustomized chart	Choose **Gallery, Combination**, double-click on desired chart format
Create a combination chart from a customized chart	Choose **Chart, Add Overlay**, double-click on desired overlay chart

Desired Result	How to Do It
Change the distribution of the data series between the main and overlay charts	Choose **Format, Overlay**, under **Series Distribution** click on **First Overlay Series**, enter number of first series to appear on overlay chart
Add a second value axis to a combination chart	Activate combination chart, choose **Gallery, Combination**, select format that has both left and right value axes, click on **OK**, if necessary use **Format, Scale** to scale each axis
Attach a data-point label to a data marker	Hold down **Ctrl** and click on desired data marker to select, choose **Chart, Attach Text**, verify Series Number and Point Number values, click on **OK**

In the next and final chapter of this book, you will expand your Excel printing skills by learning how to print a large, multipage worksheet.

IF YOU'RE STOPPING HERE

If you need to break off here, please exit from Excel. If you want to proceed directly to the next chapter, please do so now.

CHAPTER 15: PRINTING A LARGE WORKSHEET

Until now, you have printed relatively small, single-page worksheets. Eventually you may need to create and print larger, more complex worksheets. This chapter introduces various techniques to help you manage the printing of multipage worksheets.

When you're done working through this chapter, you will know

- How to reduce or enlarge a worksheet printout

- How to remove headers, footers, cell gridlines, and row and column headings from a worksheet printout

- How to paginate a worksheet by setting and removing page breaks

- How to print a selected part of a worksheet

- How to set print titles (repeat row and column titles) in a multi-page worksheet printout

- How to print and preview a document using the Standard toolbar's Print button

REDUCING OR ENLARGING A WORKSHEET PRINTOUT

When printing a large worksheet, you may wish to reduce the printout size in order to fit more data on a page. Excel allows you to do this by using the File, Page Setup (or File, Print Preview, Setup) command.

To reduce or enlarge a worksheet printout,

- Choose File, Page Setup... (or choose File, Print Preview, Setup...).

- Enter the desired reduction/enlargement percentage in the *Reduce/Enlarge To box* (100 percent is normal size, 50 percent is half size, 200 percent is double size).

- Click on OK.

Note: If your printer does not support reduction/enlargement (that is, if it is not a PostScript-type printer), this option will be unavailable (dimmed) in the Page Setup dialog box, and all your documents will be printed at normal (100-percent) size.

If you are not running Excel, please start it now. If there is a worksheet on your screen, please close it. Your screen should be empty except for a maximized Excel application window. Now let's practice reducing the printout size of a worksheet:

1. Open **CHAP15.XLS** from your EX4WORK directory and maximize it, if necessary.

2. We won't be working with charts in this chapter, so let's remove (hide) the Chart toolbar to tidy up the screen and increase the display space. Choose **Options, Toolbars...** , select **Chart**, and click on **Hide**. Note that the document window expands to fill the free space.

3. Take a moment to scroll through CHAP15.XLS. Note that this worksheet is significantly larger than the others you have used in this book.

4. Choose **File, Print Preview** to preview the printout of CHAP15.XLS. Use the magnifying tool, if necessary, to determine the heading letter of the rightmost column in the page-1 preview. Determine also the heading number of the bottom row in page 1. (Note: On our system, the rightmost column is J and the bottom row is 48. Depending upon which printer you are using, your results may differ slightly.)

5. Click on **Close** to return to your worksheet. Observe the page break (dashed line) between columns J and K; this marks the beginning of a new printed page (see Figure 15.1). Scroll down to observe the page break between rows 48 and 49. (Again, depending upon your printer, your page breaks may differ from those in this chapter's activities.)

6. Choose **File, Page Setup...** .

7. Select the current value (**100**) in the **Reduce/Enlarge To box** (in the **Scaling** section at the bottom of the dialog box) and type **80** to reduce the printout size of CHAP15.XLS to 80 percent. If your printer does not support reduction/enlargement (that is, if the Reduce/Enlarge To option is dimmed), please skip this step. Be aware that the page breaks in an unreduced printout will differ from those in the printout described in the following activities.

8. Click on **OK** to accept your reduction value and return to the worksheet. Observe that the page break has moved from between columns J and K to between columns O and P (see Figure 15.2; compare this with Figure 15.1). Scroll down to observe the page break has also moved from between rows 48 and 49 to between rows 61 and 62. Now that the print size has been reduced, more of the worksheet fits on a page.

Figure 15.1   Page break in CHAP15.XLS, before reduction

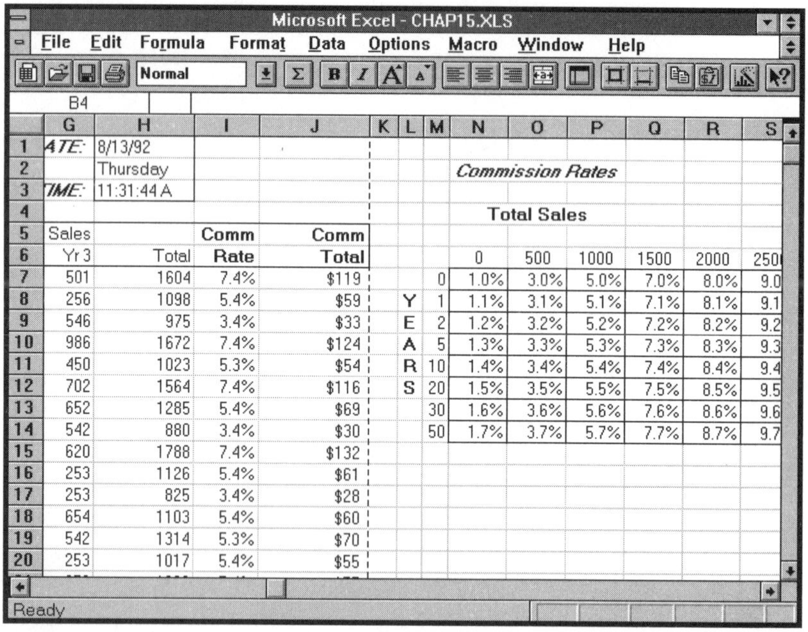

Figure 15.2   Page break in CHAP15.XLS, after reduction

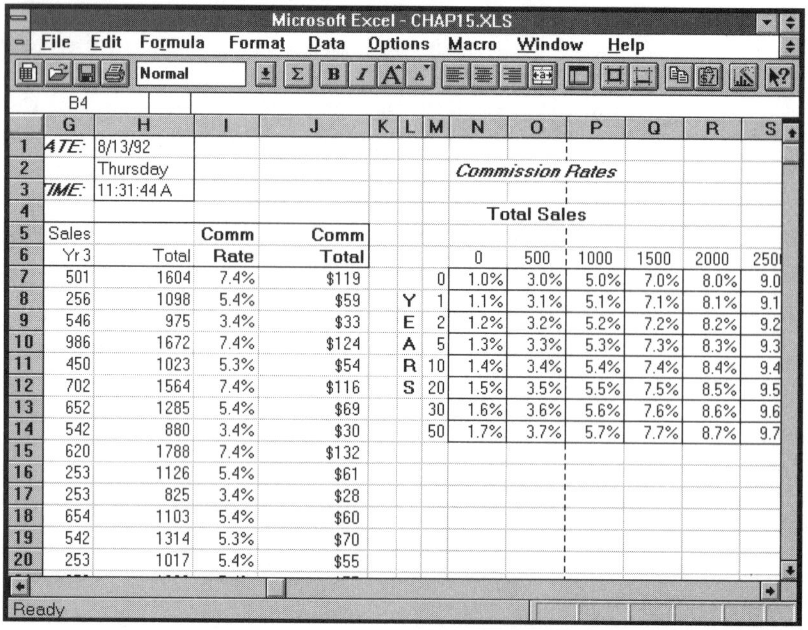

9. Preview the worksheet printout. Examine the right-hand side of page 1. Note that several columns to the right of column J are included in the printout.

10. Observe the standard header and footer, the row and column headings, and the cell gridlines. As you learned in Chapter 6, you can remove any or all of these items from your printout.

REMOVING HEADERS, FOOTERS, GRIDLINES, AND ROW AND COLUMN HEADINGS

Another way to fit more data on a printed page is to remove any or all of the following from the printout: headers, footers, gridlines, and row and column headings. You can do this by using the File, Page Setup (or File, Print Preview, Setup) command.

To remove headers, footers, gridlines, and row and column headings from a worksheet printout,

- Choose File, Page Setup... (or choose File, Print Preview, Setup...).

- Delete the contents of the Header and/or Footer text boxes.

- Uncheck the Row & Column Headings and/or Cell Gridlines boxes.

- Click on OK.

Let's remove the header, gridlines, and row and column headings from the CHAP15.XLS printout, leaving the footer intact to display page numbers:

1. From within **Print Preview**, choose **Setup...** .(Choosing Setup... from Print Preview is equivalent to choosing File, Page Setup from the normal Excel worksheet mode.)

2. Click on **Header** to open the Header dialog box. Double-click on the **&f** code in the **Center Section text box** to select it, and then press **Del** to delete it. Click on **OK** to return to the Page Setup dialog box.

3. Uncheck **Row & Column Headings** and **Cell Gridlines**.

4. Click on **OK**. Note that the page header, row and column headings, and gridlines have all been removed (see Figure 15.3). Note also that the first three columns of the commission-rates table are now displayed. (Only two columns were displayed before this step.) The extra column has

moved into the space you freed up by removing the row headings.

Figure 15.3   Preview of CHAP15.XLS, after removing the page header, gridlines, and row and column headings

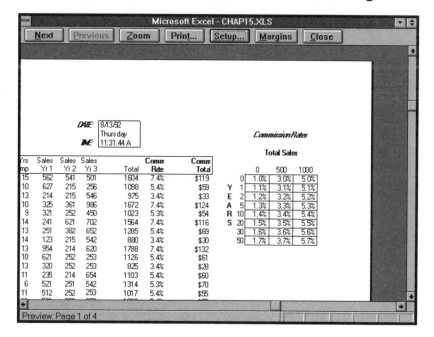

5. Use the **Next button**, magnifying glass, and scroll bars to examine pages 2 through 4 of the preview.

6. Click on the **Close button** to exit from Print Preview.

PAGINATING A WORKSHEET

When you print (or preview) a multipage worksheet, Excel automatically *paginates* the worksheet, arranging its pages according to the current print settings (margins, header, footer, reduction/enlargement, and so on). You may, however, wish to modify this arrangement—for example, to avoid breaking up a table into two pages. Excel allows you to repaginate a worksheet by specifying its page breaks (the points at which new pages will begin).

SETTING A PAGE BREAK

To set a page break,

- Select the row or the column that you want to appear at the top or the left edge of the new page. Or, select the cell that you want to appear in the upper-left corner of the new page

- Choose *Options, Set Page Break*.

Let's practice setting a page break:

1. Observe the commission-rates table of CHAP15.XLS (columns L through S). The current page break splits the table into two parts, an undesirable division.

2. Select column **K** (click on the column heading); choose **Options, Set Page Break**. Note the dashed line denoting a page break to the left of column K. (You may need to deselect the column to see this.) Column K will now appear at the left edge of a new page.

3. Scroll down to examine the area below the commission-rates table; it is empty. The table will appear on a page by itself.

4. Preview the printout. Note that the commission-rates table has been removed from page 1 (see Figure 15.4; compare it to Figure 15.3).

5. Click on **Next** to preview page 2. Click on **Next** again to pre-view page 3. Note that the commission-rates table now appears alone on this page. (You may have to scroll.)

6. Click on **Next** to preview page 4. Click the mouse pointer any-where on the page to demagnify the view. Note that this page is blank; as you saw in step 4 above, it contains the empty cells below the commission-rates table. Unless you specify other-wise (see below, "Printing a Selected Part of a Worksheet"), Excel prints the entire active area of your worksheet: every-thing from cell A1 to the intersection of the furthest active row and column. (You can see this intersection by pressing Ctrl-End from within the worksheet.)

7. Click on **Close** to exit Print Preview.

Figure 15.4   **Preview of CHAP15.XLS, after setting a page break**

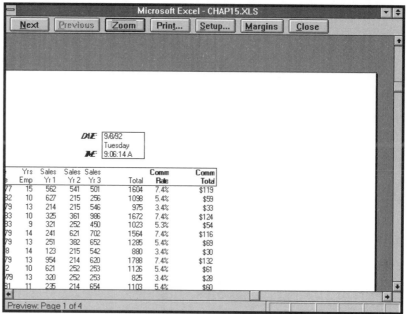

 REMOVING A PAGE BREAK

To remove a page break,

- Select the row or column immediately below or to the right of the page break, or select the cell in the upper-left corner of the page to be changed.

- Choose *Options, Remove Page Break*.

Note: Excel does not allow you to use Edit, Undo to undo a page break that you just set. You must use the above procedure instead.

Now let's remove the page break you just set:

1. Select column **K**, the column immediately to the right of the page break.

2. Choose **Options, Remove Page Break**.

3. Examine the worksheet. Note that the page break has moved from between columns J and K to between columns P and Q.

PRACTICE YOUR SKILLS

1. Try using **Edit, Undo** to undo the Remove Page Break command you just issued. (Edit, Undo will not undo a Set Page Break or Remove Page Break command.)

2. Reset the page to break between columns **J** and **K**.

PRINTING A SELECTED PART OF A WORKSHEET

Yet another way to fit more data on a printed page is to select and print a specific area of the worksheet. This enables you to avoid printing empty cells or superfluous data. As you learned in Chapter 6, to print a selected area of your worksheet (rather than the entire active area), you must use Options, Set Print Area.

SETTING A PRINT AREA

To set a print area,

- Select the area of the worksheet you wish to print. This can be a single, contiguous range (A1:F25) or several, noncontiguous ranges (A1:F25, M1:P6, A30:F34).

- Choose Options, Set Print Area.

Let's set a print area that consists of two noncontiguous ranges, the database proper and commission-rates table of CHAP15.XLS:

1. Select cells **A1:J107**. (Press **Ctrl-Home** to select cell A1; press and hold **Shift**; scroll down and click on cell **J107**.)

2. Use the mouse to scroll right and up until the entire commission-rates table is on screen (L1:S14). Do not click anywhere within the worksheet while you are scrolling or your range (A1:J107) will be deselected.

3. Press and hold **Ctrl**, then drag from **L1** to **S14**. Your noncontiguous selection now comprises A1:J107 and L1:S14. Note that the empty cells beneath the commission-rates table have not been included in this selection.

4. Choose **Options, Set Print Area**.

5. Preview the printout. Click **Next** to preview page 2. Click **Next** again to preview page 3 (see Figure 15.5).

Figure 15.5   **Page 3 of CHAP15.XLS, after setting a print area**

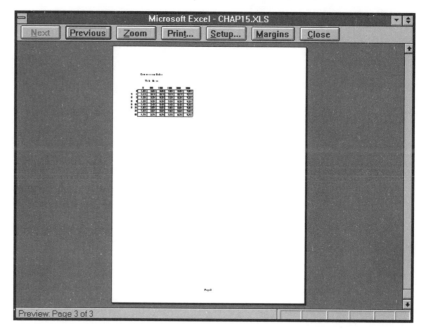

6. Note that the Next button is now dimmed. Click **Next** again; nothing happens. As you know, a dimmed button or menu option means that item is currently unavailable. Observe the status message at the bottom of the screen:

```
Preview: Page 3 of 3
```

By excluding the empty cells beneath the commission-rates table from the print area, you prevented Excel from printing a blank fourth page.

7. Click on **Close** to exit Print Preview.

DELETING A PRINT AREA

To print the entire active area of your worksheet, you must delete the current print area. In Chapter 6, you learned to do this by using the Options, Remove Print Area command. To use another method for deleting a print area,

• Choose Formula, Define Name.

- Select Print_Area.

- Click on Delete, then click on OK.

If Print_Area is deleted, the current print area will be permanently lost. If you think you may want to reuse this print area at a later date, make a copy of it before deleting it. When you want to reuse the deleted print area, use this copy to recreate it.

Let's experiment with copying and deleting a print area:

1. Choose **Formula, Define Name...** .

2. Select **Print_Area**.

3. Press **Tab** to select the Name text box and type **My_Print_Area**. (As mentioned in Chapter 7, defined names cannot have spaces; use underlines instead.)

4. Click on **OK** to create My_Print_Area, an exact copy of Print_Area. Now that you have a copy, you can safely delete the original.

5. Choose **Formula, Define Name...** again. Verify that Print_Area and My_Print_Area reference the same cell ranges.

6. Select **Print_Area**. Click on **Delete**. Note that Print_Area has been removed from the list of defined names. (Take care when you delete a defined name; you cannot use Edit, Undo to retrieve it.)

7. Click on **OK** to return to the worksheet.

8. Preview the printout. Use **Next** to display page 4. Note that this page is once again blank; without a defined print area, Excel prints the entire active area of the worksheet.

9. Click on **Close** to exit Print Preview.

Now let's use My_Print_Area to recreate the deleted print area:

1. Press **Ctrl-Home** to reorient the screen.

2. Choose **Formula, Goto...** . Double-click on **My_Print_Area** to select the range this name refers to—the same noncontiguous range as the print area you just deleted (A1:J107, L1:S14).

3. Choose Options, Set Print Area.

4. Preview the printout. Click on **Next** to display page 2. Use the magnifying glass tool, if necessary, to enlarge the page to actual size. Note that without column titles, it is difficult to interpret the

data on this page. In the next section you will learn how to include row and/or column titles on every printed page.

5. Click on **Next** to display page 3. Note that the Next button is once again dimmed; the print area you set in steps 2 and 3 above (the same print area that you deleted in the previous activity) includes only three pages.

6. Click on **Close** to exit Print Preview.

SETTING PRINT TITLES

As you just saw, it can be difficult to interpret a page of unlabeled data. To clarify such a printout, Excel allows you to include row and/or column titles on every page by using the *Set Print Titles* command.

To set print titles in a worksheet,

- Select the row(s) and/or column(s) that contain the titles that should be printed on each page. You must select entire rows or columns, not just the cells containing the print-title data. You can select multiple rows or columns, but they must be adjacent: rows 1 and 2 are okay; rows 1 and 4 are not.

- Choose Options, Set Print Titles to open the Set Print Titles dialog box.

- Verify that the Titles for Columns and/or Titles for Rows ranges are correct.

- Click on OK.

Note: Your print area should not contain the rows or columns that define your print titles. If it does, the titles may be duplicated on some pages.

Let's set print titles to clarify the printout of CHAP15.XLS:

1. Press **Ctrl-Home** to reorient the screen.

2. Select rows **1** through **6**. (Remember to select the entire row(s) or column(s) when preparing to set your print titles, not just the cells containing the desired titles.) We want the titles in these rows to appear at the top of every printed page to make it easier to understand the contents of the worksheet.

3. Choose **Options, Set Print Titles** to open the Set Print Titles dialog box. Verify that the Titles for Columns range is correct ($1:$6). Click on **OK** to accept this range.

4. Preview the printout. Examine page 1; the titles are duplicated (see Figure 15.6). As mentioned above, including the print titles in your print area may cause duplication. To fix this, the titles must be removed from the print area.

Figure 15.6   **Preview of CHAP15.XLS, with duplicated print titles**

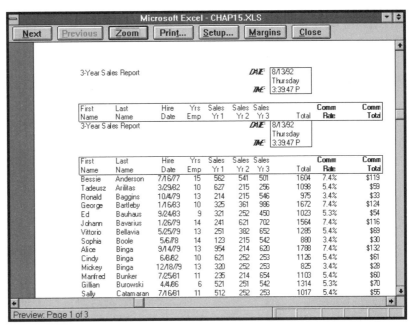

5. Examine page 2. The correct print titles appear there.

6. Examine page 3. This page has the same problem as page 1; the titles have been duplicated.

7. Click on **Close** to exit Print Preview.

Examine the worksheet. Rows 1 through 6 must be removed from the print area to avoid title duplication. We will do this by modifying My_Print_Area, then using it to create a new Print_Area.

1. Choose **Formula, Define Name...** . Select **My_Print_Area**. In the **Refers To box**, remove the references to rows 1 through 6 by changing $A$1 to **$A$7** and $L$1 to **$L$7**. (If you intend to use the Arrow keys to move through the Refers To box, make sure to first press the **Edit** key (**F2**). If you do not do this, your arrow keystrokes will change the actual contents of the box.) The Refers To box should now contain

   `=$A$7:$J$107,$L$7:$S$14`

2. Click on **OK** to accept the new My_Print_Area range.

3. Choose **Formula, Goto**.

4. Double-click on **My_Print_Area**. Note that rows 1 through 6 have been removed from the selection.

5. Choose **Options, Set Print Area**.

6. Preview the printout. Note that the print titles are not duplicated anymore.

7. Click on **Print**, and then on **OK** to print the worksheet (see Figure 15.7).

PRACTICE YOUR SKILLS

1. Make a copy of the print-titles range you set in the above activity, using the name **My_Print_Titles**.

2. Verify that My_Print_Titles and Print_Titles refer to the same ranges.

3. Delete **Print_Titles** from the list of defined names.

4. Use **My_Print_Titles** to reset the print-titles range you just deleted. This three-step procedure (copy, delete, reset) is the standard method you would use to save the current Print_Area or Print_Titles and later—after they have been deleted or changed—to retrieve them.

5. Verify that the print titles are correctly reset. (Hint: use **Print Preview**.)

6. Save the worksheet as **MYCHAP15.XLS**.

Figure 15.7   **Printout of CHAP15.XLS**

3-Year Sales Report

DATE: 8/14/92
Friday
TIME: 11:42:13 A

First Name	Last Name	Hire Date	Yrs Emp	Sales Yr 1	Sales Yr 2	Sales Yr 3	Total	Comm Rate	Comm Total
Bessie	Anderson	7/16/77	15	562	541	501	1604	7.4%	$119
Tadeusz	Arilitas	3/29/82	10	627	215	256	1098	5.4%	$59
Ronald	Baggins	10/4/79	13	214	215	546	975	3.4%	$33
George	Bartleby	1/16/83	10	325	361	986	1672	7.4%	$124
Ed	Bauhaus	9/24/83	9	321	252	450	1023	5.3%	$54
Johann	Bavarius	1/26/79	14	241	621	702	1564	7.4%	$116
Vittorio	Bellavia	5/25/79	13	251	382	652	1285	5.4%	$69
Sophia	Boole	5/6/78	14	123	215	542	880	3.4%	$30
Alice	Binga	9/14/79	13	954	214	620	1788	7.4%	$132
Cindy	Binga	6/8/82	10	621	252	253	1126	5.4%	$61
Mickey	Binga	12/18/79	13	320	252	253	825	3.4%	$28
Manfred	Bunker	7/25/81	11	235	214	654	1103	5.4%	$60
Gillian	Burowski	4/4/86	6	521	251	542	1314	5.3%	$70
Sally	Catamaran	7/16/81	11	512	252	253	1017	5.4%	$55
Edna	Cheese	8/12/81	11	521	252	253	1026	5.4%	$55
Uriah	Chips	12/30/79	13	324	252	253	829	3.4%	$28
Wilbur	Choong	12/21/79	13	321	252	253	826	3.4%	$28
Connie	Conners	2/6/79	14	215	252	253	720	3.4%	$24
Robyn	Creep	9/24/83	9	361	251	230	842	3.3%	$28
Earl	Duke	9/4/77	15	214	214	310	738	3.4%	$25
Isaac	Dune	9/18/82	10	314	316	876	1506	7.4%	$111
Errol	Duque	7/9/84	8	325	213	558	1096	5.3%	$58
Elwin	Ellmore	1/28/79	14	212	252	253	717	3.4%	$24
Woody	Epstein	11/22/81	11	253	523	654	1430	5.4%	$77
Albert	Feinstein	9/28/80	12	214	562	654	1430	5.4%	$77
Zenobia	Finch	5/7/79	13	245	252	253	750	3.4%	$26
Walter	Fish	5/5/85	7	459	709	685	1853	7.3%	$135
Linda	Flannery	2/6/79	14	215	541	253	1009	5.4%	$54
Phineas	Frank	2/3/79	14	214	252	253	719	3.4%	$24
Marvin	Gardener	7/10/81	11	510	252	253	1015	5.4%	$55
Carmine	Gladiola	1/2/80	13	325	252	253	830	3.4%	$28
John	Goodbar	2/6/79	14	215	252	253	720	3.4%	$24
Edsel	Goodyear	7/4/77	15	21	252	253	526	3.4%	$18
Theresa	Hall	1/11/84	9	315	262	698	1275	5.3%	$68
Kermit	Heiser	6/23/75	17	214	251	510	975	3.4%	$33
Bjarni	Herjolfsson	3/17/83	9	325	562	654	1541	7.3%	$112
Sam	Hill	4/5/74	18	243	406	893	1542	7.4%	$114
Ken	Hoodis	12/3/79	13	232	311	654	1197	5.4%	$65
Joy	Juno	2/6/79	14	215	888	253	1356	5.4%	$73
Willie	Kawasaki	2/4/86	7	412	214	254	880	3.3%	$29
Keith	Keith	11/27/80	12	215	324	253	792	3.4%	$27
Julia	Kids	2/6/79	14	222	652	546	1420	5.4%	$77
Julie	King	12/18/79	13	320	252	253	825	3.4%	$28
Wilhelm	Konrad	2/2/77	16	642	542	540	1724	7.4%	$128
Helmut	Krank	5/16/83	9	154	523	658	1335	5.3%	$71
Julius	Lemon	2/4/86	7	421	21	214	656	3.3%	$22
Ross	Limburger	5/2/77	15	214	673	321	1208	5.4%	$65
Mark	Lindham	3/16/68	24	145	345	453	943	3.5%	$33
Hubert	Long	4/27/78	14	120	252	253	625	3.4%	$21
Ashley	Longworth	2/6/79	14	215	424	253	892	3.4%	$30
Thurman	Muenster	10/5/77	15	52	252	253	557	3.4%	$19
Ellison	Munk	10/13/80	12	420	252	253	925	3.4%	$31
Ozzie	Nielsen	12/18/79	13	320	252	253	825	3.4%	$28
Lily	Nipper	2/4/86	7	512	325	482	1319	5.3%	$70
Harriet	Nolan	2/6/79	14	215	542	253	1010	5.4%	$55
Lori	O'Binney	1/26/81	12	321	211	654	1186	5.4%	$64

Page 1

Figure 15.7 **(Continued)**

3-Year Sales Report   DATE: 8/14/92
                                                             Friday
                                                       TIME: 11:42:13 A

First Name	Last Name	Hire Date	Yrs Emp	Sales Yr 1	Sales Yr 2	Sales Yr 3	Total	Comm Rate	Comm Total
Sean	O'Kleogh	8/5/83	9	235	536	876	1647	7.3%	$120
Jimmy	Olson	8/9/81	11	520	252	253	1025	5.4%	$55
Kay	Osborne	2/6/79	14	215	214	845	1274	5.4%	$69
Paulus	Paulus	9/23/81	11	125	252	654	1031	5.4%	$56
Warren	Peace	2/1/80	13	152	256	645	1053	5.4%	$57
Pete	Perdue	11/12/83	9	153	251	587	991	3.3%	$33
Mert	Perdy	2/19/85	7	950	252	253	1455	5.3%	$77
Kathy	Prince	9/7/84	8	235	652	584	1471	5.3%	$78
Rocky	Puglist	2/24/79	13	221	252	253	726	3.4%	$25
Tyrone	Purvis	12/30/79	13	324	252	253	829	3.4%	$28
Jack	Quick	4/1/80	12	32	352	763	1147	5.4%	$62
Karen	Randazzo	3/11/84	8	316	325	695	1336	5.3%	$71
Tom	Raven	5/31/80	12	215	214	888	1317	5.4%	$71
Nellie	Rivera	3/27/81	11	625	255	654	1534	7.4%	$114
Hyman	Roethke	11/2/74	18	400	930	234	1564	7.4%	$116
Kieran	Runidian	5/25/79	13	251	252	253	756	3.4%	$26
Samolo	Samolian	5/26/81	11	624	214	655	1493	5.4%	$81
Ben	Sampers	3/4/78	14	102	252	253	607	3.4%	$21
Laurie	Sanchez	7/30/80	12	326	217	654	1197	5.4%	$65
Leo	Shumacher	6/5/82	10	620	252	253	1125	5.4%	$61
Sidney	Slong	7/4/77	15	21	252	253	526	3.4%	$18
Mickey	Smith	2/3/86	7	124	235	342	701	3.3%	$23
Yitzhak	Solomon	2/2/77	16	214	242	845	1301	5.4%	$70
Horatio	Spelunque	6/3/83	9	518	214	214	946	3.3%	$31
Isaac	Steelman	6/23/77	15	231	430	653	1314	5.4%	$71
Aaron	Stool	7/15/83	9	263	241	564	1068	5.3%	$57
Jack	Streech	9/13/83	9	325	251	589	1165	5.3%	$62
Tad	Tadmore	7/20/82	10	332	214	845	1391	5.4%	$75
Mort	Thomas	5/2/77	15	452	214	652	1318	5.4%	$71
Abram	Turlowe	4/4/83	9	98	214	312	624	3.3%	$21
Terrance	Typhus	6/8/82	10	621	252	253	1126	5.4%	$61
Felix	Unger	4/1/75	17	123	567	901	1591	7.4%	$118
Dizzy	Unitas	7/19/81	11	513	252	253	1018	5.4%	$55
Mary	VonTrapp	3/22/82	10	32	214	645	891	3.4%	$30
Wayne	Wentworth	4/15/86	6	232	124	545	901	3.3%	$30
Jo	Wieser	1/2/82	11	213	214	450	877	3.4%	$30
Wilma	Willard	9/4/79	13	285	252	253	790	3.4%	$27
Willard	Williams	8/12/81	11	521	252	253	1026	5.4%	$55
William	Willis	2/2/77	16	214	217	420	851	3.4%	$29
Wilbur	Willison	5/28/79	13	252	252	253	757	3.4%	$26
Mick	Yaeger	2/6/79	14	555	252	564	1371	5.4%	$74
	Total Sales			17915	18731	26963	63609		
	Average			303.6	317.5	457.0	1078.11864	4.7%	$54
	High Sales			950	930	901	1724		
	Low Sales			21	21	214	526		

Page 2

Figure 15.7   **(Continued)**

Commission Rates

Total Sales

		0	500	1000	1500	2000	2500
	0	1.0%	3.0%	5.0%	7.0%	8.0%	9.0%
Y	1	1.1%	3.1%	5.1%	7.1%	8.1%	9.1%
E	2	1.2%	3.2%	5.2%	7.2%	8.2%	9.2%
A	5	1.3%	3.3%	5.3%	7.3%	8.3%	9.3%
R	10	1.4%	3.4%	5.4%	7.4%	8.4%	9.4%
S	20	1.5%	3.5%	5.5%	7.5%	8.5%	9.5%
	30	1.6%	3.6%	5.6%	7.6%	8.6%	9.6%
	50	1.7%	3.7%	5.7%	7.7%	8.7%	9.7%

Page 3

USING THE STANDARD TOOLBAR'S PRINT BUTTON

You already know two methods for printing your worksheets and charts: the File, Print command and the Print button in the Print Preview window. Here you'll learn a new, convenient method: the Print button in the Standard toolbar. You can use the Standard toolbar's Print button both to print and to preview your documents.

To print a document using the Standard toolbar's Print button:

- Activate the document window. If you are printing a chart, the chart must be in a window, not embedded in a worksheet.

- Click on the Standard toolbar's Print button (the fourth button from the left, it shows a miniature printer). One entire copy (all pages) of the active document is printed according to the current Page Setup dialog-box settings (orientation, paper size, margins, scaling, and so on).

To preview a document using the Standard toolbar's Print button,

- Activate the document window. If you are previewing a chart, the chart must be in a window, not embedded.

- Press and hold Shift, and then click on the Standard toolbar's Print button. The active document is previewed according to the current Page Setup dialog-box settings.

Let's use the Standard toolbar's Print button to preview and then print MYCHAP15.XLS:

1. Press and hold **Shift**, then click on the **Print button** (the fourth button from the left in the Standard toolbar). The Print Preview window appears.

2. Use **Next** and **Previous** to page through the previewed document. Use the magnifying glass to zoom in and out. Note that Print Preview functions exactly the same whether you activate it by choosing File, Print Preview or by Shift-clicking on the Standard toolbar's Print button.

3. Click on **Close** to exit Print Preview.

4. Choose **File, Page Setup** to open the Page Setup dialog box. Observe the settings: portrait orientation, no row and column headings, no cell gridlines, 80% scale reduction. These are the same settings that you just viewed in Print Preview. Click on **Cancel** to close the dialog box.

5. Click on the Standard toolbar's **Print button** to print one entire copy of MYCHAP15.XLS according to the current Page Setup settings.

6. Use **File, Save** to update the worksheet.

7. Close the worksheet and exit from Excel.

CHAPTER SUMMARY

In this chapter, you learned various techniques to help you manage the printing of a large, multipage worksheet, including:

- How to reduce/enlarge the size of a printout

- How to remove headers, footers, cell gridlines, and row and column headings from a printout

- How to paginate a printout

- How to print a selected part of a worksheet

- How to include print titles on a printout

- How to print or preview a document using the Standard toolbar's Print button

With this chapter, you have completed your foundation of Excel skills. Congratulations! You may now venture out into the real world to create and print handsome, sophisticated Excel worksheets, databases, and charts.

Here is a quick reference guide to the Excel features introduced in this chapter:

Desired Result	How to Do It
Reduce or enlarge a printout	Choose **File, Page Setup...** (or **File, Print Preview, Setup...**), enter desired reduction/ enlargement percentage, click on **OK**
Remove headers, footers, gridlines, and row and column headings from a printout	Choose **File, Page Setup...** (or **File, Print Preview, Setup...**), delete contents of **Header** and/or **Footer** (text boxes), uncheck **Row & Column Headings** and/or **Cell Gridlines**, click on **OK**

Desired Result	How to Do It
Set a page break	Select row or column to appear at top or left edge of new page (or cell to appear in upper-left corner of new page), choose **Options, Set Page Break**
Remove a page break	Select row or column immediately below or to right of page break (or cell in upper-left corner of page), choose **Options, Remove Page Break**
Set a print area	Select worksheet area to print, choose **Options, Set Print Area**
Delete the current print area	Choose **Formula, Define Name...**, select name **Print_Area**, click on **Delete**, then click on **OK**; or choose **Options, Remove Print Area**
Set print titles	Select entire, adjacent row(s) or column(s) that contain titles you want printed on each page, choose **Options, Set Print Titles**, verify title ranges, click on **OK**
Print a document using the Standard toolbar's Print button	Activate document window, click on Standard toolbar's **Print button**
Preview a document using the Standard toolbar's Print button	Activate document window, hold down **Shift**, click on Standard toolbar's **Print button**

Following this chapter are four appendices:

Appendix A
"Installation" walks you through Excel 4.0 installation and printer selection.

Appendix B
"Keystroke Reference" lists the keystroke equivalents of the mouse/menu commands in this book.

Appendix C
"Exchanging Data between Excel and Other Applications" discusses Excel's compatibility with other current spreadsheet programs.

Appendix D
"Upgrades from Excel Version 3.0 to Version 4.0" lists the differences between Excel 3.0 and 4.0.

IF YOU'RE STOPPING HERE

If you need to break off here, please exit from Excel. If you wish to review material from an earlier chapter or proceed to one of the appendices, please do so now.

APPENDIX A:
INSTALLATION

Installing Excel 4.0
on Your System

Selecting a Printer
for Use with Excel

This appendix contains instructions for installing Excel 4.0 on your system and for selecting a printer for use with Excel.

INSTALLING EXCEL 4.0 ON YOUR SYSTEM

There are two requirements that must be met before you begin to install Excel 4.0. First, Windows (version 3.0 or higher) must be installed on your computer. If it is not, please install it now. (For help, see your Windows reference manuals.) Second, there must be enough free space on your hard disk to hold the necessary Excel program and data files.

Perform the following steps to meet this second requirement:

1. You need to be running in DOS. If Windows is running, please exit to DOS (choose **File, Exit** from the Program Manager window). The DOS prompt (C:>\ or similar) should be on the screen.

2. Type **c:** (or, if you intend to install Excel on another hard drive, type the letter of this drive followed by a colon) and press **Enter** to log onto your hard drive.

3. Type **dir** and press **Enter**. DOS lists the files contained in the current directory and, at the very end of this list, reports the number of free hard-disk bytes.

4. Observe this number. You need at least 6 megabytes (6,000,000 bytes) of free hard-disk space to install the minimum Excel configuration needed to perform the hands-on activities in this book. You need at least 12 megabytes (12,000,000) of free hard-disk space to install the complete Excel program. We strongly recommend installing the complete Excel program, as this will include several advanced Excel options that—although not covered in this book—may prove very useful to you at a later date.

5. If necessary, delete sufficient files from your hard disk to free the space required for your desired Excel installation (6 or 12 megabytes). Be sure to back up any files that you want to save before deleting them!

6. Type **dir** and press **Enter**. DOS should now report at least 6,000,000 or 12,000,000 free hard-disk bytes. (If not, repeat step 5.)

Now that you've met the two requirements, you can begin the actual Excel 4.0 installation:

1. Start Windows.

2. Insert the disk labeled "Setup" in the appropriately sized disk drive.

3. Activate **Program Manager**. (If Program Manager is running in an icon, double-click on the icon to open it into a window. If Program Manager is running in a window, click on the title bar of the window to activate it.)

4. Choose **File, Run...** from the Program Manager.

5. Type **a:setup** (if the Setup disk is in drive A) or **b:setup** (if the disk is in drive B). Press **Enter** to start the Excel installation program.

6. If you are prompted to enter your name and organization, follow the on-screen directions to do so. Click on **Continue** when you are done.

7. Follow the on-screen instructions to enter the hard-disk directory where you will install Excel. Click on **Continue** when you are done. If asked whether you wish to create this directory, click on **Yes**.

8. A dialog box appears, showing three installation options: Complete, Custom, and Minimum. If you want to install the complete Excel program (as discussed in the previous section) and you have freed up the necessary 12 megabytes of hard-disk space, click on the **Complete Installation icon**. If you want to install the minimum Excel program and you have freed up the necessary 6 megabytes, click on the **Minimum Installation icon**. (Note: The dialog box says that 11 MB (megabytes) are needed for complete installation and 5 MB for minimum installation. The extra megabyte that we had you free up is for the PC Learning Lab data files that you'll use in the hands-on activities of this book.)

9. The next dialog box asks whether you would like information on a tool that helps people with Lotus 1-2-3 experience learn to use Excel. If you are a Lotus 1-2-3 user and are interested in this feature, click on **Yes**. If not, click on **No** and proceed directly to step 11.

10. If you clicked on **Yes**, a dialog box appears describing the Lotus 1-2-3 learning tool. Read the description, decide whether you want to enable this option, and then click on **Do Not Enable** or **Enable**.

11. The next dialog box asks if you want to update your system's PATH statement. (DOS uses the PATH statement to locate the files it will need to run Excel and other programs.) Click on **Update**.

12. At this point, the installation program begins to copy files from the Setup floppy disk onto your hard disk. A dialog box appears to inform you of the progress of the installation procedure; the procedure is complete when it reaches 100 percent. (You can click on Cancel at any time to cancel the installation.)

13. When you are asked to insert a new Setup disk, please do so.

14. When the installation procedure is complete, you are returned to Windows. To start Excel, simply double-click on the newly created Microsoft Excel 4.0 icon.

The first time you start Excel after installing it, Excel automatically loads a program entitled "Introducing Microsoft Excel" that provides an overview of the features of Excel 4.0. To use this program,

- Select (click on) the desired topic: "The Basics," "What's New?," or "For Lotus 1-2-3 Users."

To exit to normal Excel operating mode,

- Click on "Exit to Microsoft Excel."

SELECTING A PRINTER FOR USE WITH EXCEL

Before you can print from Excel, you must select a printer. To do so,

1. Start Excel. Do not close the startup worksheet, Sheet1. (If you are starting Excel for the first time after installing it, you will be automatically placed in Preview mode. Please click on **Exit to Microsoft Excel** to exit to normal operating mode before proceeding.)

2. Choose **File, Printer Setup...** . A dialog box appears, displaying a list of the printers currently installed on your system.

3. If your printer appears on the list (you may have to scroll), select it and click on **OK**. You can now use this printer with Excel.

4. If your printer does not appear on the list (even after scrolling), install the printer on your system—for instructions, refer to your Windows documentation—then begin again with step 1 of this printer selection procedure.

APPENDIX B: KEYSTROKE REFERENCE

In Excel, virtually any action that can be performed with the mouse can also be performed with the keyboard. Choose whichever method—or combination of methods—that works best for you.

The following table lists Excel actions and the corresponding keystrokes required to perform them:

Moving around a Worksheet

Action	Keystroke
Move left, right, up, down	**Arrow** keys
Move to beginning of active row	**Home**
Move up one screen	**PgUp** key
Move left one screen	**Ctrl-PgUp**
Move down one screen	**PgDn** key
Move right one screen	**Ctrl-PgDn**
Move to cell A1	**Ctrl-Home**
Move to farthest active cell	**Ctrl-End**
Go to a specified cell or range	**F5**

Selecting a Cell Range

Action	Keystroke
Extend selection left, right, up, or down	**Shift-Arrow**, or **F8** then **Arrow** key
Extend selection to end of data block	**Ctrl-Shift-Arrow**
Add another range to the current selection	**Shift-F8**
Select active row	**Shift-Spacebar**
Select active column	**Ctrl-Spacebar**
Select entire worksheet	**Ctrl-Shift-Spacebar**

Editing

Action	Keystroke
Edit formula bar	**F2**
Cancel an action	**Esc**
Repeat last action	**Alt-Enter**
Undo last action	**Ctrl-Z** or **Alt-Backspace**
Insert cells	**Ctrl-+**
Delete selection	**Ctrl--**
Clear selection	**Del**
Cut selection	**Ctrl-X** or **Shift-Del**
Copy selection	**Ctrl-C** or **Ctrl-Ins**
Paste selection	**Ctrl-V** or **Shift-Ins**
Fill selection down	**Ctrl-D**
Fill selection right	**Ctrl-R**
Find a formula	**Shift-F5**
Toggle formula reference between absolute and relative	**F4**
Delete the preceding character in the formula bar	**Backspace**
Delete the next character in the formula bar	**Del**
Paste a function into a formula	**Shift-F3**
Define a name	**Ctrl-F3**
Create sum formula	**Alt-=**

Formatting

Action	Keystroke
Apply currency format with two decimal places	Ctrl-$
Apply percentage format with no decimal places	Ctrl-%
Outline border	Ctrl-&
Remove all borders	Ctrl-_
Remove bold, italics, and underline	Ctrl-1
Toggle bold on/off	Ctrl-2
Toggle italics on/off	Ctrl-3
Toggle underline on/off	Ctrl-4

Working with Files

Action	Keystroke
Create a new worksheet	Shift-F11 or Alt-Shift-F1
Create a new chart	F11 or Alt-F1
Save a file using the Save As command	F12 or Alt-F2
Save a file using the Save command	Shift-F12 or Alt-Shift-F2
Open a file	Ctrl-F12 or Alt-Ctrl-F2
Print a file	Ctrl-Shift-F12 or Alt-Ctrl-Shift-F2

Working with Windows

Action	Keystroke
Select menu bar	**Alt** key (or **/** if Lotus 1-2-3 Help was enabled during Excel installation)
Choose a menu item	**Alt-*letter*** (or **/-*letter*** if Lotus 1-2-3 Help is enabled), where *letter* is the letter underlined in the menu item
Maximize/restore document window	**Ctrl-F10**
Select next document window	**Ctrl-F6**
Select previous document window	**Shift-Ctrl-F6**
Close document window	**Ctrl-F4**
Close all document windows	**Shift-Alt-f-c** (or **Shift-/-f-c** if Lotus 1-2-3 Help is enabled)

Working with Charts

Action	Keystroke
Move to next item	**Right Arrow** key
Move to previous item	**Left Arrow** key
Move to next class of items	**Down Arrow** key
Move to previous class of items	**Up Arrow** key

Miscellaneous

Action	Keystroke
Activate the Help window	**F1**
Get context-sensitive help	**Shift-F1**
Select next item in a dialog box	**Tab**
Select previous item in a dialog box	**Shift-Tab**
Check or uncheck a check box	**Spacebar**
Exit Excel	**Alt-F4**

APPENDIX C:
EXCHANGING DATA
BETWEEN EXCEL AND
OTHER APPLICATIONS

Opening a
Document From
Another
Application

Opening a Text File
From Another
Application

Saving an Excel
Document for use
in Another
Application

Saving a Text File
for use in Another
Application

Parsing Imported
Data

Among the greatest conveniences of Excel 4.0 is its compatibility with other software. You can easily import files from other programs into your Excel worksheets and export your Excel worksheets for use in other programs. This appendix lists the various formats in which Excel can open and save files, and shows you how to make the file conversions you need.

OPENING A DOCUMENT FROM ANOTHER APPLICATION

Excel 4.0 opens files in the following application formats:

File Format	Document Type
MS Excel	Excel versions 2.*x* and 3.0
Lotus 1-2-3	Lotus 1-2-3 releases 1, 2, and 3 and Lotus Symphony
Text	Text for Macintosh, ANSI text for Windows, ASCII text for DOS or OS/2, column delimiter (tab, comma, space, semicolon, none, custom)
CSV	Comma-separated values
SYLK	Symbolic link (Multiplan)
dBASE	dBASE II, III, and IV
DIF	Data interchange format (VisiCalc)

To open a document from another application,

- Choose File, Open... .

- Change the drive and/or directory if necessary.

- Type the name of the document you wish to open (include the filename extension) in the File Name text box; or select the file type in the List Files Of Type box and select the document in the File Name list box.

- Click on OK to open the document.

You can then analyze, chart, format, and print the imported data, exactly as if you had opened an Excel document.

OPENING A TEXT FILE FROM ANOTHER APPLICATION

To open a text file from another application,

- Choose File, Open... .

- Click on Text... .

- Select under Column Delimiter the character used to divide columns of data in the file you are about to open.

- Select under File Origin the operating environment the file was created in: Macintosh, Windows, DOS, or OS/2.
- Click on OK.
- Change the drive and/or directory, if necessary.
- In the File Name list box, select the name of the file you wish to open; or type the name in the File Name text box.
- Click on OK.

Opening a text file from another application is especially useful when working with database files. Each line in a text file represents one row (record) in an Excel database worksheet. Within this row, cells (fields) are delimited (separated) by a comma or a tab.

SAVING AN EXCEL DOCUMENT FOR USE IN ANOTHER APPLICATION

Excel 4.0 saves files in the following application formats:

File Format	Document Type
Normal	Excel 4.0
Excel 3.0	Excel version 3.0
Excel 2.1	Excel version 2.1
SYLK	Symbolic link (Multiplan)
Text	ANSI text for Windows
CSV	Comma-separated values for Windows
WKS	Lotus 1-2-3 release 1 and Lotus Symphony
WK1	Lotus 1-2-3 release 2
WK3	Lotus 1-2-3 release 3
DIF	Data interchange format (VisiCalc)
DBF2	dBASE II
DBF3	dBASE III
DBF4	dBASE IV

File Format	Document Type
Text (Macintosh)	Text for Macintosh
Text (OS/2 or MS-DOS)	ASCII text for DOS or OS/2
CSV (Macintosh)	Comma-separated values for Macintosh
CSV (OS/2 or MS-DOS)	Comma-separated values for DOS or OS/2

To save an Excel document in a file format that can be used in another application,

- Choose File, Save As... .
- In the Save File As Type box, select the file format you want.
- Observe the File Name box—Excel chose a filename extension based on the file format you just picked.
- Type a new name for the document, if necessary.
- Change the drive and/or directory, if necessary.
- Click on OK.
- Start the other application and open the file you just created.

You can then analyze, chart, format, and print the Excel data from the other application.

SAVING A TEXT FILE FOR USE IN ANOTHER APPLICATION

To save an Excel document as a text file for use in another application,

- Choose Files, Save As... .
- Select in the Save File As Type box the format you want: Text, CSV, Text (Macintosh), Text (OS/2 or MS-DOS), CSV (Macintosh), or CSV (OS/2 or MS-DOS). "Text" choices cause Excel to use tabs to delimit cells; CSV (comma-separated values) choices use commas to delimit cells.
- Change the drive and/or directory, if necessary.
- Observe the File Name text box. Excel chose a filename extension based on the file format you just picked.

- Type a new name for the document, if necessary.
- Click on OK.
- Start the other application and open the file you just created.

PARSING IMPORTED DATA

When you import data into Excel from another application, multiple columns (fields) of data will sometimes be condensed into a single column. If this happens, you can use the Data, Parse command to *parse* (arrange) these data back into their separate columns.

When you parse data, Excel fills one or more cells to the right of the column being parsed. In doing this, it erases the previous contents of these cells. For this reason, you should always double-check that there are enough blank cells to the right of the column to accommodate the parsed data.

To parse imported data,

- Select the range of cells containing the data you wish to parse. This range must be only one column wide.
- Choose Data, Parse... . The Parse dialog box appears, displaying the contents of the first selected cell. The parse settings you enter for this cell will apply to all the cells in the selected range.
- Click on Guess. Excel will "guess" how to parse the data, using a set of brackets [] to represent a single column.
- Change Excel's guess by adding or deleting these brackets, if necessary.
- Click on OK.

APPENDIX D: UPGRADING FROM EXCEL VERSION 3.0 TO VERSION 4.0

General Features

Formatting and
Presentation
Features

Analysis Features

Printing Features

Charting Features

Database Features

Customizing and
Automating
Features

Features for Lotus
1-2-3 Users

This appendix describes the enhancements and new features of the Excel Version 4.0 upgrade that were not available in Version 3.0. The following list is intended as a comprehensive reference and includes features not covered in this book.

GENERAL FEATURES

Feature	Description
AutoFill	Enables you to create a series by dragging.
Automatic freeze panes	Enable you to split the worksheet window into panes.
Automatic number formatting	When you create a formula, it is displayed in the number format of the first cell referred to in the formula.
Automatic parenthesis completion	If you omit the closing parenthesis in a formula, Excel automatically enters it for you.
Enhanced Arrange All	Enables you to arrange windows in different ways.
Enhanced Number Format dialog box	The Number Format dialog box enables you to list number formats by category.
Enhanced Paste Function dialog box	The Paste Function dialog box enables you to list functions by category.
Enter returns and tabs in formulas	Carriage returns and tabs can be entered within cells and formulas to make text and formulas easier to read.
Goto command lists four previous locations	The Goto dialog box lists the last four locations that you selected using the Formula, Goto command.
Moving and copying data with the mouse	Enables you to move or copy data by dragging.
New Standard toolbar	The Standard toolbar has been redesigned, and contains tools for the most frequently used commands and actions. The original Microsoft Excel 3.0 toolbar is also available.

Feature	Description
New styles	The style list on the Standard toolbar includes comma and currency number formats with no decimal places.
New toolbars	Several new, built-in, movable toolbars are available.
New tools	A wide selection of new tools is available. Tools that are not assigned to a toolbar can be added to an existing toolbar or to a toolbar that you create.
Open multiple files	Enables you to open more than one file at the same time.
Reference area name display	When a named range is selected, the name is displayed in the reference area of the formula bar.
Shortcut menus	Pressing the right mouse button displays a shortcut menu appropriate to whatever you are working on at the time.
Spell checking	Enables you to spell-check Microsoft Excel worksheets, macro sheets, and charts.
Support for Microsoft Mail for the Personal Computer	Enables you to use Microsoft Mail to send copies of Microsoft Excel documents to other Microsoft Mail users.
Workbooks	Enable you to work with groups of documents.
Zooming views of the worksheet	Enable you to view your worksheets at different levels of magnification.

FORMATTING AND PRESENTATION FEATURES

Feature	Description
Automatic range formatting	Enables you to apply a range-formatting combination to a selected range.
Centering text over columns	Enables you to center text within a selected range.
Color palettes	Microsoft Excel 4.0 includes 15 worksheets containing various color palettes.
Create on-screen slide shows	Enables you to create on-screen slide-show presentations of Microsoft Excel worksheets, charts, and graphic objects, along with graphics imported from other applications.
Sound notes	Enable you to record and play sound notes in your documents. (You must be working with Microsoft Windows 3.0 with MultiMedia Extensions, or with Microsoft Windows 3.1.)
Vertical text in cells	Enables you to control the vertical or horizontal appearance of text in cells.

ANALYSIS FEATURES

Feature	Description
Analysis ToolPak functions and procedures	The Analysis ToolPak that comes with Microsoft Excel 4.0 includes statistical analysis tools. These range from analyses that can be applied to many types of data to analyses specifically designed for financial, engineering, and scientific applications.

Feature	Description
Assign names to work-sheet views	Enables you to assign names to print settings and other display options that apply to worksheet ranges.
Scenario Manager	Enables you to vary input values in a model and to view the results. Also, automatically creates a table of all the input values and results produced.

PRINTING FEATURES

Feature	Description
Controlling the direction of printing	Enables you to control whether several pages of the printout are printed from the top of the print area down, or from the left of the print area to the right.
Header and footer improvements	Separate buttons in the Page Setup dialog box provide you with greater ease and flexibility when you enter, edit, and format text in the header and footer.
Printing reports	Enable you to define and print reports consisting of views and scenarios that you define in a document.
Starting page numbers	Enable you to specify a starting page number in the header, footer, or both.

CHARTING FEATURES

Feature	Description
3-D bar chart types	3-D bar charts can be created to compare items.
3-D surface area chart types	3-D surface charts can be created to show optimum combinations between two sets of data.

Feature	Description
Changing 3-D chart orientation	Enables you to drag the floor or walls of a 3-D chart to change its orientation.
Chart toolbar	When a chart is created or selected, Excel displays the Chart toolbar, which contains tools for formatting and editing charts.
ChartWizard	Excel automatically leads you through a series of steps that allow you to easily create or edit a chart.
Radar chart types	You can create radar charts to show changes or frequencies of data relative both to a center point and to each other.

DATABASE FEATURES

Feature	Description
Crosstab	ReportWizard enables you to summarize and compare information in the fields of a database by using crosstab tables.

CUSTOMIZING AND AUTOMATING FEATURES

Feature	Description
Add-in Manager	Microsoft Excel 4.0 contains various add-in macros. In addition, you can create your own add-in macros.
Additional arguments for functions	Enable you to enter up to 30 arguments for functions that accept a variable number of arguments.

Feature	Description
AutoActivate and AutoDeActivate	You can assign either of these built-in names (AutoActivate or AutoDe-Activate) to macros that you would like to run whenever a particular Excel document is activated.
Customizable toolbars	Enable you to move tools between toolbars and to add tools to built-in toolbars or to toolbars that you create.
Global macro sheet	Enables you to create macros and save them on the global macro sheet, which is hidden whenever you start Excel.
Improvements to CALL and REGISTER	Enhancements include the ability to call Excel functions from other applications.
Macro tools	The Macro toolbar contains tools for recording and running macros, for creating new macro sheets, and for pasting functions and names.
Macros with attached objects use automatic links	Excel 4.0 automatically updates links when the name or location of a macro sheet is changed.
New ON functions	Two new functions (ON.ENTRY and ON.DOUBLECLICK) can start macros when certain triggering events occur.
Pausing macros	You can temporarily suspend running a macro in order to perform data entry or editing, and then resume running the macro.
Record button in the Assign To Object dialog box	The Assign To Object dialog box now contains a Record button.

FEATURES FOR LOTUS 1-2-3 USERS

Feature	Description
Added file format support	Enables you to open and save files in a variety of 1-2-3 file formats.
Entering Lotus 1-2-3 formulas and names	Enables you to enter formulas and work with range names in Excel in the same way that you would in 1-2-3.
Evaluating Lotus 1-2-3 formulas	Enables you to perform operations— such as database criteria evaluation, Boolean evaluation, or the calculation of VLOOKUP and HLOOKUP functions—as you would in 1-2-3.
Running Lotus 1-2-3 macros in Microsoft Excel	Enables you to open 1-2-3 worksheets and run the macros that they contain.

INDEX

A

■ TO RECEIVE 3¹/₂-INCH DISK(S)

The Ziff-Davis Press software contained on the 5¹/₄-inch disk(s) included with this book is also available in 3¹/₂-inch (720k) format. If you would like to receive the software in the 3¹/₂-inch format, please return the 5¹/₄-inch disk(s) with your name and address to:

Disk Exchange
Ziff-Davis Press
5903 Christie Avenue
Emeryville, CA 94608